Simplicity Marketing

End Brand Complexity, Clutter, and Confusion

Steven M. Cristol
Peter Sealey

THE FREE PRESS

New York   London   Toronto   Sydney   Singapore

fP

THE FREE PRESS
A Division of Simon & Schuster, Inc.
1230 Avenue of the Americas
New York, NY 10020

Designed by Brady McNamara

Manufactured in the United States of America

10   9   8   7   6   5   4   3   2   1

Figure 4.1, the iMac advertisement, is reproduced with permission from
Apple Computer, Inc., and TBWA/Chiat/Day.

Figure 10.1, the brand equity diagram, is adapted from *Managing Brand Equity*
by David A. Aaker, © copyright 1991 by David A. Aaker. Reprinted by permission.

Library of Congress Cataloging-in-Publication Data

Cristol, Steven M.
    Simplicity marketing: end brand complexity, clutter, and confusion / Steven M.
    Cristol, Peter Sealey.
        p.   cm.
    Includes bibliographical references and index.
        1. Marketing. 2. Customer relations—Technological innovations.   I. Sealey, Peter.

HF5415.C6993 2000
658.8—dc21
                                                                    00-042188

ISBN 13: 978-1-4165-7644-0
ISBN 10: 1-4165-7644-4

To Elaine and Steffie, my anchors in the wind.

— *Steven M. Cristol*

To Donald R. Keough, retired president of The Coca-Cola Company, and Peter F. Drucker, Clark Professor of Social Science at the Claremont Graduate University, for their seminal contributions to the discipline of management and great inspiration to me.

— *Peter Sealey*

Contents

I AM INDEBTED to many for enabling this book. First, my thanks to Frank Cespedes at the Center for Executive Development for his wisdom, encouragement, and early feedback on the concept of Simplicity Marketing. My thanks to Carolyn Neal for her role in publishing our original article on which the book is based. I am also grateful to Professor Kevin Lane Keller at Dartmouth College—both for his guidance in leading me to The Free Press with this project, and for the inspiration provided by his extraordinary book, *Strategic Brand Management*.

Special thanks to Bob Wallace, senior editor at The Free Press, for his enthusiasm about the project from day one. It has been a privilege to have the benefit of Bob's vast experience from editing many of the business books that I have most respected over the years. Anne-Marie Sheedy at The Free Press was also a pleasure to work with as she helped bring the project to conclusion in a multitude of ways. Giorgio Stenner, my research assistant, provided diligent support in excavating data to augment, and sometimes modify, my judgment. Tracy Barrett provided the computer graphics to help our readers visualize strategies and ideas.

Among the many who helped bring the book's examples to life, I'd especially like to thank Ralph Drayer and Allen Olivo for being so giving of their time. Thanks also to Mark Nielsen and Lynn Upshaw for their invaluable counsel and insights along the way. Finally, I want to deeply thank Elaine and Stephanie, my wife and daughter, for seeing me through, and my trusted friends Lee Franklin and David Brandt for their moral support in my decision to undertake this book at a very busy and challenging time.

—*Steven M. Cristol*

L IKE CAPITALISM ITSELF, contemporary marketing has been based on an unflagging belief in giving customers more and more choices. The choice curve ramped up in the post-World War II economy, when packaged goods manufacturers set in motion a relentless juggernaut of product proliferation and line extensions. The cumulative result of a half century of bombarding customers with an overload of options is that their mental circuit breakers are beginning to trip—in both the consumer and business worlds. In a pressure-packed buying and selling environment, the line between choice and overchoice has become increasingly fine.

By the early 1970s, marketers were already desperately hungry for ways to ensure that their brands could stand out amidst the swelling marketing noise created by more choices and more media pervasiveness. It was then that the concept of *positioning* rippled through the marketing world. Positioning focused on the importance of differentiating a product, service, or company from its competition. It brought to the marketing planning process a new sense of focus on carving out a proprietary space in the customer's mind. During the three decades since, sustained success has come to those brands with a unique, relevant, and credible positioning consistently supported by aggressive marketing.

But many such successes are now threatened by overchoice. A new imperative for the positioning discipline has emerged: that marketers look for ways to connect their brands to *simplicity*. The interaction of two forceful tides—extreme choice proliferation and an exponentially increasing pace of change—creates a combustible combination that at once brings customers unprecedented opportunities and unprecedented anxiety. This book hypothesizes that, in the most developed economies of the twenty-first century, *the next generation of positioning successes will belong to those brands that relieve customer stress.* That means simplifying customers' lives or businesses in ways that are inextricably tied to brand and product positioning. It means *becoming the customer's partner in stress relief.*

Brands that do this will be the customer's heroes. Brands that don't will be nuisances.

Since the authors' initial published work in this arena appeared in *Marketing Management* (American Marketing Association) in 1996, much has been written about simplification. In concept, addressing simplicity in marketing might seem fairly straightforward, intuitive, and not exactly rocket science. But if you have ever tried to build a credible brand positioning strategy on simplification, you already know that it is much easier said than done. A strategic framework is needed—a framework that provides a new set of filters through which products and brands can be passed to distill the kernels of simplicity that will reduce customer stress.

Simplicity Marketing is that framework. With Simplicity Marketing, choice and innovation need not incrementally clutter the customer's mind but can instead be positioned to *de-clutter* it. As the rhythms of innovation further compress and customer demand for stress relief continues to grow, this de-cluttering will translate to stronger sales, customer loyalty, brand equity, and competitive advantage.

This book is divided into three parts. Part I examines the impact of customer stress on the buying and selling environment and introduces foundational concepts for understanding it and addressing it as marketers. Part II provides a suite of stress-reducing strategies that are the linchpins of effective Simplicity Marketing. It then explodes those strategies into their actionable components. Part III is a guide to managing simplicity strategies, leveraging information technology, and integrating all the tools in this book into an executional blueprint. Finally, it explores the linkages between customer stress reduction, brand equity, and share-holder value.

Simplicity Marketing also aims to help you evaluate the significance of trends, and to do so before your competitors. For example, after you read it we believe you will see why those who were late to grasp the strategic impact of the Internet would have likely grasped it earlier in a Simplicity Marketing context.

If you are a marketing strategist, we hope you will use the book as an action-oriented handbook. If you are a senior executive presiding over marketing, or the CEO of a marketing-oriented company, we hope you will use it to help rethink your company's fundamental relationship with your customers—and how making those relationships less stressful can enhance shareholder value. And if you are a marketing academic, market researcher, or consumer psychologist, we hope you will use it to challenge those existing methodologies that overchoice is rendering less and less effective.

A final note on using the book: Although we recognize that, in some industries such as consumer packaged goods, "customer" means *trade* customers and not "consumers," throughout the book we have used the word *customer* to be inclusive of both consumers/end users and distribution channel customers. Simplicity and stress are not unique to either the consumer or business-to-business marketplaces, and *customer* is the only word broad enough to encompass both.

The mission of *Simplicity Marketing* is to facilitate value-creating brand and product strategies. We also hope to ignite the debate about the merits of choice proliferation versus choice simplification. Though we are not alone in having identified the hunger for simplicity as the under-pinnings of a watershed marketing trend, we have tried with this book to both illuminate that trend and bring discipline to leveraging it. Our best hope is that by mixing your talents with the concepts presented here, we can produce an alchemy that makes your customers' lives easier, fortifies your brand, and strengthens your company's financial performance.

—*Steven Cristol and Peter Sealey*

PART I

The Buying and Selling Environment in the Digital Age

Chapter 1

Too Much Choice

In the three short decades between now and the twenty-first century, millions of ordinary, psychologically normal people will face an abrupt collision with the future.   —ALVIN TOFFLER, opening statement, *Future Shock*, 1970

DEVELOPED ECONOMIES were largely built on proliferation of choices. The notion of "more is better" became genetic code among twentieth-century consumers growing up in these economies. Now, with each passing day, more and more of these same consumers find that they have run headlong into a wall. The wall is their manageable threshold for the sheer number of decisions they are being asked to make, and they are throwing their hands up in despair. But in this frustration is a win-win opportunity to de-stress customers and, in so doing, to build brand equity and shareholder value.

How did we get to a consumer world of 40,000 products in a supermarket, hundreds of long distance and cellular calling plans, 52 versions of Crest toothpaste, magazine ads that show 37 available configurations of a Dodge Caravan on a single page, and the distribution of a thousand coupons *per human being* each year in the United States? How did we get to a business world confronted by more than 200 different brands of conference room chairs, 225 different models of mobile phone handsets, and 100-plus brands of desktop and laptop computers—all marketing for mindshare above the daily din of the purchasing manager's voice mail and e-mail messages? Can the human brain sustain its ability to cope with such overwhelming choice in an age of a networked economy, higher productivity expectations, and shrinking leisure time? Is the resulting level of customer stress really such a big deal?

You bet it is.

■ Digital-Age Stress: A Day in the Life

To glimpse how radically purchase decisions have changed since publication of Alvin Toffler's seminal *Future Shock* in 1970, one only needs to peer into the digital-age lives of two people who could be *your* customers. Meet John Braxton and Lucy Chavez. John is a middle manager in a Fortune 500 company, the father of first- and fourth-grade children, and the husband of a real estate broker who works long hours. (John's wife is among the ranks of 75% of U.S. wives under age 65 who work—compared to less than 40% in 1970.) Lucy is a thirty-something superstar director of information systems at one of the world's largest banks; her career has been all-consuming, and she hasn't yet had time for marriage or family (though lately she's been all too aware of the ticking of her biological clock).

Note that neither John nor Lucy, though technologically savvy, are bleeding-edge early adopters of new technologies in their personal lives. Like so many readers of this book, they are users of mainstream digital-age technologies like voice mail, cell phones, e-mail, and the Internet, but have not yet plunged deeply into the post-PC world of information appliances. So as you read about their day, remember that still awaiting them in the short-term future is the prospect of learning about and sorting through the burgeoning milieu of home computer networks, digital VCRs, portable Internet music players, wireless Web tablets, wristwatch phones, "smart" picture frames, networked washing machines, personal portable bar code scanners, and the next generation of handheld organizers. Forgetting for a moment that the post-PC world will bring even more clutter and confusion into the picture, let's first look in on John's day.

Before leaving to drive the kids to school on the way to his office, John has only a few minutes to glance at the morning paper while standing at the kitchen counter to wolf down some breakfast cereal. Seeing the business section reminds him that he really ought to invest that $7,000 bonus check he received over the holidays. He doesn't have time to evaluate individual stocks or bonds, so he's been thinking about mutual funds as a simpler approach. Today's newspaper happens to have an article on mutual funds, reporting on the fact that there are now more than 13,000 funds worldwide to choose from. Thirteen thousand! John had no idea, and suddenly what he thought would be an easy way out seemed formidable. What he had hoped could reduce his anxiety had just produced more. (Mutual funds, originally known as investment trusts, have been around for more than a century in the United Kingdom and nearly 80 years in the United States. Yet as recently as 1970, even with all that evolution, there were still only about 500 open-end funds to choose from compared to today's 13,000-plus.)

At the office, John overhears his assistant making airline reservations for his trip to London next month for a trade show. He rushes out from behind his desk to say, "Wait! Let me check my frequent flier miles before you commit to an airline. I think I'm close to a free ticket to Hawaii with either Delta or United, but I can't remember which. And one of them is having that big bonus miles promotion right now on overseas flights. You'll have to call them back after I log onto the Web and check my mileage plan account balances. (When *Future Shock* was published, there were no frequent flier programs. American Airlines launched the first in 1980.)

At lunch, John and a colleague only have enough time to run across the street to McDonald's. The menu board fills the wall with Value Meals, Chicken McNuggets with a choice of four sauces, Arch Deluxe with or without bacon, Happy Meals with action toys, two kinds of fish filet sandwiches and two kinds of chicken, fat-free Apple bran muffins, multiple salads with multiple dressings, and a host of additional menu variations. The number of choices is sufficiently incomprehensible that John hears himself ordering a number 2 Value Meal even though he doesn't really want or need the large order of fries that comes with it. (When *Future Shock* was published, "fast" food also implied "uncomplicated." McDonald's 1970 menu board was certainly uncomplicated compared with its nearly 60 different items in 1999—not counting nine Value Meal combinations. In contrast, the thriving and popular regional Los Angeles-based In-N-Out Burger chain still had the same menu in 1999 as in 1988; just burgers, cheeseburgers, fries, drinks, and shakes—not that different from McDonald's 1970 menu.)

After lunch, John's assistant reminds him that today is the enrollment deadline for choosing an HMO in the company health plan, now that Human Resources has added more options for next year with different coverages and different levels of co-payment. (When *Future Shock* was published, John's company was simply telling employees, "Here is your health benefits package. Your coverage is with ABC Insurance." No HMOs, no co-payments.)

Before leaving the office, John picks up a voice message from his wife asking him to stop at the supermarket to pick up a few simple items to get the family through to the weekend: orange juice, bagels, Philadelphia cream cheese, Crest toothpaste, Coke, and some fresh lettuce for salads. John enters a Safeway supermarket on his way home; it contains about 37,000 different products with distinct SKUs (stockkeeping units).[1] Inside the store, his little 2-inch Post-It Note-size shopping list becomes a 25-minute obstacle course as it explodes into more than *250 choices* for only those six items on his list. (In 1970, the same six items combined offered just over 50 choices. The average supermarket contained only about 8,000 SKUs; the approximate number of new grocery product introductions in the United States was 800 in 1970, compared to more than 11,000 in 1998.) Table 1.1 shows a comparison of what John sees this evening, compared to what might have been a typical 1970 selection.

Table 1.1

	1999	1970
Crest Toothpaste	45 SKUs (including tubes and pumps of gel, paste, tartar control, baking soda, glitter for kids, mint or original flavor)	15 SKUs (mint or original, one formula in tubes only)
Orange Juice	70 SKUs (six brands; from concentrate or not from concentrate, No Pulp, Some Pulp, Lots of Pulp, Double Vitamin C, Calcium-Fortified, frozen or fresh or fresh squeezed in the store; cartons or plastic bottles or 16-oz. glass bottles or single-serving six-packs or frozen tins; 70 SKUs is orange juice only, not counting blends like orange-pineapple, orange-tangerine, orange-mango, etc.)	20 SKUs (two or three brands plus private label; mostly from concentrate in frozen tins or cartons)

Bagels	35 varieties, in the adjacent bagel shop (ranging from sugar-free sesame to whole wheat cranberry-orange)	4 varieties (plain, egg, onion, poppy seed)
Philadelphia Cream Cheese	30 SKUs (block or soft or whipped; regular or light; 15 flavors, ranging from Roasted Garlic to Apple Cinnamon to Jalapeno)	3 SKUs (three sizes of one flavor in one foil-wrapped block cheese form)
Coke	25 SKUs (5 sizes: 12-oz. cans or bottles, plus 16.9-oz., 1-liter, 20-oz., or 2-liter plastic bottles; regular, cherry, diet, diet cherry, caffeine-free diet, caffeine-free regular, etc.)	6 SKUs (just classic Coke in cans or glass bottles; Diet Coke, cherry and caffeine-free versions were not introduced till the 1980s)
Lettuce	9 varieties of whole lettuce plus 40 SKUs of packaged, fresh pre-cut lettuce/salad (among 433 total items in the fresh produce section)	4 varieties of whole lettuce; no packaged, pre-cut product (only about 100 total items in the fresh produce section)

John finally gets to the checkout counter, only to be asked, "Do you have your Safeway Club card? Do you want paper or plastic bags this evening? Credit card or debit card?"

Home at last, John is putting the groceries on the counter next to a large bowl of fresh fruit when he notices the stickers on the bananas are carrying button-size micro-ads for ABC Television. The phone rings. MCI WorldCom is calling to tell him about a new long distance calling plan that is only available to customers of John's bank. With his and his wife's combined income and credit history, they qualify for a Platinum Visa card. The telemarketing rep tells John that if he moves his long distance service from Sprint to MCI and fills out an application for the Platinum Visa before a certain date, he will qualify for a preferred-customer lower APR on his Visa and for MCI's special Platinum calling plan. He responds, "Sorry, I can't deal with this now." (In 1970 there was only one class of BankAmericard before it later became Visa, one class of Master Charge before it later became MasterCard, and one class of American Express until it launched an exclusive Platinum card in 1983). For consumers at the end of the '90s, cards were regular, Gold, and Platinum Visa and MasterCard, branded not only by banks but co-branded as well, plus a Titanium Visa, plus American Express's 20+ options (green, gold, platinum, Optima, Optima Grace, etc.). Together they accounted for the lion's share of nearly 4 billion mail and phone credit card solicitations a year in the U.S. Visa estimates that in the U.S. alone, beyond single-bank cards there were co-branded Visa cards bearing more than 6,000 different brand names by 1999. (And relative to the call John just answered, in 1970 there was only one long distance provider—AT&T—and no packaged calling plans; today there are nine brands of long distance service available in his area, each with its own spin on calling plan options and pricing.)

One reason John couldn't deal with that call was because he had just spent two grueling hours the previous evening trying to figure out the best solution for upgrading his wireless phone service from his old analog cellular to digital PCS—until the formidable tangle of handset features and battery types, pricing plans, calling areas, and special promotions from six different wireless carriers in his area finally led him to conclude, "I'll just keep what I have." (According to a 1998 Wirthlin Worldwide/Ameritech survey, 86% of consumers interested in wireless phone service said they were confused by the choices.)

After dinner, John quickly shuffles through the stack of today's 13 pieces of mail on the table. He notices a Gateway Computer ad on the back cover of *PC World* magazine. This single page ad contains five logos: Gateway's, the Intel Inside logo, the *PC Magazine* Editor's Choice seal, Pentium III, and Microsoft Windows. (The clutter of "ingredient branding" barely existed in consumer markets in 1970 beyond Dolby in stereo and DuPont's pioneering ingredient brands like Teflon and Lycra. But after NutraSweet and Intel in the '80s, the floodgates opened and today we have countless ingredient brands splattering their logos on the advertising, packaging, and promotional materials of countless host brands. Sometimes we now see even three layers of branding on the same product. One new personal TV receiver, for example, carries the Philips brand name alongside both the TiVo brand name (the company that licenses its personal TV service and technology to Philips) and the Quantum Quick-View brand name (the branded enabling storage technology). The consumer buys a box with three brands emblazoned on it, all vying for mind-share even as they endorse each other.)

On his way to the trash can to throw away the plastic bag that the evening paper came wrapped in, John puts the discardable mail in the paper recycling container and the empty bottles from dinner in the glass recycling container. Later he'll put yesterday's newspaper in the separate newspaper recycling container. (In 1970, in the house that John grew up in, his parents didn't think about recycling—much less using separate containers for sorting different materials every day—so everything John just now did would have been one simple trip to the trash can. Today's scenario is certainly progress, but like many other forms of progress has mental clutter consequences.) John then remembers that tomorrow evening he needs to get some new tennis shoes before this weekend's tournament, so he reaches for the Yellow Pages—only to be faced with a choice between the GTE Everything Pages and the Pacific Bell SMART Yellow Pages. (In 1970, there was only one Yellow Pages brand per market in most U.S. markets. Some now have four different brands distributed to the same household.)

When the kids are finally in bed, John and his wife decide to unwind by vegging out in front of the TV for a little while. John flips on the remote to see the TV Guide Channel's scrolling list of what's on—on the nearly 300 channels they now get via digital cable. After using up 10 minutes of TV watching time just to sort through some of the choices, John sees that the year's first Monday night football game is on. But his wife thinks that the 1,050 hours of football programming available on ESPN alone this season (not counting the previously broadcast games on ESPN Classic) should provide enough choices for John without her having to watch a game on a work night. (After all, the traditional fall football "season" we faintly recall from 1970 now stretches to six months from early-August preseason opener to the early-February Pro Bowl, overlapping with the extended seasons and expanding leagues of other professional sports to create exponentially more event choices in any given week than ever before.) So John's wife opts instead for a CBS special on stress reduction. During that hour of prime time, 47 commercial/nonprogram messages run—not including a *one-second* commercial for Master Locks—the broadcast equivalent of the banana sticker micro-ads mentioned earlier. (In 1970, there were four TV channels in the average U.S. market.

Today's fragmentation of programming explains why *Seinfeld*, the top-rated sitcom of the '90s, drew only one-third the audience of *The Beverly Hillbillies*, a top-rated sitcom of the '60s. The average number of commercials in a 1970 prime time hour was 16, less than half of today's number.) Forty minutes later, John has fallen asleep sitting up.

The next morning, in another city on the opposite U.S. coast, Lucy Chavez wakes at 5:15. She feels behind if she's not at the office by 7 A.M. sharp. On days when there's no immediate fire raging, she gives herself the first hour at the office to answer e-mail, check voice mail, skim *The Wall Street Journal* and 2 or 3 of the 23 trade publications she regularly receives (not counting newsletters). She then jumps on the Internet to scan her customized daily news summary and 3 or 4 of the online information technology magazines out of the 30 or so such sites that she will visit during the course of the week. Since she used her cell phone while driving home from work last night to answer most of the 47 voice messages she received yesterday, there are only 6 new messages so far this morning. But there are 61 new e-mails because she hasn't checked e-mail since 2 P.M. yesterday on her way to a four-hour meeting. (By 1998, the average U.S. office worker received more than 160 messages a day via e-mail, fax, voice mail, and conventional mail, according to a study conducted for Pitney Bowes and The Institute for the Future. Similar statistics were reported in the United Kingdom and Canada. In 1970, fax machines barely even existed—the successors to the first commercial fax introduced in 1964 at $29,500 were still unaffordable for most companies.)

Tasting the sludge-like remains at the bottom of the office coffeepot, Lucy asks her assistant if he would mind getting her a tall decaf vanilla latte from the espresso cart in the lobby. He queries back, "Nonfat, 1%, 2%, or regular?" When it arrives, Lucy takes it with her to her 9 A.M. briefing of the CIO staff, where she delivers her piece of the updated global status report on how the bank is stretching systems and human resources to simultaneously cope with conversion to the euro and post-Y2K deferred infrastructure upgrades. After her presentation and a brief discussion about how they are doing with merging the organizations and data centers of another sizable bank they recently acquired, she races back to her office, 10 minutes behind schedule, to apologetically begin her 10:30 meeting with an outsourcing consultant. Lucy passes her business card across the desk. In addition to her mailing address, the card shows her company's main phone number, her direct line, fax number, cell phone number, pager number, e-mail address, and Web site URL. (In total, it contained nearly a hundred more alphanumeric characters—including 40 more digits—than would have appeared on the business card of one of the same bank's managers in 1970.)

We will spare you the rest of Lucy's day, which is not yet even one-third over. You get the idea without suffering the details of her hectic afternoon and her late evening return to her high-tech condominium. After all, her day probably wasn't that much different than yours.

TOFFLER'S PRESCIENT PREDICTION

The world of John and Lucy was foreshadowed three decades ago by Alvin Toffler, who we believe coined the term *overchoice* in the 1960s. There had been mounting fear then that the super-industrial revolution would result in people progressively losing their freedom of choice, as mighty corporations became ever more powerful and the Orwellian vision of Big Brother took hold. Yet, counter to the conventional wisdom of the time, Toffler wrote:

> Ironically, the people of the future may suffer not from an absence of choice, but from a paralyzing surfeit of it. They may turn out to be the victims of that peculiar super-industrial dilemma: overchoice.[2]

Only now is it clear how right he was, though there were early clues. Even then Toffler cited the findings of the President's Commission on Mental Health that, by the late '60s, one-quarter of all Americans were suffering from some form of severe emotional stress. And this was before the digital age divorce rates, traffic congestion, and the percentage of people addicted to dangerous drugs all roughly doubled from 1970 levels. It was also well before the corporate downsizing of the 1980s and 1990s that caused so much stress in the many families that lost jobs and in the families of survivors who kept their jobs but had more work to do than ever before. It was also before the average American couple spent less than 6 minutes a day playing with the kids and only 12 minutes a day talking to each other. So imagine today's stress level compared to the level reported in 1970. (Oops—we don't have to imagine it; we're living it!)

Just how bad is it? In the world's most advanced economies, stress levels ushering in the millennium are staggering. Studies in the '90s showed that 65 to 90% of all American visits to physicians are stress-related.[3] Is it really that much worse now than just 30 years ago? During the first two decades of *Monitor,* the ongoing consumer research study by Yankelovich Partners that is the longest-running annual survey of American psychographics (launched, coincidentally, in 1970), stress was an also-ran on the list of American preoccupations and concerns. But by the '90s, it was at the top—dubbed "the number one 'thorn' that consumers are trying to remove" in a recent Yankelovich report. Around the same time, chair massages started popping up everywhere from airports to outdoor festivals.

Meanwhile, the day-to-day complications of customers' lives were occurring against an increasingly dynamic backdrop, where not just technology was spiraling ahead at a dizzying pace, but the very fundamentals that define the world around us were destabilizing. Even maps of the world changed dramatically since 1970 as the number of nations in the United Nations mushroomed from 144 to 185 by 1998. By today's standards, in 1970 telemarketing calls interrupting dinner were rare; by 1999, more than 20 million telemarketing sales calls poured into U.S. homes each day, and the average U.S. household was receiving about 150 pieces of mail a month (far more in affluent Zip codes) to add to the 18 pieces already received at the office each *day* by the average worker. For homeowners, those calls and mail are coming into houses averaging 2,000 square feet that are almost twice as large as in 1970 (and twice as much to take care of and fill up with stuff).

During the '90s, the simplicity movement in general and the voluntary simplicity movement in particular became a groundswell of determination to reverse the direction of "more is better." An increasing number of middle- and upper-middle-class people began to look at moderating consumption and reducing both physical and emotional clutter as strategies for relieving stress and improving quality of life. The first week of August became Simplify Your Life Week and, by 1995, surveys were showing that 60 to 80% of working people would take a pay cut to be able to work fewer hours. A spate of similarly themed books suddenly crowded the shelves, ironically even pushing the threshold of overchoice on simplicity books (consider Larry Roth's *The Simple Life,* Deborah Deford's

The Simpler Life, and Elaine St. James' *Living the Simple Life* and *Simplify Your Life*—all published or rereleased within the one-year period ending July 1998, and all selling in spite of the confusion because people were sufficiently desperate for relief).

Customers certainly don't have to be actively involved in the simplicity movement for stress to manifest in their shopping behavior. Just look at "cross-shopping"—the phenomenon of more and more upscale consumers shopping at discount stores such as Target. In spite of a strong economy and negligible inflation, a 1998 survey by WSL Strategic Retail found that 90% of U.S. shoppers with household incomes exceeding $70,000 shop in discount stores—twice as many as five years before. In reporting on this survey, *The New York Times* cited the Vanilla Candle Syndrome: "Tired overworked shoppers prefer to save their paychecks for bigger thrills like vacations and massages than to spend them on baby clothes and placemats; and if they cannot afford the vacation or the massage, they go for a scented candle instead."[4]

Meanwhile, the enormous popularity of video games—an industry whose revenue surpassed that of movie theater box offices during the '90s—is increasingly due to the need for stress relief. In recent consumer research asking men why they play video games, gamers in their 20s and 30s cited key reasons as "relieving the stress of my workday" and "it relaxes me and helps me unwind."[5]

TIME: MORTAL ENEMY OF PEOPLE AND COMMERCE ALIKE

Why did we subject you to John's and Lucy's daily war? In a word, *empathy*. Can you honestly say as a marketer that you have fully taken into account such scenarios—even though you're likely living some variation of them yourself—when planning the next battery of customer choices that you will thrust into the marketplace? If so, congratulations! You're in the minority, as many marketers either haven't heard customers' cries for help or have underreacted in adjusting their product development and marketing philosophies.

A key building block of empathy with the customer is fully tapping into *time* issues. In reporting on the voluntary simplicity movement's growing head of steam in 1997, National Public Radio reporter David Molpus used the phrase "time famine" to introduce the relevance of the subject matter. Time *famine*. Looking beyond the commercial realm, psychotherapist and author Dr. David Kundtz summed up the stress-producing relationship we have with time in his recent bestseller, *Stopping*:

> Most of us in this hurry-up, e-mail world of instant response are feeling the same sense of overload. . . . Indeed, the primary challenge of successful human life in the postmodern millennial world is the challenge of too much: too much to do; too much to cope with; too much distraction; too much noise; too much demanding our attention; or, for many of us, too many opportunities and too many choices. Too much of everything for the time and energy available.
>
> We all have been feeling, at least on a subliminal level, the choices, demands and complexities of life increase with every passing year. We have more to be, more to do, more places to go, and more things we want or need to accomplish. But the day remains twenty-four hours; the year, the same twelve months. The amount of activity constantly increases, but both the amount of time into which it must fit and the human energy with which it must be met, at best, remain the same.[6]

Commerce is just one contributor to these feelings—and to the cluttered, burdened psyches to which you are trying to market. Too much choice in commerce is compounded by proliferating choice in noncommercial arenas. Consider just two cornerstones of life in an evolved democracy: schools and elections. In the United States only about 4% of parents sent their kids to private schools in 1970. Usually, the neighborhood school (or a designated school across town where forced busing programs were in effect) was the obvious and only choice. No decision was involved. Today, parents are nearly four times more likely to send their kids to private schools, choosing among as many as two dozen different schools in a metropolitan area—and first having to decide between secular versus religious, co-ed versus not, how far they are willing to commute, and whether to choose a primary school that goes all the way through high school (or at least middle school) versus only through fifth grade. Meanwhile, even those in the public school system may have to decide whether to apply to an "alternative" public school, get on the waiting list for one of the better public schools outside the neighborhood, or apply for an accelerated program school for a smarter child.

Elections were generally held every two years, with a ballot that could be digested quickly, and perhaps there would be a very occasional special election. But like items in the supermarket, local elections and special referenda have fragmented and proliferated. The November 2000 U.S. presidential election may be the 25th time since the prior presidential election in 1996 that a voter in a large U.S. city has been asked to go to the polls—and often for a ballot laden with so many arcane measures that the election pamphlet mailed to the home is more than a hundred pages of fine print that many conscientious voters feel obligated to study. (In another National Public Radio report, registered voters in post-election surveys cited "time crunch" as the number one reason for not voting in the 1996 presidential election.)

If it were just the once-in-a-while noncommercial choices like schools and elections adding to the commercial clutter, we would probably be managing better—but it's also the countless little day-to-day things. More than 300 million Western Europeans must muddle through the unsettling daily challenge of putting aside the currencies they grew up with, adjusting to living and working with, and thinking in terms of, a new monetary unit. As the most developed economies attract more and more language-dependent immigrants, ever larger sectors of the consumer populations in countries like the United States face the daily stress of transactions and buying decisions outside the comfort of their native languages. Meanwhile, it appears that within the next dozen years the United States will run out of 10-digit telephone numbers—resulting in the need to change all numbers to perhaps 14 digits (e.g., a 5-digit area code and 9-digit number) and, along with that, structurally as well as numerically change countless databases and software applications that involve the use of phone numbers. With such mind-numbing data intake woven into the fabric of each day, it's almost unspeakable to contemplate the 15,000 channels that may become available to a single TV set via satellite technology.[7]

So it isn't just commerce that's stealing time. But the noncommercial clutter certainly makes conducting commerce all the more challenging for customer and marketer alike. No wonder so many Baby Boomers find themselves pining for the simplicity of their parents' lives. When of child-rearing age, their parents not only didn't have to choose a long distance company or a brand of electricity and gas or choose one of those 37 different models of Dodge Caravan but also may have never had to choose an elementary school, sort out myriad child care issues and options, or even live through a single area code split. We won't even think about the contrast of their grandparents' lives, when Coke was available in only one variety and one size (before 1955), and when the prospect of 2-liter plastic bottles of Caffeine-Free Diet Cherry Coke adding more visual clutter to the task of navigating supermarket aisles would have been questioned as perhaps unnecessary.

Time is not a solitary enemy; rather, it is the alchemical stew of time and *confusion*—both from commercial and noncommercial overchoice— that simmers to produce the stressful bewilderment which new marketing strategies must address. This is further compounded by sleep deprivation since, when Americans need more time, nearly half take it out of sleep.[8] The catalysts that convert time into stress, exacerbated by 4 out of 10 Americans admitting they are so sleepy during the day that it interferes with their activities, will be further explored in Chapter 2 as additional clues to what marketers can do to be heroes rather than villains.[9]

On one hand, more and more customers are addicted to speed and insistent on immediacy; on the other, they are desperately searching for ways to slow down or even step off the treadmill. No one likes to acknowledge their own limitations. But with the futility and frustration that would come from trying to stuff the Internet through an old 2,400 baud modem, we try to stuff ever-expanding options into a nonexpanding brain that simply wasn't bioengineered for this. Computer processor speed doubles every 18 months but, as Nobel laureate Arno Penzias points out, "Even Albert Einstein could take only 300 bits per second. No human being can take in more."[10] Natural complexity will continue to increase with the tide of innovation, technology, and infrastructure. Without help from marketers, customers will increasingly find themselves swimming upstream.

The growing gap between what we are *able* to take in and what we are *confronted* with taking in has not only emotional and physical costs but a dollar cost as well. The stress epidemic is levying a hefty stress tax on all of us—costing industry more than $300 billion annually, or nearly $8,000 per worker, in increased health insurance outlays, absenteeism, reduced productivity, burnout, costly mistakes and accidents in the workplace, high employee turnover, poor morale, and problems in the family and with alcohol and drugs."

■ It's the Number of Decisions, Not Just the Number of Products

Overchoice backlash, of course, is not only propelled by proliferation of products and line extensions but also by any other choices offered elsewhere in the marketing mix that require incremental decision making. As we saw with John and Lucy, the increasing number of product categories—and options within each category—not only represent more decisions that customers are being asked to make; they also drive exponential increases in outbound telemarketing calls, direct mail, Web marketing, traditional media advertising, and point-of-sale promotions that all ask customers to react, respond, or make incremental "sub-decisions" in some way. And it's not just decisions on purchase options or whether to enter a sweepstakes. It's also monitoring the decisions already made. (Uh-oh, have I reached the number-of-stays threshold to keep my Swissotel Club Swiss Gold card for next year? Have I exceeded my home office Internet service provider's fixed 50-hour monthly maximum before I start incurring the variable per-additional-hour charge for the rest of this month? If I write this check, will my checking account balance be high enough to avoid those pesky per-check charges and keep my free safe deposit box? The tracking requirements are endless.)

This does not imply that when a customer contact presents a well-targeted offer of real value, it is not a valuable and welcomed service to the customer. But even valuable offers and splintering of options still contribute to the noise that in turn contributes to customer stress and overchoice. And, tragically, sometimes even life-simplifying products come along, only to sabotage themselves with complex pricing schemes, arcane short-term promotions, and less-than-clear advertising. All of this in the aggregate can add insult to injury for overstressed customers—even for the most passionate champions of capitalism.

The message for marketers is clear: *Human capacity for choice is not an infinitely expandable commodity.* This is as true for the purchasing vice president of a large corporation as for a housewife or househusband. But empathy for the customer's plight is still lacking. Choice must be proactively managed in the twenty-first century, and this puts contemporary marketing at a crossroads. Those who succeed will increasingly have to market new products and services as replacements for, or consolidators of, existing choices rather than merely as something new.

WHOLE LIFE CONTEXT

One key to excavating stress-reducing customer solutions is the concept of a *whole life context;* that is, placing more emphasis on how a marketer's product category interacts with other product categories in the customer's life, and less emphasis on analyzing the category in a silo. Ostensibly, in most categories, customers continue to demand an abundance of choices. Different needs and lifestyles have naturally led to the call for products and services tailored to the individual, with more and more customization. But customers' lives are a complex quilt of hundreds of product categories that they use or are solicited about. And customers' minds are not neatly segregated into separate compartments the way marketers compartmentalize their definitions of product and service categories, sales channels, and communications vehicles. What may be good and desirable in one category compounds over many categories to create dysfunctionality for the individual customer.

A central cause of this is that customers are generally interrogated by market researchers about their preferences within the confines of a *single* product or service category. But the customer's real life is not so neatly segregated. So while customers continue to demand choice and customization when asked about preferences within that single category, it is the exponential impact of choice in multiple categories that produces most ongoing overchoice stress. Unfortunately, the brand marketer conjures up the inevitable outcome: If you tell me you want more choice in my product category, and then you also tell my peers you want more choice in their categories, we will collectively flood you with an avalanche of decisions. The result is stress-compounding reverse synergy, where more is less as the customer tries to cope.

■ What Can Be Done

The good news is that there are nearly endless possibilities for creative ways to reduce customer stress.

THE ROLE OF BRANDS

Brands can play a core role in stress reduction, especially when brand managers understand and fully leverage brands as time savers and simplifiers.

Overchoice backlash explains why Yankelovich Partners, based on the findings of *Monitor,* talked during the '90s about the emerging importance of brands as "one-think shopping." In the context of too much choice, *brand* becomes the shortest, most efficient path to potential satisfaction and tension release. *Monitor* found that brands were playing a bigger role as the exasperated consumer's simplified shortcut to a purchase decision; in essence, the prevailing thought was, "I've hit my threshold for comparing all these features; this is the company (brand) I want to do business with (based on my brand perceptions), so let's just get on with it!" Hence, one-think shopping—the safest way to cut corners in making choices.

This attitude coincided with the consumer losing faith in support systems and thus having to be more self-reliant. As *Monitor* continued to show waning consumer confidence in everything from travel agents to doctors to advertising, this put more pressure on making choices for one's self. So the one-think shopping that a strong brand can offer has become even more appealing as choices pile up with less reliance on third-party assessment of those choices. More than ever, *strong brands are simplifiers.* Weaker brands promotionally shouting for attention are not.

THE STREAMLINING WAKE-UP CALL

Beyond ongoing strengthening of their brands, some leading marketers have already acted on the simplicity imperative. The mid-1990s marked the first wave of blue-chip marketers not only questioning their long-standing more-is-better momentum, but actually beginning to do something about it. IBM's PC Division was struggling in 1994, building an almost incomprehensible number of different models, racking up a billion-dollar operating loss in one year, and getting leapfrogged by Compaq for market leadership. But during the next three years, IBM slashed its number of models from 3,400 to 150, options from 750 to 350, and number of different parts in inventory from 56,000 to 15,000. By 1997, IBM's PC business was growing faster than the industry for the first time since the 1980s.[12]

Meanwhile, Procter & Gamble (P&G) had already turned to simplification to begin reversing its long history of unbridled line extension and product proliferation. When P&G cut its marketing staff by 30% between 1993 and 1995, it did so as the first major packaged goods marketer to commit to weeding out unnecessary variations of products and packaging around the world. Among the first categories in which P&G decided to reduce customer choice was hair care products. Starting from a place where there were more than 30 varieties of Head & Shoulders shampoo alone, P&G reduced formulas and packaging variations until the company's total number of hair care SKUs were cut by half. Less choice for consumers, yet P&G market share has increased steadily every year since. So what may have begun as a cost-cutting measure at P&G became a win-win for consumer and marketer alike. (See Chapter 10 for a more comprehensive look at P&G's Efficient Consumer Response initiative and its impact on shareholder value.) When fewer than 10% of household and personal care products account for more than 80% of sales, that's a pretty strong clue that shoppers' (and retailers') lives are unnecessarily cluttered with product variations few people really care much about.[13]

While P&G was passing out marketing staff pink slips, Burger King eliminated 27 menu items in one year. Refocusing on core products and a simpler menu ended a series of marketing missteps and was considered a key driver of the reversal of Burger King's fortunes, generating double-digit revenue growth internationally by 1997. Also during the mid-1990s, companies as diverse as Sunoco, Nabisco, and General Motors had begun reducing product variations in significant parts of their businesses, and in 1999 Unilever announced a five-year plan to slash its brand portfolio from 1,600 to 100.

Still, as P&G, IBM, Wal-Mart, and Burger King led the way on simplifying, most marketers continued to crank out an unprecedented number of new products, line extensions, and complex promotions. This is somewhat understandable in rapidly evolving technology categories where product cycles are short, obsolescence is quick, and many new brands are vying for market entry, but less understandable in established, more stable categories where sophisticated brand marketers have ruled. Yet Kraft introduced 38 new cheese products in 1997 alone.

It's easy to overemphasize product proliferation as the culprit, when in fact much of the stress issue relates to customer service at least as much as to products. While one company's customer care policies and selling tactics may not change a customer's life that much, many companies—one company at a time—can. *Telecosm* author George Gilder comments on the digital age's state of affairs, and the impending backlash:

> The entire economy is riddled with time-wasting routines and regimes that squander much of the time of the average customer. Suffice it to say that the concept of the customer's life span as a crucially scarce resource, indeed the most precious resource of the information economy, has not penetrated to many of the business and governmental institutions. . . . The customer who is well fed, sheltered, and capable of purchasing most of the material boons of life, the customer who grasps the possibilities of the new technologies of the speed of light, is no longer going to put up with standing in unnecessary lines, filling out gratuitous forms, (or) telling telemarketers whether he has had a nice day.[14]

This certainly pertains to after-sale service as well. As a member of United Airlines' Mileage Plus program, this author recently received an account statement in the mail that was accompanied by a 12-page newsletter, a fine-print insert about blackout dates, and no fewer than 13 separate special-offer promotional pieces from MCI, rental car companies, hotels, credit cards, and real estate services—each with their own special restrictions and instructions. I am a member of several frequent flier programs; what if I received such a formidable, mind-numbing package every month from each of them? In the whole life context of anyone busy enough to be a frequent flier, this "loyal customer" mailing made me feel worse—not better—about my relationship with the United brand.

A Stress-Relief Framework: Simplicity Marketing

It seems increasingly clear that simplifying customer decision making can help you survive the inevitable overchoice shakeout that will occur in materially rich but time-starved societies. But there are at least two good reasons why most marketers haven't been more responsive to the customer's plight. One is that, as long as there are shareholder expectations for revenue growth—which there most always will be—it seems antithetical to eliminate products and risk that competitors will be left to offer something that some customers may still be interested in buying. But the other reason is that reducing customer stress is a tough, complex job without much of a road map. There have been theoretical frameworks for years on how to strategically extend a product line, but how many road maps have you seen for customer stress reduction?

The remainder of this book provides that road map and dissects Simplicity Marketing as a framework for effective stress relief. Chapter 2 begins by offering fundamental concepts that help you assess the degree to which you're part of the problem or part of the solution, and lays the foundation for the specific Simplicity Marketing strategies that follow.

■ Summary

In this chapter we have brought into focus how more choices in the marketplace, against a backdrop of new technologies and rapid change, can cause a backlash of customer confusion and frustration. We looked into the daily lives of two intelligent, capable people and saw some of the challenges that overchoice can present to them as customers—and to you as marketers. We explored how the ever-increasing flow of required decisions in choosing and using products can create stress, even for products designed to make life easier. We discussed the aggregate impact of marketing across the many product categories and brands in any one customer's life, and why sensitivity to stress in a *whole life context* is increasingly important to any brand trying to sell or service that customer. Finally, we glimpsed power in the simplifying role of brands as anchors in the customer's chaotic life, and described how streamlining product lines can improve business performance while bringing more clarity to the customer's world.

Chapter 2

Becoming Part of the Solution

When a new technology rolls over you, you're either part of the steamroller or part of the road. 	—STEWART BRAND, *The Media Lab*, 1987

STEWART BRAND'S OBSERVATION was about technology but it could just as well have been about any new product category or tidal wave of product variations. If your brand is not part of the overchoice solution, it's part of the problem. If it's not reducing customer stress, it's probably creating it. And if your brand is creating stress, it's vulnerable to losing market share to more customer-empathetic competitors.

The more stressed your particular target market, the more vulnerable you are. In the face of change and the anxiety that waves of new choices bring, customers will be paying much more attention to which brands are helping them become part of the steamroller rather than part of the road. There is little gray area in between, partially explaining why by the late '90s an average of nearly 400 U.S. businesses were failing *every business day* in spite of a very strong economy.[1] With survival of the fittest, *fittest* may increasingly mean *simplest*.

■ Assessing Your Brand's Stress Quotient

How can you assess your brand's current situation in this black-and-white, hero-or-villain context of stress-producing versus stress-relieving? Beyond your own customer research designed to confront stress issues head-on, two fundamental concepts can serve as guideposts to assessing where your brand sits on the stress spectrum. The first is the concept of "replacement" versus "incremental"; the second is the concept of maximum choice versus *optimum* choice. Let's delve into both.

REPLACEMENT VERSUS INCREMENTAL

Just as brand positioning is not an optional activity (if you don't position your brand, your competitors will position it *for* you), neither will Simplicity Marketing be optional in the era of overchoice. Every product or service will fall into one of two mutually exclusive, zero-sum categories: *replacement* or *incremental*. Any product or service that doesn't *replace* something else for the customer or consolidate multiple solutions into a single solution is, by default, incremental. Introducing something as "new"—once a positive, automatic attention grabber—is less and less likely to be automatically perceived as a plus and more likely to be perceived as clutter (something *additional*) unless the product's positioning allows the customer to forget about or eliminate something *old*. There is precious little room in the customer's psyche to add things without taking something away. As with a personal computer, if you keep adding and saving files without ever purging old files from your hard drive, performance can suffer over time.

Consider "smart cards," which store various amounts of money as well as storing customer information that can be read/captured by marketers. Smart cards were heralded in the '80s and early '90s as the future of small-purchase financial transactions. Yet, as 2000 dawned, the value of using a smart card over cash was still lost on most consumers. Smart cards can't replace cash except in a limited circumstance, and therefore are a hard sell when perceived as something incremental to cash in the customer's whole life context.

Consider also consumer electronics. A new model or even a new generation of VCR ostensibly will *replace* an old model VCR (unless the customer is a first-time VCR buyer). But an incremental technology like MiniDisc audio CDs, introduced in 1992 with much fanfare from very credible brands like Sony and Sharp, still met great resistance (especially in the United States) in spite of marketers' hopes that it could replace audiocassettes—largely because many consumers saw it as an incremental product that didn't really replace anything. MiniDisc offered yet another way to access digital audio content, but this new, incremental piece of consumer entertainment hardware for audio playback also had a new, incremental software format incompatible with the old. As choices continue to proliferate, it is increasingly likely that incremental products will fail or, at best, erode their perpetrators' brand equity.

The true power of Simplicity Marketing, however, is in products that go beyond merely placement and actually reduce the number of products, brands, or decisions in a customer's life. Such reduction, or de-cluttering, may take various forms of consolidating, aggregating, or integrating multiple functions into a single product or service. De-cluttering strategies are discussed in detail in Part II of this book.

De-cluttering may occur at the product development stage—as a guide to streamlining product lines, features, and variations, as well as allocating more resources to those products and features that have stress-reduction potential. Or, it may occur in positioning strategy, branding, or even logo design.

In positioning strategy, some marketers will choose to directly leverage customer stress in their advertising tag lines that try to communicate a "brand soul" which is simplicity-sensitive. Honda was early to market with this approach, with "Honda. We Make It Simple." Gateway Computer did it more subtly, differentiating itself by using cows for its brand imagery in stark contrast to the whiz-bang, fast-moving high-tech glitz of the PC category. By the late '90s, we began seeing and hearing more advertising tag lines like "Life Simplified." for Dasani mineral water from Coca-Cola Co., "Simplifies your life." for Safeway.com, and "The Power to Simplify" for both Delphi Automotive Systems and ALLTEL Corporation.

Other marketers will de-clutter in branding, using stress-sensitive names to brand their products. Some will name products in ways that speak directly to stress or anxiety (Stressless Recliners, CareFree Sugarless Gum), while others will choose names that describe products or services in ways that imply simplicity (Onebox.com for integrated e-mail, voice mail, and fax in a single mailbox). Another de-cluttering approach to branding is reducing the number of sub-brands (Acura reversed a market share decline after replacing sub-brands like Legend and Vigor with simple model numbers attached to the Acura name). Still other brands will de-clutter their identities with logo design. A recent study published in the *Journal of Marketing*, in which cognitive response to 195 logos was analyzed, found both greater memorability and appeal of simple logos (like Nike's swoosh) than detailed ones (such as Green Giant and Land O' Lakes in packaged goods).[2] In the late '90s, logo redesigns for greater simplicity started becoming more commonplace, with cleaner, simpler designs introduced by brands ranging from Oldsmobile to Planter's Peanuts.

The more dimensions on which de-cluttering occurs, the more likely a brand's identity can represent simplification and reside in the hero compartment of the customer's mind. Unfortunately, even highly regarded marketers may end up in the villain compartment when they take their eyes off the simplicity ball. On the brand positioning front, in contrast to Honda, history may ultimately show that "Take Pictures. Further."—while very clever and memorable—may not have helped Kodak's brand identity in the mass market where, in the context of stress reduction, more people still may just want to take pictures simply than take them further.

And then there's Fresh Chef. When Campbell Soup introduced the Fresh Chef line of fresh salads and soups, which had a shelf life of one week, they thought customers would appreciate having an in-between alternative to fresh foods that needed to be used right away and canned or frozen foods with long storage life. But Fresh Chef was an incremental introduction to the food category, rather than a replacement, and the customer (as well as food retailers) resented the pressure represented by a new subcategory of packaged foods that needed to be consumed within a week—and resented the spoilage that occurred if the consumption deadline wasn't met. After this costly failure, Campbell pared back product lines to stay closer to its core competencies of canned soups and sauces, and reduced its average number of new product introductions by some 30 launches a year.[3]

Sometimes, entire new industries are successfully born because of their replacement value, though they usually will initially appear to be incremental until people adjust to them, use them, and discard the old. Certainly that is what cars did to the horse and buggy almost a century before the stresses of the digital age, not just because of comfort and excitement but also because of saving time. Fast forward to today, when even the veins of national infrastructures are being replaced as Internet-based networks carrying data and voice transmissions are gradually replacing century-old public switched telephone networks. Certainly one reason that the Internet mainstreamed so quickly during the late '90s is that its this-instead-of-that value was inherently visible to both consumers and information technology managers alike.

Still, when considering the customer's whole life context, remember that the overlap of old and new—during the period that they coexist— produces additional stress. Cars were at the same time simplifiers and complicators: they saved time, enhanced freedom and, on Main Street, reduced the amount of horse dung that had to be constantly dodged and cleaned up. But they also simultaneously introduced new challenges, including the automobile purchase decision, learning to drive, gasoline replenishment, maintenance and repair, and how to insure against the risk of accidents. The transition was awkward. For most of the years when cars and horses coexisted on Main Street, roads were not optimized for either while the infrastructure was in prolonged transition to pavement and to the signage and signals required to safely accommodate a growing number of cars.

Similarly, coexistence of IP (Internet Protocol) networks and the established services of the public switched network has created temporary, but considerable, duplication and complexity that increases whole-life-context customer stress. Most believe, however, that this is a replacement worth enduring, because Internet technology's potential to simplify things over time is so great. As bandwidth replaces switching, it enables product development for whole new generations of simplifiers. This, of course, assumes that marketers will use bandwidth to simplify rather than complicate, which is exactly what customer-empathetic marketers will do.

So, when introducing a new product or line extension, or repositioning your brand, ask yourself to what degree your strategy is—from the customer's perspective—replacement or incremental. If replacement, which hopefully it will be both for your sake and the customer's, then ask what can be done to minimize the overlap between what you're selling and what it's replacing. The goal is to make the replacement as clean and swift as possible, with a minimum of duplication and temporary additional complexity and adjustment. You'll find many examples among the specific replacement strategies covered in Part II (Chapters 4–7).

The replacement mentality becomes an ongoing way of thinking about your entire marketing mix. Customers will thank you for it.

MAXIMUM CHOICE VERSUS OPTIMUM CHOICE

The next question is whether you are offering customers maximum choice, or *optimum* choice. The persistent goal of maximum choice has fueled the proliferation of products and line extensions since the 1940s. World War II scarcities deprived people of choice, so the postwar era brought with it a reactionary swing to more-is-better excess. As layer upon layer of multiple categories have since clogged the customer's brain, even within individual categories we find more frequent evidence that less is more—whether in the number of choices actually available or in the positioning and packaging of those choices. Each category has an optimum level of choice within the customer's whole life context beyond which there are diminishing returns. With the buildup of incremental categories, the customer's maximum capacity for choice within individual categories is diminished.

In 1992, CEOs of large cable TV and telephone companies waxed eloquently about the "500-channel information superhighway" that so-called full-service broadband networks would soon deliver. But by the time the Web had trumped interactive television, it was clear that 500 channels were not exactly what consumers wanted. For more and more customers in the Simplicity Marketing era, 500 channels was an anxiety-producing, incremental, maximum-choice positioning. The real Holy Grail was in a different perspective on the same offer: *one* personal megachannel that has only what the consumer wants to see, and when he or she wants to see it. *Optimum* choice, rather than maximum choice.

In that subtle difference of orientation lies the appeal of mass customization. By making maximum choice and flexibility look like optimum choice, the choice appears deceptively simple. This is not to say that ordering a customized touring bicycle doesn't involve a number of careful decisions. But it's still far less overwhelming (and yet more likely to produce a satisfying purchase and postpurchase experience) than walking into a large specialty bike shop and seeing 40 models from seven different brands—and still not finding one that really feels like it was made for your particular body.

Let's say that you take daily nutritional supplements and, for a variety of reasons, need to take individual pills (rather than a single multivitamin) to get the desired dosage of each vitamin and mineral. The shelves of nutritional supplement specialty stores are lined with several different brands of each substance, multiplied by different sizes and multiplied again by different forms (tablets, capsules, gelcaps, powder, etc.) and sometimes yet again by additives (vitamin C plus rose hips). This maximum-choice environment is at once both overwhelming and comforting: overwhelming because of overchoice in a relatively high-risk category (health), and comforting in the flexibility and belief that, if you work hard enough, you can find the right combination of separate pills to satisfy your individual needs. But the result is still a need to take six different pills a day, and replenish six different products each time you run out (and you will run out of each at different times, since pill-count bottle sizes are not uniform). Recognizing that the price for maximum choice is often paid as much in time as at the cash register, Acumin Corporation was founded in 1996 as a mass customizer of nutritional supplements. Customers decide how much of each vitamin or mineral they want and in what form; Acumin manufactures each unique formula in a single pill and ships the order directly to each customer. Delivering optimum choice, like one customized megachannel of TV, spelled rapid success for Acumin.

So what is known about the customer's limits on dealing with choice? Plenty, and we've known it for a long time. The concepts of *bounded rationality* and *satisficing* were introduced by Dr. Herbert Simon more than 50 years ago in his classic management treatise, *Administrative Behavior*.[4] Simon was talking about managers making decisions, but could just as easily have been talking about consumers (managers are people, too) when he pointed out that managers cannot contend with all the factors influencing a decision because the information flow is too great. He suggested bounded rationality as a practical approach: delimiting reality by bounding it into comprehensible bundles. He contended that because we can't know the optimal solution to a problem with perfect precision, we should choose a solution that satisfices, or reaches a certain standard of acceptability. (As Simon pointed out, we satisfice in business every day with concepts such as *reasonable* profit, *fair* price, and even *share* of market—because we know it's unrealistic to maximize any of these variables to the ultimate degree. Consumers, likewise, must make similar compromises in decision making just to get through the process.) As life stress increasingly causes bounded rationality to become an even more predominant dynamic for customers, optimum choice may mean fewer rather than more—and may ultimately mean single, customized solutions that balance choices and limits.

We have also learned much about the manageable limits of choice from the marketing research technique known as conjoint analysis. Sometimes referred to as trade-off analysis, conjoint analysis is used to quantify customers' priorities when evaluating alternative product features. For example, in shopping for an exercise treadmill, one consumer may be willing to trade off a built-in heart rate monitor for a quieter motor; another may be willing to trade off a longer-term warranty to get the heart-rate monitor; still another is willing to trade off a lower price and pay more to get the longer-term warranty. What's instructive about the thousands of conjoint analyses that have been conducted since the technique was commercially deployed around 1970 is this: To provide reliably predictive results, trade-offs have been most effectively measured by exposing the consumer to only two product features at a time. This is because consumers are not very capable of evaluating multiple features independently of each other, but *are* capable of making a choice between one or the other when confronted with a single pair of features. This is why "pairwise" trade-off analysis is now so commonly used. If only real life was so simple!

In the treadmill example, a real-world purchase decision may involve trading off among dozens of factors to stay within a budget, ranging from those mentioned above to multiple design aspects of the treadmill's running/walking surface, the digital display panel (that shows speed, elapsed time, etc.), or whether or not the treadmill can be folded up for storage. If the consumer decides to trade off budget (that is, to spend more), fewer features will have to be traded off—so price can exponentially compound the complexity of the decision process for products with lots of different features, especially if the customer's commitment to staying within a budget is wavering. Yet if consumers are asked to rank their preference for all of these treadmill features, or their willingness to trade off one for another, they could not deal with the entire list at once. They instead trade off within pairs, two features at a time.

According to Dr. William Deaton of ConStat, Inc., a marketing research firm, "Given what we've learned from conjoint [analysis] over the years, we see the extreme degree to which customers must find shortcuts through purchase analysis in order to survive the decision. Seeing the difficulty that customers have in choosing among even three features instead of two is a sobering reminder of how complex even everyday purchase decisions can be, except for highly commoditized products which are so much alike that price and brand identities are the only real differentiators."[5] In the whole life context of many purchases multiplied by many categories, this is all the more so. As conjoint analysis has taught us, maximum choice is almost never *optimum* choice for the human brain.

In the Simplicity Marketing era, smart marketers will be using techniques like conjoint analysis not just to determine trade-offs within a product feature set but also to fine-tune the threshold of optimum choice for an entire product category. For example, Toyota used trade-off research to significantly limit the number of options and configurations offered on its first full-size pickup truck, the Toyota Tundra. When launched for model year 2000, the Tundra—offering far fewer options than competitors' trucks—was so enthusiastically received for cutting through the category's buying complexities that it recorded the fastest sales start of any new product in Toyota's history.[6]

Likewise, Marriott made extensive use of trade-off analysis to simplify hospitality options. The result was the creation of its Marriott Fairfield properties to appeal to the significant segment of travelers who want the Marriott brand at an affordable price, but who don't choose hotels based on the availability of exercise mini-gyms, complete business services, or extended-hours room service. As with both Toyota and Marriott, the simplification value possessed by strong brands will allow the marketers behind such brands to be more confident in *limiting* choice. This can be another shareholder value creation strategy, since limiting choice can significantly reduce operating costs (see Chapter 10, especially the Procter & Gamble case).

Finally, as challenging as it is for customers to sort out multiple features within a single product, it is challenging in different ways to evaluate one competing product versus another in categories where similar "me-too" products proliferate. The irony of this was not lost on the former director of the MIT Laboratory of Computer Science, Edward Fredkin, who observed, "The more equally attractive two alternatives seem, the harder it can be to choose between them—*no matter that, to the same degree, the choice can only matter less.*"[7] (Italics added.) Customer tolerance for undifferentiated products will continue to shrink as tolerance for clutter shrinks, placing more burden than ever on products to have a readily perceived reason for being—and on brands to have uniquely relevant brand identities.

■ Follow the Stress: A Common Denominator for Resonating with Customers

On closer inspection, seemingly disparate phenomena such as the creation of the European Money Union, the overhaul of Procter & Gamble's product management organization, the rise of personal finance software, and the revenue growth of systems integration services in information technology markets, all have a common thread—the demand for simplicity. Since the customer's need to reduce stress is driving that demand, acknowledging this tells us where to look for marketing opportunities in the digital age: *Follow the stress.*

The truly stress-sensitive marketer will continually conduct a "stress scan" of the market. The stress scan addresses three key aspects of following the stress: (1) locating stress pockets in both the existing and prospective customer bases, (2) identifying the drivers of stress that create those pockets, and (3) identifying customers' own strategies for coping with stress (in order to tap into those strategies). These are each discussed below.

DEMOGRAPHICS, PSYCHOGRAPHICS, FIRMOGRAPHICS—WHAT ABOUT STRESSOGRAPHICS?

Markets are routinely segmented by identifying and profiling groups of customers that have certain characteristics or affinities in common. Traditionally, most market segmentation attention has been focused on demographics (such as age, gender, income, occupation, family life cycle, geographic location), firmographics (such as business size, industry classification, job title of purchase decision makers and influencers, country/region), psychographics (attitudes, opinions, perceptions, beliefs), and product usage (such as heavy, medium, or light usage of the product category). The popularity of these approaches has been largely based on the fact that certain of these characteristics have repeatedly shown strong correlation with preference for a particular product type or brand. But as customer stress and the simplicity imperative continue to grow in parallel importance, stress levels and stress types become more and more predictive of buying preferences. We will see a growing number of cases in which stress—encompassing both the *level* and *nature* of stress—eclipses traditional variables in determining purchase behavior and brand relationships.

Technically, attitudes and beliefs about stress and simplicity might fall under the psychographics umbrella. But for the immediate future, they risk getting lost there. Until managing stress becomes an integral day-to-day part of what marketers do, stress is sufficiently complex and poorly understood that it requires its own area of focus. We call it *stressographics*— if perhaps only until the day comes when it's such an obvious part of psychographics to all sophisticated marketers that it can be subsumed by the psychographics moniker.

The simplicity-astute stress scan will routinely measure both the level and nature of stress across the market, looking for hot spots where stress levels are most pronounced and where the nature of the stress is such that the marketer's product or brand can be made relevant to stress relief. This will be especially beneficial for marketers in higher-anxiety categories. Stressographics are likely to yield greater dividends for, say, a pharmaceutical company or mainframe computer manufacturer than for a marketer of impulse items.

IDENTIFYING DRIVERS OF STRESS

Locating stress pockets in the marketplace requires measuring and tracking customers' "drivers of stress" (*stressors*, in psychology parlance), where the customer has articulated the sources of stress and how stress is impacting her life or business. This is best done on an open-ended basis; that is, asking customers in qualitative research to talk freely about stress and its causes and then ultimately focusing that discussion on the specific product category of interest (but *not* before understanding in general what the customer's stress is like and where it's coming from in her whole life context). After all, stress is a universal experience that cuts across all cultures, ages, and even species, but what actually evokes anxiety varies greatly by cultural and demographic context—and each individual experiences stress differently.

Once the stress of any particular market segment is better understood through qualitative research, quantitative research can be used to track the presence and relative importance of these stress drivers in the context of specific purchase decisions and brand perceptions. Both qualitative and quantitative research can also help establish linkages between the customer's feelings of discomfort and behavioral changes. The old adage about how no information technology manager ever got fired for buying IBM (referring to IBM's reputation as the reliable, safe choice) also implied that it was incumbent upon IBM's competitors to understand the nature of customer discomfort produced by buying a different brand. With that understanding, the competitor could better show how they would help the customer through whatever behavior modification would be required in the wake of a non-IBM purchase decision.

Short of doing custom research, some of the more obvious drivers of stress can often be deduced even from a basic demographic perspective. For example, common sense tells us (as well as many research studies) that, all other things being equal, in most cases stress in the consumer marketplace is likely to be higher in households with children (especially young children) than in those without.[8] Among two-parent households with children, stress is likely to be higher when both parents work full time. Stress will also be higher in households with dire money issues or where significant illness or injury is present. And stress will certainly be higher among households that are surviving recent life-change events, including divorce or separation, moving, or a job change.

There are also direct links between age, gender, and stress. According to Yankelovich Partners' *Monitor* research cited in Chapter 1, the two most stressed groups of Americans are Baby Boomers (and especially working mothers in this group), and Generation Xers (born between the mid-'60s and mid-'70s).[9] Ostensibly, the Simplicity Marketer might look at the incidence of these groups within any otherwise-defined market segment as an indicator of how ripe the segment may be for stress-reducing solutions—or how insistent they may be that new products be replacements rather than incremental. But in scanning the market for stress, the *nature* of the stress is at least as important as the amount.

For example, the nature of stress differs markedly between Baby Boomers and Generation X. Baby Boomers' stress is principally driven by complexity in their daily lives while Gen Xers' stress is driven by the personal challenges they face. Boomers tend to work and play aggressively, be very competitive, and are the most likely to be dual-career housholds with children (or single-parent households after separation or divorce). With above-average disposable income and above-average appetites for both status and technology, their lives can be a complex swirl of multiple credit cards and the latest in electronics, computers, and cell phones, overlaid with a steady stream of higher-stakes purchasing such as home buying, remodeling, or refinancing, and thinking about their next car purchase or lease while evaluating trade-offs for an expensive overseas vacation. So anything that reduces complexity has a running start as a product that can be perceived as highly relevant by this group.

Not necessarily so for Generation X consumers. Consider their primary sources of stress: ongoing anxiety about a happy, meaningful future, their career, or the opportunity to become at least comfortably middle class on their own—while many fend off hopelessness about any or all of these things. Entire books have been devoted just to the stress of Gen X customers, many of whom haven't been able to find good jobs after college, who worry that Social Security will vanish before they retire, and who keep hearing that they are part of the first generation since the industrial revolution to earn less money than their parents.[10] Complexity is not nearly as much the core stress issue as for Baby Boomers, even though Gen X stress may be as great or greater both in intensity and pervasiveness. So products and brands will certainly be perceived differently in the different whole life contexts of these two groups, as largely defined by the nature of their stresses.

Such differences carry through across other stressed market segments. For Generation Y consumers, primary sources of stress may be the disproportionate weight of teen peer pressure, alienation from mainstream society, or the struggle to meet parental expectations. The primary source of working mother stress is the conflicting expectations between going out and making money and still being the nurturer in the family. According to *Monitor*, 74% of all men and 81% of all women believe women have as much responsibility to support a family as men, yet even higher percentages of both genders believe women are still supposed to be the main nurturers. Working mother stress is escalated by the ongoing effort to balance these dual roles and effectively fulfill both. So, in households where the responsibility for getting a good-tasting but nutritionally balanced meal on the table falls to the working mother, any product that helps deliver that meal more easily is a highly relevant stress-reducer. For this customer, such a product may be more relevant to core stress issues than, say, an easier-to-understand telephone bill—while the converse may be true for a Baby Boomer who is not a working mother.

In the business marketplace, stressographics might include job security concerns (or disproportionate presence in the customer base of companies that are downsizing), the pace of technological change and other changes in the customer's specific industry, the length (or compression) of product development cycles and accompanying time-to-market pressure, the level of shareholder pressure on short-term business results, or pending mergers or acquisitions. Stress levels and the nature of stress may also differ geographically because of the concentration of stress-intense industries in certain areas, or because of how evolved a particular economy may be. If you're selling business services in Silicon Valley, Simplicity Marketing and stress reduction strategies are obviously likely to be more important and more effective than if you're selling agricultural equipment in rural areas (which is not to say that agriculture can't be stressful and won't hold Simplicity Marketing potential, but rather speaks to the wisdom of adding the stress dimension to how you compare vertical markets or geographic regions in business-to-business targeting). Similarly, in global perspective, just as in comparing urban with rural stress, the differing nature of stress in First- and Second-World countries (not to mention Third) will define Simplicity Marketing opportunities.

Deftly used, stressographics can provide real competitive advantage in accurately assessing market opportunity, segmenting, and targeting markets in the digital age. Once targeted, an even greater marketing tailwind can be generated by tapping into the customer's own ways of dealing with stress.

TAPPING THE CUSTOMER'S OWN STRESS REDUCTION STRATEGIES

Every customer has personal strategies for coping with and reducing stress, whether premeditated or haphazardly done on the fly. It's part of the survival instinct, with both biological and mental dimensions. By keenly observing these strategies among your customers, you can position your products and brand to be enablers rather than obstacles in the customer's private war against stress, time, and bewilderment.

Imbedded in the following quote from *Monitor's* findings is a useful starting point for how to do this in marketing: "Whether consumers are busy dodging it or dealing with it, there's no question that stress drives most lifestyle choices, day in and day out."[11] As "dodging or dealing with it" suggests, all the ways customers cope with stress fall into one of two categories: *tackling* stress or *escaping* stress. This provides a simple construct for the marketing purposes of empathizing with customers and tapping into customers' methods of coping, both in consumer and business marketing.

Tackling rather than escaping stress corresponds to what psychological researchers often refer to as *problem-focused* instead of *emotion-focused* coping strategies.[12] In problem-focused coping, the customer tackles stress proactively in an effort to gain control. This may be done by immediately confronting the source of stress head-on, by making a plan to deal with the stress and following it, or by seeking support from someone who can influence the source of stress. In emotion-focused coping, the customer does not confront the stress but rather tries to avoid it. Among the variety of ways this may be done are by trying to distance from it (pretend it never happened), by keeping feelings in instead of acknowledging them (Freud established that repressing anxiety-producing thoughts or memories is a means of coping), or by escapism (just wishing the source of stress would go away, which may lead to behaviors including smoking, drinking, or drugs if the stress is significant enough). Though most people handle stress through some combination of problem-focused and emotion-focused coping, in many people one or the other approach is dominant as a personality trait.

How do *your* customers cope with stress? Coping styles may provide a basis for market segmentation in the digital age. For example, target markets can be divided into stress-tackling or stress-escaping subsegments. Each of these subsegments may have greater propensity to engage in certain antistress behaviors that you as a marketer can help enable with products or promotions. (If you have trouble identifying Tacklers versus Escapers, an indirect route is to identify optimists and people who agree with a statement such as, "I have a lot of control over my life"—since both of these traits characterize Tacklers. Pessimists and people who don't believe they have control over their lives are more likely to be Escapers. (You can learn more about coping styles in *Stress Management* by Stephen Auerbach and Sandra Gramling, where much of the above material on coping is covered in greater detail and with more attention to clinical accuracy than we are qualified to provide.)[13]

Here is an example of marketing implications: Two closely related stress-*tackling* behaviors are clearing clutter and getting organized. Among the most popular stress-*escaping* behaviors, besides sleep, are watching TV and listening to music. The retail chain Hold Everything, which sells personal storage and organization solutions, might find it more effective to segment and target Tacklers than to segment and target based on demographics alone. Conversely, Windham Hill Records, purveyor of relaxing New Age instrumental music, might find it effective to target Escapers beyond the demographic targeting it has already done so well. Or, a brand that has little obvious direct connection with either of these coping styles may still temporarily borrow interest with targeted special promotions that use as incentive premiums, say, relaxing music CDs (or vanilla candles)—or, by contrast, Hold Everything coupons—depending on whether the target audience is more likely to be comprised of Tacklers or Escapers.

Such stress sensitivity provides a point of entry into Simplicity Marketing. The stress scan can point the way, giving Simplicity Marketers a competitive advantage in following the stress down the path to stronger brand relationships. How stressographics can be incorporated into the brand planning process is covered in Chapter 9.

■ Caveat: Two Simplicity Traps

Finally, before we introduce the core Simplicity Marketing strategies in subsequent chapters, a word of caution about two traps on the road to becoming part of the stress solution: market economics, and knowing when the cure is worse than the disease.

MARKET ECONOMICS AND SIMPLICITY PRICING

Market economics can trip up simplicity strategies because even simplicity must be reasonably priced. Sounds obvious. But with the hue and cry for simplicity, it's easy for marketers to get swept up in the fervor when establishing pricing—and wind up with simplicity that customers love but is just plain too expensive.

Apple Computer's initial success was based on making wonderfully simple-to-use computers relative to the alternatives available. But Apple's subsequent decline and fall (prior to its 1999 resurgence) was largely due to pricing those machines significantly higher than PC alternatives. Furthermore, Apple long refused to license its operating system to other manufacturers who could make Apple clones that would have put more affordable Apple-powered machines into the market. So the only alternative to paying the Apple premium was buying a PC that was more complicated to use. Only a small fraction of the market was willing to pay that premium, especially as the price spread grew while PC prices came down faster than Macintoshes' through the '90s.

Another market economics trap is not recognizing that it is harder to cost-justify simplicity when there is already a large, entrenched customer base for a more complex alternative. This means that even competitive pricing may not be enough to sell simplicity if the cost of switching—that is, the perceived cost of abandoning the currently used product—is perceived to be too high.

Consider the QWERTY keyboard—the standard typing keyboard layout that has graced typewriters since their commercialization and is universally found today on Roman-alphabet PCs. In debating the behavior of free markets, some economists and historians have found evidence that an alternative keyboard layout known as the Dvorak (for its inventor), which placed frequently used pairs of letters in a single row, is much simpler to use than the QWERTY. (The QWERTY keyboard was purportedly designed to *increase* complexity and *slow down* typists of more than a century ago, when manual typewriters were still very prone to jamming if keyed too rapidly.)[14] But even though the Dvorak is arguably simpler in both concept and utility, most people have still never heard of it in the nearly 70 years that it has been around. When the Dvorak came along in the 1930s, there was simply too large an installed base of QWERTY keyboards for companies to be willing to spend the money to retrain its typists—even for a simpler, superior design. Recent anecdotes in the business press have disputed some aspects of this historical account (and Dvorak design superiority), but this keyboard conundrum is still a useful metaphor for reminding us that there will be cases where sunk costs in established complexity are significant enough to prevent the economic success of simplicity.[15]

Sometimes, when complexity is extremely entrenched, even significantly underpricing the competition isn't enough. It's likely that Dvorak keyboards could have been given away free and still not have gained a sustainable foothold in the market. The Linux computer operating system—which *was* given away free throughout the '90s—still took years to meaningfully transcend the world of hobbyists and even begin to make marginal inroads in business against the broadly entrenched alternative known as UNIX. Yet the technical community widely acknowledged that Linux was easier to install than UNIX and that it ran on a greater variety of hardware, while being just as reliable. It's true that Linux was not aggressively marketed during those years, especially relative to the marketing muscle of UNIX vendors (like Hewlett-Packard, Sun Microsystems, and IBM), and that software developers long resisted building applications for a platform with little market penetration. But Linux's slow adoption prior to 1999, in spite of giving away the product, was also because the customer's perceived cost of switching from UNIX was monumental in terms of its impact on training and internal systems.

In most situations, simplicity will likely continue to command higher premiums as long as chaos and confusion continue unabated in the marketplace. In becoming part of the stress solution, it is important to conservatively evaluate the degree of price elasticity that the level and nature of stress in your particular target market will drive in buying a replacement product. Likewise, if there is a more complex—but firmly and widely entrenched—alternative, the relationship between perceived switching costs and the demand for stress reduction will be a key input to successful pricing strategies.

WHEN THE CURE FOR COMPLEXITY IS WORSE THAN THE DISEASE

A final caveat is that the stress-reducing cure can be worse than the complexity disease, and that can spell failure for even the most useful of replacement products. Replacing anything—even with something much simpler—involves *change* in status quo, so each replacement is still a portal of adjustment that the customer must pass through. Since any adjustment can produce stress, even en route to simplification, even replacement products can act like incremental ones during the transitional period in which customers must adjust to their use.

As whole life contexts continue growing in complexity and stress, more demonstrable advantages may be required of a replacement product to get customers to be willing to experience the temporary disequilibrium of adjusting from old to new. When it replaced the horse and buggy, the automobile brought improvements so dramatic and obvious that people were able to overcome the initial complexities discussed earlier in this chapter. Also, the world was a simpler, less stressed place, so whole life context could be more accommodating to change. But today, in cases where those improvements are less obvious than with the automobile, the initial adjustment hurdle must be lower.

Consider "unified messaging," championed during the late 1990s as the salvation of beleaguered victims of the daily avalanche of messages via voice mail, e-mail, paging, and fax. Unified messaging promised to aggregate all of these messages into a single, integrated e-mail box, voice mailbox, or Web browser page, depending on customer preference. Companies large and small, from Lucent and Motorola to high-profile startups like JFAX, rushed to market with unified messaging solutions in the name of simplifying communications. But since customers spent much of the '90s finally getting used to e-mail, voice mail, cell phones, and paging, unified messaging on the heels of all that was just one more thing to get used to all over again. Besides, its ostensible simplicity was offset by the ways in which it compromised the functionality of each messaging component (for example, having to endure listening to a robotic voice reading back your e-mails and faxes, including punctuation). Yes, customers were indeed screaming for help in managing the message avalanche. But in the long view of how much change and complexity people endured in the '90s just to acclimate to core messaging technologies, is it any wonder that adoption of unified messaging got off to a slow start?

For most, the cure was still worse than the disease. But that also speaks to the importance of market timing for replacement products: Time is a great healer, and when customers have had more time to recover from assimilating new communications technologies, solutions that aggregate them will seem less formidable.

■ Summary

This chapter has discussed two essential concepts for developing a Simplicity Marketing mentality: *replacement versus incremental,* and *optimum choice versus maximum choice.* With those providing both a practical and philosophical foundation, we suggested identifying and following the stress in the marketplace via a stress scan of the potential customer base to determine the level and nature of stress that is present. We emphasized the importance of profiling customer stressographics—the causes of customers' stress, their attitudes toward stress, and the customer's coping behaviors—to understand how to ensure that your brand becomes part of the simplicity solution rather than part of the complexity problem. To leverage that understanding for competitive advantage, the next chapter lays down the basic strategies for building brand loyalty through Simplicity Marketing and the resulting customer stress relief.

Chapter 3

The 4 R's of Simplicity Marketing

'Tis a gift to be simple, 'tis a gift to be free.

—JOSEPH BRACKET, 18th Century Shaker Hymn

F OR A BOOK about simplicity, this is not a simple book. No apology for that: If it appears that the authors aren't practicing what we preach, it's worth a reminder that this book is more about *delivering* simplicity than receiving it. Delivering simplicity is a deceptively complex business in the extreme, much like the seemingly effortless grace of world-class ballet belies the extreme rigor and development effort underneath.

The relationship can be starkly inverse: The simpler you make it for customers, the more complex it can be for you—huge financial rewards notwithstanding. So at the risk of offering new ideas that by Chapter 2's definition appear to be incremental to what you already have to think about in marketing and brand equity management, we find great utility in simplifying the range of Simplicity Marketing strategies by reducing it to what we mnemonically call The 4 R's: *Replace, Repackage, Reposition,* and *Replenish.*

Why 4 R's? We already have the time-honored 4 P's in marketing; do we really need to make alphabet soup? Well, yes, and here's why. There are so many ways to build brand equity by delivering simplicity that this discipline begs to be broken apart into digestible, manageable components. Part II of this book—its strategic core—lays out the spectrum of possibilities in 10 specific strategies for reducing customer stress through Simplicity Marketing. But 10 is a lot to keep track of, and the 4 R's provide a higher-level way to organize and think about these strategies by sorting them into four buckets. These four strategy groups interact with each other in powerful ways and may be executed in combination or individually to build brand loyalty through stress relief. The 4 R's encompass complementary approaches to excavating the "simplification value" of a product, service, or even an entire company and incorporating that value into an effective positioning strategy. We define each of the 4 R's in this chapter, and then bring them to life with a dedicated chapter on each.

REPLACE

Replace is developing and positioning products as replacements either for multiple products, or for more complicated products or processes. To reduce customer stress, Replace may be as basic as substituting a simpler product for a more complex one, or may focus on consolidating the number of products or steps required by the customer to accomplish a particular task or goal.

One of the simplest, most obvious examples of Replace among more firmly established categories predates the digital age: conditioning shampoo. For consumers who use hair conditioner, conditioning shampoo provided the opportunity to simplify by substituting one product for two—and save time both in purchasing and using hair care products. Until Procter & Gamble introduced Pert Plus in 1987, shampoo and hair conditioner were two separate purchases, two separate packages, and sometimes even two separate brand choices for the same customer. Yet the two products are largely co-dependent and almost always used together. For that substantial (and growing) market segment that is more concerned with saving time and effort than with purist fashion and cosmetic sensibilities, conditioning shampoo has become a must-have staple and is now a $5 billion-plus category worldwide that accounts for more than 30% of the total shampoo market. (The original Pert, launched in 1979, was not a 2-in-1 product, and its market share had dwindled to less than 2% before Pert Plus saved the brand.)[1]

In supermarket produce departments, the phenomenal success of

packaged salad, or salad kits containing fresh, pre-washed, pre-cut let-
tuces and other salad vegetables, takes the Replace strategy a step further. Where conditioning shampoo replaced two products with one,
packaged salad replaced several different fresh produce purchases and
also eliminated the time-consuming processes for cleaning, chopping,
and mixing different salad ingredients. This product was such a time-
saver/stress-reducer that it truly revolutionized the fresh produce category in just a few short digital-age years, spawning all sorts of fresh
pre-cut fruits and vegetables in both stand-alone and combination convenience packaging. Time-starved consumers have sustained this
"value-added fresh produce" category well beyond 20% growth per year
through the late '90s, and it is expected to account for nearly $20 bil-
lion—nearly a quarter of the entire fresh produce market—by 2003 as
stress continues to mount.[2]

Replacing complex processes with simpler ones also spelled tremendous success for Intuit Corporation's Quicken personal finance software. Quicken initially set out to replace the complex process of paying
bills. Complex? On one hand, paying bills seems just a basic fact-of-life
process that almost everyone engages in at frequent intervals throughout adulthood. On the other hand, compared to lathering up and rinsing
out conditioning shampoo, consider all the steps, thinking, and effort
required to "simply" pay bills and support the process: manually writing
checks, addressing envelopes, making entries in a check register, calculating the impact of each check on the checking account balance, organizing payments by category for tax purposes and keeping track of
category totals, and monthly reconciliation of a bank statement. Quick-
en not only eliminated some of these steps (when a check is written on
the computer in Quicken, the check register entry is made automatically, the payee's address is already positioned for a window envelope, and
the tax-related organization and calculations are automatically done) but
also simplified the steps that it didn't eliminate. For example, Quicken
automates the writing of a check after recognizing the first few letters
typed in as the payee's name and substantially simplifies bank statement reconciliation.

With QuickBooks, TurboTax, Quicken.com services and beyond, Intuit continues finding ways to extend its brand into related new ways to
reduce customer stress. In a Simplicity Marketing context, it's no sur-

prise that customer gratitude for time and effort saved has fueled Intuit's ability to thrive for more than 15 years amidst the much-larger, deep-pocketed titans of the financial services and software industries.

The Replace strategy and its component parts are the focus of Chapter 4.

REPACKAGE

Repackage is bundling together a number of products or services that were previously only available from multiple sources (or as separate purchases from the same source), offering integrated solutions with a single point of contact for the customer. In some cases, Repackaging may principally focus on aggregating a multitude of related customer solutions in one place at price points that deliver obvious value; in other cases, the focus is on the integration required to make the individual products/solutions work better together. In either case, the result is value-added one-stop shopping. Done effectively, Repackaging will increase "share of customer" as well as attract new customers.

Before Simplicity Marketers such as Yahoo! used Repackaging strategies to build significant brand loyalty by aggregating information on the Web, Bloomberg L.P. built a highly successful digital-age business based on its core competencies in pulling together vast amounts of financial information for professional investors. From many different sources, the Bloomberg Service aggregates into a single source comprehensive worldwide securities information, news, research and analysis, and real-time, historical, and projected prices—and delivers it all to subscribers' desktop PCs, with the value-added replacement of PC keyboards with special keyboards that are color coded for fast, easy use of Bloomberg applications. With inventive Repackaging, Bloomberg has not only become the share-of-customer leader in professional financial information services, but has built a strong enough brand to successfully extend it beyond the professional market into television, radio, and the Internet.

In the airline industry, Star Alliance aggregates priority check-in service as well as baggage handling on behalf of eight major international airlines. Positioning itself as "The airline network for Earth," Star Alliance provides its Gold members with a number of services including guaranteed priority check-in for any airline in the network and with interairline baggage check-through as if flying a single airline. For the global traveler who might be flying United from Chicago to Frankfurt, Lufthansa from Frankfurt to Rio de Janiero, and Varig from Rio back to Chicago—but who may be a VIP frequent flier member of only one of the three airlines—the Star Alliance Gold package is a real stress reducer. (In fact, in one Star Alliance ad, the traveling customer was portrayed, if perhaps a bit tongue-in-cheek, as a stress authority who was conducting a seminar called "Living Well by Avoiding Stress.")

An example of effective Repackaging by value-added integration of complementary services is Union Bank of Switzerland's (UBS) Art Banking service launched in 1997. Recognizing that the same wealthy individuals who collect and invest in fine paintings, antiques, jewelry, and other high-value collectibles are also the most desirable customers for traditional core banking services, UBS bundled together its Art Advisory Service, Numismatic Service, and Private Banking services into one comprehensive, reliable, and discreet package with a single coordinating point of contact for the customer. Services beyond monetary included such specialties as art search and valuation, advice in sale and purchase of art and coins and precious metals, art transportation and insurance, art safekeeping, estate divisions, facilitation of coin auctions, and credit on auction consignments. Repackaging all these services as Art Banking created an extremely appealing hook for customers whose wealth management needs and love of art intersect but had formerly been dealt with separately through multiple sets of advisors.

Approaches to Repackaging are discussed in detail in Chapter 5.

REPOSITION

Reposition, in a Simplicity Marketing context, is directly positioning a brand on the promise of simplicity, or expanding a brand's positioning to reduce the number of brand relationships that a customer requires over time.

Major brands in both the consumer and business arenas found ways during the late '90s to successfully differentiate a basic brand promise by repositioning on simplicity—with products, services, and customer care to back up that promise. "Honda. We make it simple." crisply distilled into a relevant, credible, and differentiated brand position the Honda Motors reputation for straightforward dependability and user-friendly automotive design. Likewise, Hewlett-Packard epitomized Simplicity Marketing in a complex business technology category—large-scale computer storage—with the promise of "Stress-free storage. Guaranteed." Then, in 2000, Concert (the joint venture of British Telecom and AT&T) launched its "Simplicity^n" brand campaign with the tag line promising "Global communications simplified to the nth degree." These simplicity-centered, stress-reducing repositionings were especially compelling in the context of their audiences' stressographics (Chapter 2), since busy families with children were a high-priority target market for Honda, and stress-choked CIOs and information technology managers were a target for Hewlett-Packard and Concert.

Some companies have gone a step further by branding the *company* to position on simplicity. A New York firm that markets a PC package called Enchilada Grande, which includes a PC, color printer, four years of Internet access, and in-home setup, branded its company The Simple Solution and was soon being referred to as just Simple in technology trade press. Meanwhile, a dot-com startup that allows customers to use its Web site to compare telecommunications providers and rates calls itself simplexity.com.

Another approach to Repositioning is reducing the number of brand relationships that a customer requires over time. This may involve extending an upscale brand downmarket (for example, the less expensive Mani suits from high-end fashion designer Giorgio Armani) or finding ways that products already used by the customer can satisfy additional related or unrelated needs (Tums antacid as a calcium supplement). A related strategy is reducing the number of sub-brands within a family of products. Chapter 2 mentioned Acura's improved business performance after eliminating sub-brands in favor of consistently putting only its Acura name on all its cars, modified only by simple model numbers which is what competitors such as Infiniti, Saab, Lexus, and BMW had done all along. In the early 1990s, 3M's dental division went from more than 100 proprietary brand names to fewer than 20, significantly simplifying things for 3M's dentist customer base. For both Acura and 3M, brand streamlining also yielded more effective use of marketing dollars spread over fewer brands to support.

Methods of reducing the number of brand relationships are explored in Chapter 6.

REPLENISH

Replenish is providing a readily available continuous supply of zero-defect product or service to the existing customer base at acceptable price points, resulting in the customer only having to make the purchase decision once. This is especially relevant to staple goods, raw materials, and ongoing or recurrent services.

Back to toothpaste. For loyal users of Crest, part of the appeal is knowing that the 6-ounce tube of the tartar-control variety will be virtually always available on the shelf of any retailer of health and beauty aids, regardless of which retailer, what day of the week, or what location. Formulation, flavor, and quality will not vary from purchase to purchase. With replenishment, Crest eliminates the toothpaste decision and reduces it to simply a near-automatic action with no customer forethought or analysis other than having noticed the supply at home is running low. As with other leading brands that enjoy extreme brand loyalty in staple categories, Procter & Gamble's job as a Replenisher of Crest is to execute product management at the level of zero defects and zero out-of-stocks. Missing the mark on either not only disappoints a loyal customer but also compounds decision-making time and effort as the customer weighs and selects alternatives.

Chapter 7 explores specific approaches to Replenishment as stress relief, including the role of distribution and product quality control as well as the ultimate in continuous supply: delivering fully automatic replenishment.

Before asking you to roll up your sleeves for the four individual R chapters, it's only fair that we cover two topics to help you assess how— and to what degree—the 4 R's are relevant to your business: (1) the value chain as a context for applying any simplification strategy, and (2) clues to assessing whether you can successfully ignore the simplicity imperative without serious repercussions.

■ Simplifying the Customer's Value Chain

Building on the Chapter 2 concept of "replacement versus incremental," the 4 R's address effective ways to create both real and perceived value by differentiating brands and products in the contexts of customer stress and the mandate for simplicity. In *Competitive Advantage*, a bible of corporate strategy since its publication in 1985, Harvard University Professor Michael Porter provided a useful springboard for all this—the value chain. He defined the individual consumer's value chain as the sequence of activities performed by a consumer in which the product is directly or indirectly involved, and the firm's value chain as the collection of activities performed to design, produce, market, deliver, and support its products.[3] "The starting point for understanding what is valuable to the buyer is the buyer's value chain," proclaimed Porter, and we believe it's also the best starting point for identifying strategic opportunities to simplify customers' lives in the most valuable ways. If the 4 R's are the strategic colors of customer stress relief, then the value chain provides the relevant set of canvases.

When Porter laid out the two basic ways of enhancing the customer's value chain—*lowering the buyer's cost* or *raising performance*—he acknowledged *nonfinancial costs* such as those we have discussed as drivers of stress: "the [customer's] cost of a product includes not only financial costs but also time or convenience costs. The cost of time for a consumer reflects the opportunity cost of using [that time] elsewhere, as well as the implicit cost of frustration, annoyance or exertion."[4] As a route to simplicity strategies that are value chain specific, let's look separately at business and consumer value chains and examples of reducing stress within them.

RELIEVING STRESS IN THE *BUSINESS CUSTOMER'S* VALUE CHAIN

Most business customers' value chains are teeming with opportunities for stress reduction. Using Porter's model, we find nine places to look within each firm: the firm's five primary activity areas including inbound logistics, operations, outbound logistics, marketing and sales, and customer service, and the four basic support functions including the firm's infrastructure, human resources management, technology development, and procurement. (For readers less familiar with the value chain model, inbound logistics include materials receiving, handling, warehousing, inventory, etc., while outbound logistics include storage and distribution of finished goods, order processing, and delivery. You may wish to go straight to the source for further information; *Competitive Advantage* is fully referenced in the Endnotes of this chapter.) In all but very small businesses, each of these nine arenas will likely have a different individual manager as the supplier's target customer—each with his own drivers of stress and ways of perceiving time/cost trade-offs.

From a Simplicity Marketing perspective, we can ask whether there are opportunities to reduce customer stress in any of these nine arenas by applying the 4 R's to either lower cost (including nonfinancial cost such as time) or improve performance (real or perceived). This creates a matrix (Figure 3.1) that provides a basis for brainstorming and capturing an inventory of opportunities to de-stress customers in business-to-business marketing. It is essentially a way of using the value chain to extend the customer stress scan discussed in Chapter 2. By identifying the drivers of stress for the purchase decision makers and influencers in each activity, we can ask whether lowering the buyer's cost (again, including nonfinancial costs) or raising product performance is the most fertile area in which to offer simplification solutions. Once the high-opportunity areas are agreed upon—for example, saving the customer the nonfinancial cost of time in the activity of physically delivering products (outbound logistics), we can apply one or more of the 4 R's to derive a Simplicity Marketing solution that reduces customer stress.

Filling in the empty cells on this matrix is one way to get started. You may then want to refer back to it after Part II of the book, when you will be looking for places to apply the 4 R's for competitive advantage.

Consider how a seller of corporate computer networking solutions might use such a matrix when strategizing on how to sell to a large aircraft manufacturer like Boeing or Airbus. In these manufacturers' value chains, let's say for the sake of example that the top three drivers of stress are found in the areas of inbound logistics, operations, and human resource management. The stress drivers are different in each area: anxiety about quality parts availability and speed of delivery in inbound logistics; the pressure to control costs in operations (especially during periods when the company's stock is languishing); and in human resource management, coping with the demands of gyrating cycles of layoffs and hiring with the ebb and flow of orders for new planes.

Relative to the computer networking sale, our aircraft manufacturer is certainly interested in improving communication between employees with more efficient and cost-effective connectivity between its facilities.

Stress Reduction Opportunities in the Business Customer's Value Chain (Based on Porter's Value Chain Model)			
THE FIRM'S ACTIVITIES	**Drivers of Customer Stress**	**Stress-Related Opportunities to:**	
		Lower Buyer Cost (Including Non-financial Costs)	Raise Performance (Real or Perceived)
Firm's Primary Activities:			
Inbound Logistics			
Operations			
Outbound Logistics			
Marketing and Sales			
Service			
Firm's Support Activities:			
Infrastructure			
Human Resource Management			
Technology Development			
Procurement			

Figure 3.1

But there is less stress—and therefore less urgency—associated with the continuous improvement sought in that area. So our Simplicity Marketer of networking equipment decides to demonstrate specifically how its new generation of products reduces managers' stress in the three value chain arenas where stress runs highest. For example, the vendor shows how these products make it easier to establish and maintain extranets with parts suppliers for improved inbound logistics, how they reduce overhead by making more efficient use of the customer's existing data network to control costs for expanding that network, and how they help human resource managers save time—both by more efficient use of the Internet for recruiting and by use of the customer's intranet to administer employee benefits. In value chain context, the stress reduction value that strengthens the customer's perceptions of our networking equipment vendor's brand is based primarily on raising performance in the inbound logistics arena, lowering costs in operations, and both raising performance and lowering nonfinancial costs (saving time) in human resources management.

From a simplicity standpoint, Porter's original value chain concept—which preceded the World Wide Web by nearly a decade—must be revisited through the lens of how the Internet is impacting value chains across all industries. The Internet has already made the link between the firm's internal activities and its suppliers, channels, and customers a dramatically more important source of competitive advantage. In more and more industries, the ability to efficiently move actionable information has supplanted the importance of having a vertically integrated value chain. Yet even with that in mind, whether the firm is a state-of-the-art virtual corporation of partnerships with other companies or a traditional model of vertical integration, the value chain model still holds up today as solid ground for exploring business-to-business Simplicity Marketing opportunities and applying the 4 R's.

RELIEVING STRESS IN THE *CONSUMER'S* VALUE CHAIN

The value chain also provides a comprehensive window on stress reduction in consumer marketing. Though less structured and less well-defined than in business-to-business, each area of personal or household activity relevant to a particular consumer's use of a product or brand can be assessed for opportunities to simplify with the 4 R's. As in business-to-business marketing, lowering cost (*especially* nonfinancial) and raising real or perceived performance are the arenas in which to look for these opportunities. The most obvious examples are within the realm of the first R, Replace—when new, simpler-to-use generations of products replace old, harder-to-use ones.

During the '90s, many consumers replaced their hard-to-program VCRs with newer models incorporating the VCR Plus feature that allowed one-step programming. VCR Plus both reduced nonfinancial cost in saving time and effort and improved performance by reducing programming errors so that consumers were more likely to accurately record the intended program. The stress-reducing replacement cycle continues with the next generation of television recording and playback technology, as companies like TiVo and Replay Networks set out to replace the VCR with on-demand television viewing systems that capture and digitally store programming to disks for unprecedented flexibility in playback.

In understanding the consumer value chain for any particular product, it is important that what are considered relevant personal or household activities are not so narrowly scoped as to overlook the impact of whole life context (Chapter 1). As with any performance improvement in the value chain, success may ultimately depend on whether the overall net stress impact of including a product in one's life is experienced by the consumer as positive or negative. For example, in the case of those new on-demand television viewing systems, success in the mass market will largely depend on whether the performance benefits outweigh the complexity of learning and using the new technology in the whole life context of all the other technologies consumers contend with each day. In the value chain, *actual* performance will sometimes have less impact on *perceived* performance than will the stream of activities that the product is used in conjunction with.[5]

This is certainly not just a technology issue. For a highly stressed working mother, greater value may be perceived in an adequately performing laundry detergent with a highly concentrated formula than in a superior-performing detergent that is not concentrated. The concentrated formula means the product stretches further, lengthening its use cycle, and reducing the frequency of trips to the store for replenishment (while saving shelf space at home because of the concentrated product's greater density). For this customer, drivers of stress lie more in the activities around shopping for, storing, and monitoring the supply of the product than in actually using it.

In fact, most of the consumer's product-related stress often resides outside the act of product usage. So identifying opportunities to deliver stress relief depends on understanding what is valuable not only in using the product but also in prepurchase activities, the purchase process itself, and postpurchase customer care where applicable.

In the shopping and purchase process realms, years ago music retailer Tower Records reduced stress for a key segment of its customer base when it segregated its classical music departments in separate enclosed rooms (or, at some locations, even in separate buildings). This allowed classical music to be playing for ambience in the department without being drowned out by the rock or rap music playing elsewhere in the store. Perhaps more importantly, it also addressed the fact that some conservative older buyers of classical music were uncomfortable (i.e., stressed by) shopping while rubbing shoulders with what looked to them like menacingly dressed teens with pink hair and lots of pierced body parts. From a value chain perspective, this physical segregation (which increased Tower's fixed costs) resulted in conservative classical music aficionados perceiving improved performance of Tower as a comfortable, rewarding, and less stressful shopping environment.

Beyond brick-and-mortar retail, back in 1997 Internet retailer Amazon.com reduced consumers' nonfinancial costs in the purchase process itself by introducing a feature called 1-Click℠ ordering. At the time, this was a pioneering way to allow repeat customers to order merchandise with a single mouse-click instead of the usual multistep order entry process of filling out an electronic form. This lowered the consumer's nonfinancial cost of purchasing by obviously saving time, and also enhanced Amazon.com brand perceptions on the important service attribute of "easy to do business with." As a Simplicity Marketing strategy, 1-Click ordering became a cornerstone of Amazon.com's exemplary execution of the second R, the Repackage strategy (for a more detailed account of Amazon.com's Simplicity Marketing success, see Chapter 9).

In the postsale customer care arena, this author believes that Pitney Bowes stepped in a marketing pothole in the late '90s when it replaced its home office customers' mechanical postage meters with an "improved" digital Model E700 meter (part of what was called the Personal Post Office system). The simplification value of this meter, which could refill postage by phone instead of having to be carted back and forth to the post office, was largely offset by the meter's actual performance; it was arguably slower and more difficult to use than the old meters. But the Model E700's postsale customer care issues tipped the scale further in the direction of creating more stress than it reduced, as refill ink cartridges dried out relatively quickly even if very little postage was used (the old meter inkpads lasted for hundreds of impressions no matter how many months the low-volume customer took to use them up). Outside of whole life context, perhaps customers could have dealt with the time and expense of frequently reordering and installing replacement cartridges for the "improved" meter if it were the only machine in their offices. But these same customers were already ordering, paying for, and hassling with replacing cartridges in their computer printers and fax machines. So while a fax or printer cartridge replacement might at first appear irrelevant in looking at the buyer's value chain for a postage meter, it is certainly part of the customer's stream of activities that influences postage meter brand perceptions after the sale. Such a Simplicity Marketing detail may well determine whether the brand is a stress hero or stress villain.

A COMPETITIVE CONTEXT FOR THE 4 R'S

Before we leave Michael Porter, there is one last point from *Competitive Advantage* that helps illuminate where Simplicity Marketing fits in the overall dynamics of competition. "The rules of competition are embodied in five competitive forces: the entry of new competitors, *the threat of substitutes*, the bargaining power of buyers, the bargaining power of suppliers, and the rivalry among the existing competitors."[6] (Italics added.) The 4 R's are about making substitutions in the buyer's value chain, whether a business or a consumer. These strategies and the 10 component substrategies covered in the next four chapters are alternative approaches to substituting simplicity for complexity. For market leaders everywhere defending market share, the threat of substitutes increasingly means the threat of simplicity and customer stress relief at the hands of a competitor.

■ The 4 R's Imperative: Are You Exempt?

So, how universal is the Simplicity Marketing imperative? Isn't there *some* insulation from having to deal with the 4 R's and the "replacement versus incremental" conundrum?

If you're looking for an escape route, these next couple of pages are the last freeway exit before the bridge. There are a select few companies that can probably ignore all this and still survive just fine, but *only* a select few. How do you know if you're one of them?

Your risk of losing customers (or failing to acquire new ones) due to complexity and stress may be mitigated by: (1) sources of sustainable competitive advantage that are protected from emulation, (2) low-price leadership, or (3) targeting less-developed market economies.

PROTECTION FROM EMULATION

You may get away with all sorts of transgressions—including being slower than your competition in responding to customers' cries for simplicity—if your primary source of competitive advantage comes from formidable barriers to entry such as patent protection, regulated concentration of power, entrenched distribution supremacy, or long-term ownership of a highly specialized niche. Well before the digital age, Polaroid's patent on instant photography allowed it to very effectively sell a relatively complex product that added incremental do-it-yourself steps: waiting for a photograph to come out of the camera, waiting at least another minute for the image to appear, and then having to coat the photo with a foul-smelling liquid to protect it from smudging. Few customers complained, as no competitor could launch a similar product with equal or better results and less cumbersome requirements without infringing on Polaroid's patents.

An industry's regulatory environment can provide similar protection. Until broken apart by the federal government in 1984, AT&T enjoyed the regulated monopoly power that exempted it from catering to customers the way customers will be catered to as a result of digital-age deregulation of telecom services. Before there were alternative long distance carriers available to customers without the complexity requirement of dialing a bunch of extra digits to bypass the AT&T service, there was no significant competitive pressure on AT&T to offer even the most basic of simplifiers, such as easier-to-understand bills.

Protection may also come from distribution supremacy. The recent federal antitrust suit against Microsoft was triggered in part by the distribution supremacy of the Windows operating system, which achieved a 90+% penetration of desktop computers worldwide by being preinstalled in every major brand of PC—in spite of being more complex to use than alternatives such as Apple's Macintosh operating system. In the snack chips category, it is arguably easier for Frito-Lay than for Procter & Gamble's Pringles to get retailer support for more complex promotions, because Frito-Lay has the distribution advantage of "store-door" delivering its products directly to supermarkets rather than passing them through the retailer's distribution center warehouse. Even with a greater variety of snack products on the shelf (another result of its distribution supremacy), Frito-Lay's superior control of shelf space and SKU stocking can provide superior synchronization of promotional logistics. This enables more complexity without necessarily creating an incremental burden on the retailer.

Finally, some specialized niches have become so synonymous with one dominant brand that complexity is forgiven by the customer. Rolls-Royce has long epitomized the luxury car, and customers have been willing to not only pay the premium for that luxury but also to accommodate above-average complexities in maintenance and in finding conveniently located authorized repair facilities.

LOW-PRICE LEADERSHIP

Simplicity has a cost, and lack of simplicity can raise expectations for savings. Millions of grocery shoppers routinely sacrifice packaging conveniences to save money on private label products or generics for which the sellers have reduced the packaging costs and passed on savings to the customer.

Though this chapter has said more about reducing nonfinancial costs than dollar costs in the customer's value chain, certainly stress reduction may also come in the form of saving money. Simplicity may not be so critical for brands that can occupy and defend the low-cost producer position in any category. Southwest Airlines mastered low-cost production of quality air transportation, and for years turned in superior business performance in spite of the customer inconveniences of "open seating" (no preassigned seats).

If the price is right, it may even prove irrelevant that a particular new product is incremental. Beanie Babies were incremental in that they were not really replacements for larger-size stuffed animals as much as a new category of collectibles within the toy realm. But at the retail price of as little as $5, parents showed little resistance to picking up more Beanies month after month even when dozens of them might already be cluttering up their homes.

At the extreme, FreePC.com gave away computers in exchange for customers' willingness to supply detailed personal profiling information for advertising targeting purposes, and for their willingness to have their computer desktops continuously cluttered with advertising.

Simplicity did not enter into this for the customer (other than possibly saving the aggravation of shopping for a computer for those relatively few FreePC.com takers that would have actually paid to buy one).

TARGETING LESS-DEVELOPED MARKET ECONOMIES

Once upon a time in America, overchoice wasn't a big issue. Of course, there are still places like that today—they're just fewer and farther between. But if you're a company selling to less-developed economies, or even to rural customers in developed ones, simplicity and the 4 R's may recede into the background.

When Philips sells an industrial floodlamp in highly developed countries, it best be a long-life bulb that keeps customers off the ladder or the hydraulic lift to replace it for as long a time period as possible; this is not such a big deal in Third World countries where time isn't such a scarce commodity, labor isn't so expensive, or where, in some cases, it hasn't been long since it was considered a luxury just to have the electricity to power that floodlamp. Likewise, selling local telephone service in First World countries means providing value-added features that simplify (Call Waiting, Repeat Dialing, etc.) or reduce stress (Caller ID); in Third World countries just cobbling together first-generation telephone networks, it may simply mean providing a marginally reliable dial tone.

■ Simplicity Marketing for the Rest of Us

If, like the majority of First World businesses, your business is not significantly defined by any of the above situations, welcome to Simplicity Marketing for the rest of us. As we forge ahead together into the 4 R's, Figure 3.2 depicts an overview chart that serves as a guide to specific strategy components—or substrategies—within each R. All are explained in detail in Chapters 4 through 7, which sequentially focus on the possibilities within *Replace, Repackage, Reposition,* and *Replenish.* As you read those chapters, you may occasionally want to refer back to this overview chart for context.

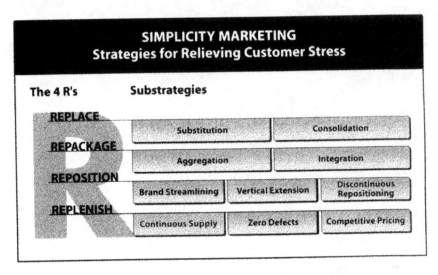

Figure 3.2

■ Summary

This chapter introduced the 4 R's of Simplicity Marketing—*Replace, Repackage, Reposition*, and *Replenish*—as a suite of strategies that may be used individually or in combination to build stronger brands by reducing customer stress. We explained that each of these strategies has component substrategies, or different approaches to the same end which also may be used in combination, each of which will be explored in greater detail in subsequent chapters. We discussed simplifying the value chain, and how the value chain can be a useful tool for identifying and evaluating opportunities to apply the 4 R's in both business-to-business and consumer marketing. And we looked at special circumstances which could mitigate the perils of an overstressed customer base for a select group of marketers.

The next chapter begins our in-depth examination of each of the 4 R's, beginning with *Replace*.

PART II

Strategies

Applying the 4 R's for Competitive Advantage

Chapter 4

REPLACE:

Substitution and Consolidation

> The sole substitute for an experience which we have not ourselves lived through
> is art and literature. —ALEKSANDR SOLZHENITSYN, Nobel Lecture, 1972

IN OUR LIVES of finite time constraints, almost anything can be positioned and viewed as a substitute for something else. In the case of Dr. Solzhenitsyn's observation above, art and literature are not only substitutes but also great savers of time, effort, and expense. It would have cost significantly more than $8 and four hours to have actually sailed and sunk on the *Titanic* rather than to have seen the movie. In the stark absurdity of that tongue-in-cheek example is a serious marketing lesson and the entryway to Simplicity Marketing: *Replace*—the first R.

Replace is the most fundamental of the 4 R's and the minimum requirement to avoid the curse of being perceived by customers as incremental. As the price of admission to becoming a Simplicity Marketer, the Replace strategy honors the imperative that—while it's often impossible to significantly reduce customer stress—at the very least it's important not to increase it. This chapter will divide the Replace strategy into executable substrategies that can change the fortunes of entire categories, and certainly the brands and products within them, in our evermore stressful digital age.

In Chapter 3 we defined *Replace* as developing and/or positioning products as replacements for either multiple products, or for more complicated products or processes (citing conditioning shampoo and Quicken personal finance software as examples). There is also the opportunity to take some existing products that have not been overtly positioned this way and reposition them for their replacement (i.e., simplification) value.

Early commercial online services such as Prodigy, CompuServe, and America Online were examples of great replacement products that were not really positioned as such. Online services were largely a discontinuous innovation, so it did make some sense to initially position the online experience—like these online pioneers did—as essentially a "whole new world of adventure, information and fun." But, by definition, a whole *new* world is an *incremental* world. And there was the rub: Beyond early adopters of such services, most people were not only intimidated by new worlds involving technology but also, more important, threatened by still another incremental *anything*. Yet, by the mid-1990s when AOL's marketing push reached fever pitch, we had already arrived at a time when the *simplification* benefits of online services may have outweighed the *adventure* benefits. (By 1998, leader AOL had built some replacement/stress-reduction value into its positioning, and aol.com's home page carried the messages, "Searching made simple. Personal news made simple. Shopping made simple.")

Still, AOL's early brand communication never emphasized the multitude of things it effectively replaced; for example, some subscriptions to printed magazines (each one representing 12 to 52 pieces of incoming mail, depending on whether it's a monthly or a weekly magazine, plus the invoice, and then another check to write); phone calls to a stockbroker for quotes (then available on AOL before any electronic brokers or financial Web sites existed); calls to airlines or subscriptions to printed airline guides (since AOL was early to offer schedules and booking via the Easy Sabre database). As hugely successful as AOL has been, we'll never know how much faster penetration might have occurred—or how much more customers would have been willing to pay—if it had been positioned as a replacement.)

When the much-hyped palmtop computer/personal organizer market remained stalled at the starting gate through the early- and mid-1990s, mobile executives and managers already had their hands full with laptop computers, cellular phones, and other small devices ranging from pagers to dictation recorders. So the idea of carrying and learning another incremental portable appliance was not only unappealing to many but almost downright distasteful. After years of major product failures in this category—even from marketing machines like Sony (Magic Link) and Apple (Newton), 3Com's Palm Pilot finally took off in 1997. This was not only because the Palm Pilot was more intuitive and easier to use. It was also because of the way it was positioned at a time when busier-than-ever businesspeople were ripe for addiction to instant information while on the go. With the Internet explosion, suddenly the Palm Pilot was no longer just a personal organizer; it became a consolidator of organizing and Internet access, since it also provided a miniature mobile gateway to the Web. Instead of the "techie" ads that other palmtop devices had used, Palm Pilot was positioned as the most important part of your PC "to go." 3Com minimized the Palm Pilot's risk of being perceived as incremental by resisting the temptation to load it up with extra features, and by demonstrating that it was as fast as using paper because of its intuitive design. And *paper* is what it actually replaced, along with replacing the need to use a PC to access the portable data.

■ Substrategies for Effective Replacement

Replace can be achieved by two specific stress-reducing substrategies: *Substitution* and *Consolidation*. *Substitution* is Replace in its simplest form: "use this (or *do* this) instead of that, and it will be easier/faster/less stressful." (The most ubiquitous, established example is using the ATM instead of the teller's window; and you can come anytime you want and likely won't have to wait in a slow-moving line.) A marketer who can at least substitute, and do it credibly, has already avoided becoming an incremental product. Increasingly, successful substitution will also require emphasizing the stress-relief quotient in the product's positioning.

Consolidation goes a major step further. It reduces the number of purchases and/or the number of steps involved in acquiring a solution (product or service) and/or in accomplishing a goal through its use. (Buy this luxury sport utility vehicle and you won't need both a luxury sedan and a separate off-road, four-wheel-drive utility vehicle.) Consolidation almost always saves the customer time and sometimes saves money, but it especially saves *thinking, effort,* and *headaches.* Combining things is certainly not a new idea, but it is much more relevant in a digital-age whole life context.

SUBSTITUTION

There are three basic approaches to Substitution that may be employed individually or in combination: (1) substitution built into the product or service itself, (2) substitution built into marketing (especially where not obviously built into the product), and (3) substitution of predictability for variability.

Substitution Built into Products and Services

At the product development stage, the simplest question that must always be asked is "This instead of *what?*" As obvious as this sounds, many product concepts without substitution value do get commercialized because they have inherent value in a vacuum, but are incremental and therefore met with resistance when introduced into the customer's whole life context. When there is a clear proposition of "this instead of that—and here's the payoff," even new products that require significant behavior modification can succeed with the advantage of Simplicity Marketing's tailwind.

As with ATMs, getting people to use voice mail in the home instead of answering machines required customers to behave differently, learn a new interface, and trust that an intangible service could reliably and confidentially capture their phone messages. So rather than being instant successes, these metamorphoses to new ways of banking and communicating took time. But their eventual acceptance—as stress levels and time pressures continued to grow in intensity—cut broad swaths through the mainstream population, respectively saving the banking industry billions of dollars and creating significant new revenue streams for phone companies.

Unlike personal organizers, voice mail was a *direct* substitution. It not only replaced the answering machine's functionality (except for screening calls), but also replaced a physical appliance with a virtual, invisible service that could do some things more quickly than an answering machine (such as fast-forwarding through messages, or "rewinding" them) and could enable other things that answering machines couldn't do at all (like changing your greeting from remote locations or forwarding a message to someone else on the network).

In the worlds of food and nutrition, substitutes are actually a *category*—in fact, multiple categories. These occur at both the ingredient brand and product brand levels. In sugar substitutes, ingredient brands like Monsanto's NutraSweet (a branded aspartame) and Hoeschst's Sunette (a branded acesulfame-K) appear in products like Equal and Sweet One, respectively. In fat substitutes, Olean (a branded Olestra) appears in Frito-Lay's Wow! brand chips and P&G's Pringles. In and of themselves, these may not seem like profound examples of Simplicity Marketing; after all, they are just substituting one substance for another in the name of health. But it's the intersection of substitution and the increasing anxiety that health concerns raise—partially because we learn more each year about the ill effects of consuming sugar and certain fats—that lets these products capitalize on their role in de-stressing the consumer. Just look at their marketing: Equal is positioned not only as helping to maintain a healthy lifestyle (including Web site tips for relaxation), but also as helping to make living with diabetes less stressful; Wow! brand chips targets calorie counters and parents concerned about unhealthy snacks for kids. Direct substitution that reduces anxiety is Simplicity Marketing at its most elementary level.

Just as food substitutes have the advantage of health anxiety to propel category interest, any sphere of high anxiety becomes a likely place to look for above-average substitution potential. Online data backup services for PCs, such as @Backup, epitomize this strategy. Reminding PC users that "a hard drive crashes every 15 seconds," @Backup offers daily automatic backups of an individual's computer data and secure off-site storage of that data at multiple locations in case of any single-facility failure. This is a substitution category married to a high-anxiety sphere—the trauma of data loss—with a clear promise that's built into the product: Use this instead of disk or tape backup, and you'll save time, money, space, potential mechanical failure hassles, and gain the added security of off-site data storage along the way (not to mention the ability to access your stored files while traveling away from home or office).

Finally, consumers' appetite for saving time has become so extreme that offering even tiny increments of time saving can be enough to successfully launch a new product in a crowded category. After Tenneco launched Hefty OneZip food bags in 1996, it became the number two brand and grabbed 22% of the market in less than two years just by offering one advantage over other sealable bags like Glad Lock. With OneZip's plastic zipper, consumers wouldn't have to fumble around for two or three seconds to line up the two sides of the bag to seal it.

Substitution Built into Marketing

For some products, the inherent substitution value is simply less obvious than for voice mail or Equal. In cases where this value legitimately exists but is not so apparent, marketing strategy must excavate it and bring it to the fore. There is often even greater opportunity to differentiate on stress reduction in such categories by virtue of the fact that substitution *is* less obvious. Remember Chapter 3's discussion of Michael Porter's point about the need for "signaling" substitution? Taking for granted that customers will just figure it out can be a big mistake.

An instructive business-to-business marketing example is at the higher end of the data storage category in the corporate market, often referred to in the computer industry as enterprise storage. In large corporations there is tremendous focus on ability to access, protect, and effectively manage huge quantities of data and mission-critical software applications. Yet, as the 1990s were drawing to a close, no major enterprise storage player in the critical UNIX and Windows NT arenas had overtly focused its positioning on stress reduction. Though Hewlett-Packard competitor brands such as Sun and Compaq made strong reliability claims, and unsurpassed reliability was already deeply imbedded in IBM's brand name, HP was first to see the opportunity to go one step further and position its entire enterprise storage solutions product family on stress reduction. The "Stress-Free Storage" promise, telegraphed with headlines such as "Relax." resonated with information systems managers whose jobs are on the line every day if storage fails.

Generally, even Hewlett-Packard—perceived as one of the most reliable brands in history—couldn't differentiate against the IBM brand on reliability. HP, however, was able to win market share in enterprise storage by preempting the stress-reduction space with a message that essentially said, "Use our storage solutions instead of whatever you're using now and the payoff will be lower anxiety as you forget about storage problems and concentrate on how to best leverage reliable data management for competitive advantage."

Another way to fortify differentiating on stress reduction is with guarantees and warranties, which essentially pledge to substitute certainty for uncertainty. With all the reliability promises in the enterprise storage category, and all the citing of uptime statistics (the key measure of reliability), no one guaranteed systemwide uptime until Hewlett-Packard first offered a 99.95% uptime guarantee in conjunction with its stress-free repositioning. (The bar has subsequently been raised even higher.) In the digital age, consumers and business customers alike are increasingly looking for reliable ways to reduce stress, so few messages are potentially more powerful than helping customers make the connection between the reliability of your product (or company) and stress reduction—and backing it up with a guarantee as a reason to believe.

Branding is another weapon in telegraphing a stress-reduction promise to get customers to use this instead of that. When women were deserting the nail polish/enamel market in the late '90s because of less time available to spend with beauty products, Revlon created Top Speed quick-dry enamel. Yes, substitution was built into the product (which dried in only 90 seconds), but the brand name did wonders to *quickly* communicate to busy women that this was a product for them. With its advertising, "Sets you free in 90 seconds," Revlon Top Speed quickly captured a double-digit market share.

Substituting Predictability for Variability

In stressful lifestyles and chaotic business environments, few things are more welcomed than *predictable consistency*. Substituting predictable for erratic can make a brand a hero. This especially applies to smoothing out variability in *pricing, timing,* and *results*—three key dimensions on which to look for opportunities to differentiate on predictability.

Pricing Guarantees. Cries for simplicity explain the increasing popularity of flat-rate pricing in a number of categories, which can de-stress in multiple ways: (1) reducing customer uncertainty about what she will be paying at different times of the day or week, (2) smoothing out the customer's cash flow over longer periods, and (3) in the case of price guarantees, reducing anxiety about exposure to future price increases.

Through the mid- to late-'90s, flat-rate pricing by utility companies proved especially popular since the value of products like electricity, telephone, and data networks are so usage-dependent and/or time-dependent. In consumer telecommunications services, flat-rate pricing first became a significant differentiator in 1995 when Sprint introduced its very successful "10 cents a minute" campaign and later when AT&T introduced its wireless phone Digital One Rate ("50 states. One rate."). In both cases, competitors quickly followed suit to retain the many customers who didn't want to keep track of what they were paying when (or constantly shift their calling behavior to save money); flat-rate long distance was the rule rather than the exception as the '90s ended.

Meanwhile, regional electric and gas utilities introduced bill-averaging programs, such as Puget Sound Energy's aptly-branded "Predict-a-Bill," which allowed customers to automatically pay the same amount every month (by automatic withdrawal if desired) for natural gas based on past average monthly usage (with periodic adjustments if the customer under- or overpaid for actual use). Around the same time, Internet service providers and online services such as AOL went to flat-rate pricing as well. And by 1998, Williams Energy was winning and keeping customers through "energy price-risk management," offering businesses "a decade of absolute price certainty" by locking in energy prices with higher-margined long-term contracts in which the customer willingly paid a premium to reduce anxiety about variability. In these inherently "variable" categories, marketers used pricing strategy as a means of satisfying growing appetites for predictability. (Incidentally, flat-rate pricing returns to the Simplicity Marketer more predictable revenue streams as well and, in some cases, reduces the cost of administering usage-based pricing.)

More can be done here, especially in the area of price promotion and couponing. The corner dry cleaner sets its list prices very high and then freely distributes 40%-off coupons 52 weeks a year—which customers have to remember to bring every time they want to save money. Instead, what about everyday value prices at 30% off, providing both predictability and the time savings of not having to constantly hassle with coupons? It's a simpler, less stressful way to manage customer relationships. And it simplifies things for the cleaners' employees as well.

Timing Guarantees. Whether in time-driven industries such as logistics management and transportation, or something as simple as a house call for cable TV repair, de-stressing customers means putting them in control by being as precise as possible in defining their timing expectations and following through with meeting them. To address this, Roadway Express launched Roadway Precision Delivery, fully guaranteeing freight deliveries within a one-hour window. Increasingly, as cable TV and local phone service become more competitive, customers are less tolerant of "We'll be there on Thursday sometime between 8 A.M. and noon." They're looking for "9:30." And why shouldn't they want proof that cable and phone companies respect their time pressures and want their business?

Within the timing realm, Ritz-Carlton Hotels even found a way to reduce the variablility of time zones for its international traveler guests. At its Asian properties, the Ritz-Carlton 24-Hour Stay program allows guests to define their stay in terms of any 24-hour period they choose. Depending on when your plane lands and what time zone you are coming from, you define when the day starts and ends at the hotel—and after check-in you pay in 24-hour increments for each day rather than paying for fixed, fractional days based on the hotel's normal local check-in and check-out times. It's a superb example of substituting guaranteed predictability for variability to reduce stress in weary, stress-prone business travelers.

Results Guarantees. Much has been written about product/performance guarantees and warranties, so we won't get into the nuances here. In a Simplicity Marketing context guarantees should maximize the degree to which customers have a reason to believe claims of stress reduction and simplicity. In general, the importance of the guarantee will be in proportion to three variables (besides the variable of how common or uncommon guarantees already are in the category): (1) the degree of stress associated with the category, (2) the degree of personal stress in the market segment being targeted, (3) the current level of customer satisfaction in the category in general and for your brand in particular.

Service level guarantees, or service level agreements (SLAs), are an increasingly popular approach to this problem. Such commitments have been around a long time but are growing in sophistication. (In 1976 Federal Express began offering service options scaled by time and price, such as next-day-noon delivery versus two business days, and instituted guarantees in the early '80s.) Simple service level approaches still have their place: In 1997 Gateway Computer not only began offering the usual free standard technical support line to its home PC customers but also was selling a three-year Gold Premium support package for $99. Gold Premium allowed Gateway buyers to save time by bypassing the long wait times on the standard 1–800 support line. Especially in more complex business-to-business marketing, demand has grown for more specific service level guarantees. By the late 1990s, leading data network and Internet services vendors began guaranteeing business customers different levels of network availability and data delivery efficiency. And technology operations departments in companies ranging from investment bankers Goldman Sachs in New York to pharmaceuticals maker Hoffman-LaRoche in Europe were even beginning to offer SLAs to their internal customers.

The challenge with variable service level guarantees is that, from a Simplicity Marketing perspective, they walk a tightrope between reducing stress and creating it. If the choices of service levels are few in number and clear in definition, there is a greater likelihood that they will reduce customer stress. However, if the choices are too many and/or confusing in definition, then they only replace the former single choice with a stress-producing array of options and more decision time and effort.

The Hewlett-Packard enterprise data storage example cited earlier reminds us of the ever-increasing importance of asking this question: What is the most compelling way to frame a guarantee to make a direct hit on the human emotion of feeling overwhelmed, anxious, hurried, and hassled? Then it's equally important to ask, How can we keep the guarantee itself as simple as possible? As with SLAs, complicated and condition-ridden guarantees can create as much stress and mental clutter as they were designed to eliminate.

In 1994, Co-operative Bank was the first bank in the United Kingdom to guarantee that the bank would pay cash to customers anytime the bank made a mistake in opening an account, paying direct debits, compiling statements, calculating charges and interest, or failing to ensure that the customer always had valid bank cards. This was a clear, black-and-white approach to service guarantees. If we goof, we'll apologize, promptly correct the error, and pay you £10 for your inconvenience (i.e., stress). Polls by British research agency MORI in 1996 showed that Co-operative Bank had more satisfied customers in the United Kingdom than any other bank. And in retail, though Nordstrom and Eddie Bauer are closely associated with accepting merchandise returns with a minimum of hassle, Men's Wearhouse went a step further by institutionalizing its guarantee in the brand's positioning with CEO George Zimmer's long-running "I guarantee it!" ad campaign driving growth to some 450 stores that approached a billion dollars in annual revenue by 1999.

Finally, as overchoice continued to intensify through the '90s, even the venerable-but-somewhat-tired Good Housekeeping Seal began experiencing a revival by 1998 as it significantly increased its license agreements and spread to more than 1,500 products. Overwhelmed consumers were responding with renewed interest in a visual shortcut to quality assurance and variability reduction.

Emphasizing a Substitution's Stress-Relief Element

Since substitution is often easy for customers to miss, nowhere among the 4 R's is it more important to make the replacement and the stress-relief element apparent. Ideally, that may mean incorporating it into brand or product positioning at the "tag line" level (à la the Hewlett-Packard and Men's Wearhouse examples). But even short of that, much can be done executionally in customer communication to telegraph substitution. In the voice mail example above, one TV commercial showed a customer throwing his answering machine into the Grand Canyon—removing any doubt that voice mail was a replacement or about what it was designed to replace. Substitute products without Simplicity Marketing are missed opportunities.

CONSOLIDATION

Substitution can lead to significant market share gains or even market leadership, but seldom leads to value-added marketing breakthroughs. Doing that usually requires something more than "this for that," and *Consolidation*—the next substrategy along the Simplicity Marketing continuum—offers the more compelling promise of *multiple* substitutions, or "this for *those*." Photochromic eyeglass lenses like Corning's PhotoGray Extra darken in sunlight to work as sunglasses outside and regular glasses inside. One pair of frames, one transaction, one trip to the optician if the nosepads need adjusting. In the context of stress, PhotoGray Extra and the plastic versions it spawned from other lensmakers are even more relevant today than back in 1967 when the original Photogray lens was introduced.

Consolidation almost always saves the customer time and sometimes saves money, but it especially saves *thinking* and *effort*. There are four ways of implementing Consolidation, separately or in combination: (1)

reduce the number of decisions, purchases, or transactions; (2) reduce the number of steps; (3) reduce the number of stops (shopping); and (4) reduce the amount of "stuff."

Reduce the Number of Decisions, Purchases, Transactions
The simplest Consolidation is generally the combination of two well-understood, closely related products or services, and the best of these provides some functionality or interoperability that is relatively seamless compared to using the two component products separately. Consolidations range from a $3 jar of Smuckers' Goober, which combines the time-honored kids' favorites peanut butter and jelly into a single spread, to a $65,000 Range Rover luxury sport utility vehicle.

The luxury SUV market, which really took off in the late 1990s, is an instructive case. As mainstream market penetration of Ford's Explorer and Jeep's Cherokee became firmly established, upscale buyers began gravitating to SUVs as a second or third car—often ending up in the driveway right next to a BMW, Lexus, or Mercedes. It seemed as if only then did Mercedes and Lexus discover what the Range Rover had already proven years before: It's possible to combine the comfort and engineering of a luxury sedan with the utility, ruggedness, and safety of an SUV. Even in the lower end of the SUV market, "best of both worlds" was a common theme with ease of handling replacing luxury as the showcased attribute of the car component (e.g., Subaru Forester's campaign, "Sport utility tough. Car easy.").

Back in the supermarket, multiple substitution manifested in Oscar Mayer Lunchables. Like TV dinners long before it, Lunchables aggregated multiple foods (like sliced ham, cheese, crackers, a fruit drink, and dessert snack) into a semibalanced meal that was a single SKU in the store, a single preparation step, served in the same container in which it was packaged, and compact enough to easily slip into a child's lunchbox and still leave room for a piece of fruit. But from a Simplicity Marketing perspective, why were Lunchables even more customer-relevant than TV dinners? Because most parents would agree that, as stressful as lunchtime or dinnertime may be in a busy household, getting kids off to school on time in the mornings is far more stressful. Lunchables responded to that stress with a highly convenient solution geared to a pressured, recurring circumstance—the last half hour at home on school mornings.

Reduce the Number of Steps

The digital-age twist on the old saw, "Cash is king," must certainly be "*Time* is king." One of the most obvious ways to save customers time is to reduce the number of steps involved in completing a task.

Digital cameras have done this both in the consumer and business markets by eliminating the step of converting images from analog to digital. In business markets, step reduction through digital cameras has eliminated time-consuming scanning of images by computer graphics artists (to convert those images to digital). It has also enabled TV news crews to capture news on a digital television camera that stores the "footage" in digital form directly on a hard disk to make it instantly available for random access and retrieval, eliminating the more time-consuming linear editing of analog video—and getting a finished product on the air significantly sooner as broadcasters race each other to be first to break a news story. In the consumer market, digital cameras eliminated the step of film processing (including the trip to drop off and pick up the photographs), and also enabled easy archiving on a personal computer (saving physical space; see "Reduce the Amount of Stuff" below).

In business conference rooms during the '90s, electronic whiteboards on which notes scribbled with a marker pen can be printed out in hard copy began popping up everywhere. They eliminated the step of someone transcribing the board's contents for capture in a computer and made the content immediately portable. At pay phones, "Express Call Completion" gained in popularity as directory assistance operators, upon giving the customer the number they requested, offered to automatically complete the call for a surcharge and eliminate the step of initiating another pay phone call with pocket change or a calling card number. Meanwhile, 3Dfx launched the first media processor for PCs that enabled PC users to play computer games inside a window on their PC screen while running other software applications, so they could switch back and forth without the extra steps of closing down and then relaunching their word processing or spreadsheet program every time they wanted to take a break with a game.

Even the other definition of reducing the number of steps—*footsteps*—can simplify customers' lives. At Nordstrom, notice how the escalators continue directly up or down at each floor rather than routing the customer through merchandise to continue their multi-level journey.

Reduce the Number of Stops

City traffic worsens, road rage approaches epidemic levels, and there is less time than ever to get to anywhere. Lost time, pressure to stay on schedule, and palpable hassle compound each other to make just the act of getting there a significant and frequent stressor. So in personal logistics lies great consolidation opportunities for Simplicity Marketers to de-stress customers by reducing their required number of destinations to accomplish a task. Pre-digital-age precedents for solving this problem ranged from the rise of shopping malls to Arco's AM/PM mini-markets, where getting gas and milk on the way home became one stop instead of two. More recently, we have seen the growing success of bank branches inside supermarkets (sometimes not far from the supermarket's own video rental store-within-the-store), as well as Sprint PCS (digital wireless phone service) stores within 6,000 Radio Shack outlets.

Technology enables many more such solutions. While some, such as bank ATMs that also sell stamps and prepaid calling cards, reduce the number of destinations to which customers must transport themselves, others reduce the number of intradestination steps once the customer is there. For example, at the fairly simple end of the continuum, "fast-pay" gas stations eliminated the necessity of two round-trip hikes from the pump to the cashier. On a more complex level, Wal-Mart used its enor-mous database to track shopping behavior and find combinations of high-volume grocery items often bought together, and it put those items physically closer together in the stores. The results were first seen in the launch of Neighborhood Markets, Wal-Mart's first stand-alone supermar-kets, in which step-saving (and, hence, time and effort saving) pairings of bananas and cereal, tissue and cold medicine, snack cakes and coffee, and flashlights and Halloween costumes all increased sales and cus-tomer satisfaction.[1]

The phenomenal success of Kinko's is also a lesson in Consolidation, especially because of how the brand positioning reinforces the Simplicity Marketing aspects of the product itself. Kinko's not only put under one roof a trip to the stationery store (to buy specialty paper, envelopes, paper clips, and markers), a trip to the copy center, and a trip to a Federal Express drop box (and many other related services), but also acknowl-edged that they knew they were in the Consolidation business when they created a single word to describe it all in the new verb, "officing." Beyond saving customers countless stops and hours, officing positioned Kinko's brand as a stress-reducing repository of services that small businesses and home office workers could depend on for simplification.

Reduce the Amount of "Stuff"
Another contributor to stress is all the physical stuff that visually clutters our homes and offices. Especially where space is an issue, every cubic foot taken up by the footprint of another piece of equipment, electronics, or an appliance, is another cubic foot taken away from a person's room to breathe. (This is further magnified in the closer quarters of dense urban dwellings, from Hong Kong to Manhattan.) And many of these items can impose another set of interactions on the customer's life—especially when something is operationally difficult or when it malfunctions, requiring some kind of technical support from the manufacturer or a third party. Herein lies another opportunity to simplify, de-clutter, and de-stress the customer.

In the previous example of voice mail, de-cluttering came through an unseen service replacing an answering machine that took up counter space and sent another unsightly cord to a wall socket. That answering machine also came with an instruction manual that had to be filed away and a warranty card that had to be filled out and mailed. As we moved toward the "teleputer," as George Gilder likes to call the convergence of television and computer, Thomson Multimedia's eTV and Microsoft's Web TV flirted with the potential for a similar effect (especially for those who would have otherwise had another PC or TV). Before PCs with 3D graphics accelerators, computer users who were also avid video gamers needed both a PC for computing and a dedicated game console like Playstation and Nintendo. But once the price of PCs with good 3D capabilities dropped below $1,000, game consoles became less of a requirement (except to play certain games that were only console compatible). And as placing telephone calls over the Internet rather than the public switched network continues to become more reliable and less expensive, computer-telephony integration removes one more piece of equipment from the desk when callers use the PC's built-in microphone instead of a telephone.

Finally, high-tech manufacturers are increasingly finding ways to consolidate multiple products that perform closely related tasks into single "all-in-one" devices—the digital-age rough equivalent of the Swiss Army knife. Hewlett-Packard's OfficeJet was a pioneer in the "all-in-one computer peripheral" category, consolidating a copier, fax machine, computer printer, and scanner into a single box (one transaction, one manual, one warranty card, one call for technical help) with a compact footprint of only about four square feet (smaller today, of course). Soon after its launch, Xerox attacked the higher end of the multifunction market with the Xerox Document Centre in the same vein.

Some of the most effective Consolidations in recent history provide customers with *every* benefit discussed above. A good example was mentioned in Chapter 3: fresh pre-cut packaged salad. This product not only consolidated at least three to six separate purchases (e.g., two or three kinds of lettuce, carrots, radishes, and, in some cases, a pouch of dressing) into one, but also saved steps (by pre-washing, pre-cutting, and pre-mixing), stops (walk over and pick up one bag instead of making multiple tracks through the produce section), and stuff (dramatically reducing the amount of stuff to take up space in the home refrigerator).

AVOIDING CONSOLIDATION'S BIGGEST RISK: GOING TOO FAR

Before there was Cuisinart, the manually-operated Veg-O-Matic sold in late-night TV infomercials was a marvel for its ability to slice, dice, chop, and grate. But as *The Wall Street Journal* reporter Thomas Weber once remarked when reviewing the performance of all-in-one devices like the OfficeJet, "If you're going to do a lot of chopping, choose a cleaver." In the zeal to be a hero for the stressed-out customer, it's tempting to go too far with Consolidation. It is paramount that product testing accurately gauge the threshold of diminishing returns. Today we still wouldn't even have conditioning shampoo if it didn't both clean and condition our hair reasonably well when compared to separate, dedicated products.

3DO, a company spun off from entertainment software leader Electronic Arts with much hoopla in the early '90s, designed an entertainment console that was a video game system, CD-ROM player, audio CD player, Photo CD player, and video disc player all rolled into one sleek tabletop package. But the complex combination of new and established technologies confused and intimidated consumers, exacerbating a high initial price and scarcity of software titles to thwart trial.

On a simpler note, even microwave-convection combo ovens ultimately failed as a category, despite the tremendous success of their toaster oven ancestors, because neither the microwave nor convection functions were competitive with stand-alone products.

Finally, sometimes Consolidation can be prone to failure in the channel. Consolidation often produces a new life form that may at first appear strange to the customer, requiring knowledgeable channel support to effectively sell it. When Huffy Corporation first consolidated a mountain bike and racing bike into a higher-priced hybrid bike called the Cross Sport, Kmart and Toys 'R' Us were not able to provide the selling expertise on the retail floor to move the product through. The adverse impact on Huffy's earnings that year was significant, but other bike manufacturers went on to have great success with hybrid bikes by focusing distribution on specialty shops where selling expertise could effectively support the consolidated product.[2]

Incidentally, going too far can be an issue in Substitution as well. Back to the Palm Pilot a few years ago: it didn't try to replace the PC, as did some earlier palmtops that positioned themselves as "sub-notebook" computers. The Palm Pilot's product managers knew it was a poor replacement for a PC, but an excellent "window to your important data." Replacement would have been overpromise, so instead the Palm Pilot capitalized on the anxiety associated with being *cut off* from important data.

■ How To *Replace*

With this chapter's examples and strategies in mind, you can now develop your own blueprint for implementing the first R of Simplicity Marketing. Step 1 is to gauge your products' and brands' potential to benefit from the Replace strategy. Then proceed to Step 2, taking inventory of all the ways you might leverage the strategy, by using the checklists that follow—one for each of the Replace substrategies, Substitution and Consolidation. These will help you articulate the specific proof points that can provide the basis for a successful Replace effort. Finally, Step 3 is to ensure that the power of Replace is incorporated into your positioning strategy, making the product's stress-reduction benefits obvious and as compelling as possible to customers.

STEP 1: GAUGE YOUR REPLACE POTENTIAL

Six variables determine the degree to which you and your customers can benefit from the first R. Audit your category, brand and products/services (including presale and postsale customer service) as follows:

1. **Assess the level of customer anxiety in the category.** Generally, the more anxiety and stress inherent in the category, the more opportunity to win and keep customers through Simplicity Marketing (i.e., the less tolerance customers will have for incremental choices, products, and brands). Three determinants of anxiety levels are (1) how inherently life-critical or mission-critical is the category perceived to be, (2) how closely aligned with customer needs is the existing array of choices and options, and (3) within the category, what is the relative stress level of one market segment compared to another?

First, regarding inherent category stress, one could safely argue that the health care category is inherently more critical than the candy category. But within health care there is still an anxiety continuum that may range from "What flavor cough syrup do I buy?" to "Which doctor do I choose for brain surgery?"

Second, there is more tension in a category in which customer needs are not currently being met very well—not only in terms of product/service quality but also in how the array of choices and options is currently scaled relative to customers' appetite for same.

Finally, for each market segment, what is the relative pace of change in the customer's whole life context? How well is he coping? In light of the number and variety of options currently available in the category, multiplied by the degree of proactive marketing (i.e., noise), does the customer have it all reasonably under control or is he really overwhelmed? (See Chapter 9 for important considerations in marketing research that will help you profile your target segments on these dimensions.)

2. **Qualify product/service as Substitute or Consolidator.** Use the checklists that follow under Step 2 to help determine if the Substitution or Consolidation substrategies are a good fit for your product, service, or brand. Remember, in some categories *customer care* may be a more important potential differentiator than the product itself in terms of where the substitution or consolidation occurs.

3. Assess your sustainable competitive advantage as a Replacement. If positioned as a Substitute or Consolidator, what are the barriers to emulation by competitors? Considering previous examples, this was not a significant issue for voice mail in the home since most local phone companies providing that service enjoyed monopoly status at the time of product launch. By contrast, however, the sport utility vehicle category became very crowded in the late '90s, raising the bar on what it would take to sustain differentiation as a Consolidator. So, relatively quickly, individual brands were finding it necessary to differentiate on dimensions like styling and price rather than on the Replace value of the category itself.

4. Assess the likely perceived economic value of stress reduction. This is especially relevant to Consolidation. It may be possible to develop a product that satisfies all other criteria for Consolidation, but cost-based pricing can drive the product beyond the threshold of what customers are willing or able to pay to reduce the associated stress. A successful business model for the Replace strategy must take into account, early on, the price elasticity associated with the Replace value proposition. Just remember that, even for conservative marketers, it's easy to underestimate the hunger for stress reduction (and the premium that it may justify).

5. Assess the degree to which simplification can be your marketing thrust without suboptimizing positioning. For some products, simplification can legitimately be the product's core reason for being. For others, a simplification-focused positioning may obscure more relevant benefits and/or differentiators. Determine whether simplification in general, or Substitition or Consolidation in particular, is more appropriately your marketing *thrust* or a secondary, enhancing message.

6. Look for preemptive reminder opportunities for products that may already be taken for granted as Substitutes or Consolidators. Everyone knew that paper plates were substitutes for dishes. But Fort James Corporation significantly boosted sales of Dixie paper plates by repositioning Dixie as the tableware component of "home cleanup replacement." Suddenly Dixie was no longer competing just on superiority to other brands of paper plates, but instead was simultaneously expanding both the category and its share of it by making the benefit of stress-reducing Substitution more obvious.

Note: Numbers 1, 2, 4, and 5 above may well require customer research.

STEP 2: INVENTORY YOUR SUBSTITUTION/CONSOLIDATION PROOF POINTS

Whether positioning as a Substitute or Consolidator, the Simplicity Marketing message will be built on stress-related reasons to believe, or proof points. To help excavate those points, answer the questions about your product or service on the following checklists.

Substitution Checklist

1. What does this replace? (This instead of _____.)

2. Does this significantly reduce customer stress? Specifically, how does it save time, thinking, effort, or headaches?

3. Where do stress/stress-related attributes rank in the category's hierarchy of drivers of brand choice?

4. How much of the Substitution value is obviously built into the product itself, versus being dependent on a Substitution marketing message?

5. Will this substitute predictability for variability? How?

6. What is the relative relevance (and the presence/absence in the category) of pricing guarantees, timing guarantees, and results guarantees, and what are we prepared to offer?

Consolidation Checklist

1. What does this consolidate? (This instead of _____ and _____ . . .)

2. Does this significantly reduce customer stress? How?

3. Are the components being consolidated already well understood as separate elements?

4. Does this reduce the number of decisions/purchases/transactions?

5. Does this reduce the number of steps?

6. Does this reduce the number of stops?

7. Does this reduce the amount of "stuff"?

Step 3: Incorporate Replace in Positioning

See how these final checkpoints clarify positioning issues in "Anatomy of a Replacement: Apple's iMac," which follows this section.

1. Is stress reduction built into the positioning? The more obvious you make it, the less hard your busiest, most distracted customers will have to work to make the connection between your brand and their stress relief.

2. What are the stress-related reasons to believe? Ensure that the stated or strongly implied promise of stress relief has teeth in it. If you're differentiating on simplicity, demonstrate it (simply!) wherever possible.

3. How does stress-reduction impact perceptions on key drivers of brand choice? This one requires a bit more explanation. If there are time-honored, traditional drivers of brand choice in your category, understand how customer stress is or isn't associated with each one. For example, the four high-level drivers of choice in many packaged foods categories are taste, nutrition, convenience, and economy. Let's say that Brand A of hot cereal is virtually at parity with Brand B on these dimensions, and Brand A's message is focused on nutrition. Brand B does some customer research and finds that, among certain key high-stress market segments, stress is associated more closely with time than with health. Brand B may then target those segments with a differentiated message focused on convenience and, in spite of parity on convenience, Brand B is perceived as the more valuable product. By virtue of emphasizing stress reduction in its message, Brand B is also perceived as being more empathetic with the challenges of these consumers' lifestyles, improving brand perceptions on softer brand personality attributes such as "Brand B understands me."

4. To what degree can you own stress reduction in the category? As with any positioning strategy, stress reduction is likely doomed to fail if you can't differentiate your message on it. That is, unless you plan to so significantly outspend your competition that it doesn't matter. The basic checkpoints here are:

- To what degree are category messages already addressing this?
- Does my brand equity afford more credibility in the stress-reduction arena than do competitor brands?
- Can a preemptive position in the stress-reduction arena be sustained in the face of emulation?

Anatomy of a Replacement: Apple's iMac

SIMPLICITY MARKETER:	**Apple Computer, Inc.**
PRODUCT:	**iMac Personal Computer**
LAUNCH:	**1998**
PRIMARY SUBSTRATEGY:	**Consolidation**

As a dramatic turning point in the then-declining fortunes of Apple Computer in 1998, the introduction of the iMac was a Simplicity Marketing tour de force. It embodied customer stress reduction from product design through all key aspects of marketing strategy and execution, and successfully struck an emotional chord with its target markets.

Though Apple's residual brand equity from its earlier glory days arguably gave it a head start on simplicity due to its user-friendly heritage, its brand situation in 1998 was anything but simple. After Apple's market share had slipped to less than 5%, it was much harder to find software applications and add-on peripheral devices for Apple than any other significant brand of personal computer. And Apple's product line had proliferated into a confusing array of 28 different models, which the company pruned to just four during the year preceding the iMac launch.

Everything about the iMac set out to kick complexity in the shins. Let's examine iMac's strategy in the context of Replacement and, specifically, the Consolidation substrategy.[3]

PRODUCT

Other networkable personal computers with iMac's level of functionality typically consisted of at least four or five separate hardware components (not counting modems, which by 1998 were usually built into the PC, and not counting a mouse, which was of relatively little consequence in terms of size and complexity): (1) the CPU (central processing unit; i.e., the box—either a vertical mini-tower or a horizontal desktop box containing the circuit boards and computer chips), (2) a monitor, (3) a keyboard, (4) an add-in networking board that had to be installed in the CPU, and sometimes (5) external speakers. The iMac consolidated these hardware components into a single box and a keyboard, returning to the original Macintosh approach of 14 years before by combining the monitor and CPU, and then building in networking, stereo speakers, and a microphone as well—and the ability to plug in anywhere in the world with a built-in AC variable-current adapter. Apple also preloaded software that connected customers directly to an Internet service provider.

CONSOLIDATION CHECKLIST

What does iMac consolidate?
CPU, monitor, networking board, and stereo speakers.

Does iMac significantly reduce customer stress? How?
The stress epicenter in the personal computer arena (especially outside of business, which was not the target for the iMac) was, for its less computer-savvy target market, getting it to work right out of the box and getting it hooked up to the Internet. The Macintosh tradition of "easy" was the perfect foil for the perceived complexity of the Internet. The iMac reduced stress first with Apple's long-standing brand promise of empowerment through simplicity, and then more specifically by promising in advertising that plugging into the wall socket and the phone jack is all one would need to do besides attaching the keyboard and mouse to be off to the races.

Are the components being consolidated already well understood as separate elements?
Except for first-time computer buyers, who accounted for the minority of iMac sales, customers were already familiar with monitors, CPU boxes, and speakers. While most were considerably less familiar with Internet connections and especially networking boards, they didn't care about what they were getting as long as the computer delivered on its promise of the ability to simply access the Internet and, where applicable, private networks. (In fact, trying to explain these invisible components would only have unnecessarily complicated the marketing message.)

Does iMac reduce the number of decisions/purchases/transactions?
Choosing an iMac means: No choosing a monitor type, brand, or size. No shopping for network boards and ensuring compatibility with the computer. No choosing speakers. No sorting out Internet service options and connection requirements (unless a customer chose to find an alternate route to the Internet).

Does iMac reduce the number of steps?
Once purchased, the iMac eliminated the steps of hooking up a monitor to the computer, installing a network card, completing multiple warranty cards, and

reading multiple owner's manuals. (And, if there was a problem requiring assistance, calling multiple vendors.)

Does iMac reduce the number of stops?

As an integrated, stand-alone product, any pre- or postpurchase needs could be satisfied in one place—be that at an Apple retail outlet, on the Web, or on the phone. As far as the purchase itself was concerned, prior to the iMac launch Apple radically simplified its distribution channel, eliminating all retailers except CompUSA. So consumers still had a big national chain that they could go to "to kick the iMac's tires," or they could buy from the comfort of home through either the Apple Store online or major catalog outlets.

Does iMac reduce the amount of "stuff"?

The footprint of the iMac was approximately 40% smaller than that of a competitive PC with a similar-size (15-inch) monitor. It also spared the space needed for external speakers, had fewer surfaces to dust, had fewer cables, and simply made for a less cluttered computing environment. This made it especially popular in college dorms and in home offices where space was tight.

POSITIONING LEVERAGE

Is stress reduction built into the positioning?

The iMac's introductory advertising attacked simplicity head on, with headlines such as:

- "Amazingly simple. Simply amazing."
- "One decision. One box. One price."
- "To everyone who thinks computers are too complicated …"

Even headlines like "Say hello to iMac." had Apple's traditionally friendly, simple, and nonthreatening tone. TV copy contrasted iMac with humorous definitions of PC, such as "Perpetually Complicated," "Profusely Corded," and "Physically Conspicuous."

Furthermore, stress reduction was built into the product's branding: the i in iMac stood for Internet, and making the Internet easy was its primary raison d'être. So, with Macintosh's reputation for ease of use, iMac as a brand name was literally a metaphor for "easy Internet" (as well as being a simple little four-letter variation on the colloquial form of the familiar Macintosh brand).

What are the stress-related reasons to believe?

Apple's advertising copy backed up the headline claims with proof points such as:

- "It's easy to buy (no extra decisions). Easy to set up (just add electricity). And easy to use (one click and hello, Internet)."
- "Lots of parts = complicated. Few parts = easy."
- "You can bring an iMac home, take it out of the box and be cruising the Internet in less than ten minutes."

This last point was further supported by a very effective publicity video called "Simplicity Shootout," in which a 7-year-old with an iMac and a 28-year-old Stanford MBA with a PC raced to take their new computers out of the boxes, set them up, and get on the Internet. The 7-year-old won handsomely.

How does stress-reduction impact perceptions on key drivers of brand choice?

Key drivers in this stratum of the PC market were performance, value, and ease of use. Stress-reduction appeal helped iMac with performance perceptions because consumers believed they had a better chance of getting what they needed out of a computer if it was truly easy to use—especially regarding the Internet. Apple's simplicity promise—not just in its messages but in the one-box design and look of the product itself—further strengthened perceptions of Apple on ease of use. This perceived combination of performance and value, along with less computer-savvy consumers' anxiety about complexity, translated to good value perceptions even though PC systems with comparable processing speed were available for less than the iMac's initial price of $1,299.

To what degree could iMac own stress reduction in the category?

No other personal computer brand at the time was making simplicity a primary part of its positioning, and no other brand had the heritage of ease of use that could trace itself all the way back to the original Macintosh's smiley-face that appeared every time it booted up. While other brands of PCs were trying to shout down each other on features and price, the iMac message of simplicity was a clear differentiator that was both relevant and credible.

Final note: In time for the iMac launch, Apple even simplified its corporate logo from the multicolored stripes to a single-color apple icon without stripes—further de-cluttering the brand personality and the endorsement logo that punctuated every iMac ad.

One decision. One box.
One price. $1,299.*

The world's easiest-to-use computer is also the world's easiest-to-buy.

iMac comes in one box, with everything you need, for one low price: $1,299.* And there are two simple ways to buy one.

You can visit your authorized Apple reseller, who can provide personalized advice and service. (Call 1-800-538-9696 for the nearest location.)

You can also visit us any time at the Apple Store™ on the web at www.apple.com or call us at 1-800-795-1000.

Think different.™

Figure 4.1

RESULTS

iMac was the most successful launch in Apple's history since the original Macintosh, and renewed much of Apple's lost luster both on Wall Street and among computer users everywhere. Its success was immediate and global. The iMac instantly became the number one-selling personal computer in the world and single-handedly doubled Apple's overall market share within four months after launch. By the beginning of 1999, an iMac was being bought somewhere on the planet every 15 seconds, and 2 million units were sold in the first year. Though widely criticized for not having an internal floppy disk drive like most PC's of the day, it was Apple's total dedication to keeping the iMac simple and affordable that traded off the floppy drive for assured compactness, minimal parts, and putting the iMac within economic reach of as many consumers and schools as possible.

■ Summary

Stress-relieving strategies covered in this chapter are summarized in Figure 4.2. This chart reminds us that the first R of Simplicity Marketing—*Replace*—can be executed as either of two substrategies: *Substitu-*

Figure 4.2

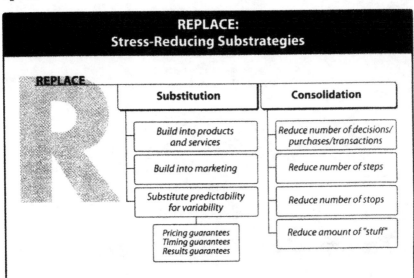

tion or *Consolidation.* For each substrategy, it recaps the key building blocks on which Simplicity Marketing effectiveness can be built. This chapter illustrated each of those building blocks with examples, and then provided checklists for each substrategy to help you gauge your product's/brand's potential for successful execution. The checklists also helped capture proof points that could be communicated to customers to give them compelling reasons to believe that your product/brand can effectively Replace something that currently occupies space and time in the customer's whole life context. Finally, we looked in depth at how Apple Computer's iMac leveraged the first R through exemplary execution of Simplicity Marketing.

Chapter 5

REPACKAGE:

Aggregation and Integration

Synergy means behavior of whole systems unpredicted by the behavior of their parts.
—RICHARD BUCKMINSTER FULLER, *What I Have Learned*, 1966

STRESS AND TIME tend to be inversely proportional; stress thrives when time is short or scarce. In the context of digital-age stress, *whole systems*—and *synergy* as defined above by Fuller—take on new importance because self-contained systems inherently save time. When marketers create whole systems that not only save time but also provide other benefits such as ease of use and less thinking and effort, the resulting value can significantly enhance customer loyalty and raise the perceived costs of brand switching. The second R of Simplicity Marketing—*Repackage*—offers ways to tap stress-reducing opportunities to win and keep customers through value-added one-stop shopping. This chapter explores those opportunities, as well as the substantial risks of failure.

BUNDLING: THE HOLY GRAIL OF OWNING THE CUSTOMER

With the digital age came the rise of "bundling"—first in the '80s with personal computers that bundled software with the PC. Then in the '90s, as telecommunications markets were deregulated and the Internet drove demand for data transport services, bundles became so de rigueur that in 1996 *The Wall Street Journal* dubbed the telecom wars the Battle of the Bundle in a report on all the new ways that telecom competition was being redefined through inventive approaches to value-added one-stop shopping.[1] Telecom marketers became obsessed with the bundling race, and within the industry even manager job titles like Integration Bundling Manager began cropping up in the more developed markets around the globe. Meanwhile, back in the PC industry, bundling has evolved way beyond hardware and software. By 2000, full-service PC vendors like IBM were—with the help of strategic partners—integrating hardware and software with networking, Internet access, Web hosting, Web site design, intranet development, and broadband services as complementary parts of one-stop PC sales and service.

Chapter 3 defined *Repackage* as the bundling together of products or services that were previously only available from multiple sources (or as separate purchases from the same source), offering integrated solutions with a single purchase and single point of contact for the customer. In fact, the burgeoning opportunities to *Repackage* across multiple industries largely drove the "fifth wave" of corporate mergers in the twentieth century (1997–2000).[2] Nearly 8,000 mergers occurred in the United States in 1997 alone, with the norm having been only 2,000 to 3,000 during the preceding 20 years. And the biggest mergers got bigger still, as Fortune 500 firms with broad product lines and large customer bases married each other to provide bundles that transcended even the substantial means of the individual partners.

Mergers and acquisitions of the prior decade had been more about economies of scope and scale (as with key mergers in the airline and banking industries) and amassing successful individual brands (in packaged goods, for example, RJR acquiring Nabisco, Grand Metropolitan acquiring Pillsbury, or Kraft marrying General Foods—only to then be swallowed up by Philip Morris). But the bundle-driven mergers of the fifth wave brought together highly complementary, rather than duplicative, products and services with the expectation of driving incremental shareholder value through Repackaging.

Consider just a few examples from 1998 alone. The creation of Citigroup married the banking, credit card, and asset management services of Citibank and the insurance services of Travelers Group with intention to create a global, one-stop financial services colossus. (About the same time, this was mirrored in Europe by the merger of Zurich Financial Services and B.A.T Industries.) AT&T acquired cable TV giant TCI as the battle intensified for control of the wires into U.S. homes, so that the combined company could control services delivered over both the phone wire and coaxial cable to offer an integrated package of telephony, high-speed Internet access via cable modem, and cable TV. And Cordant Technologies was created from a three-way marriage as Thiokol Propulsion, Howmet Corporation, and Huck International respectively combined their rocket motor technology, jet engine parts casting, and aerospace fastening systems into a single-source vendor for NASA, the military, and the commercial sector.

Fast-forward to the first megamerger of 2000—AOL Time Warner—to see a classic Repackage opportunity on a grand scale. Beyond the obvious marriage of complementary distribution channels and customer bases, bundling content (à la AOL TV) will create new revenue streams. Count on the merged colossus to repackage integrated content across the four "boxes" currently found in homes—TV, PC, stereo, and telephone.

Short of actual mergers, virtual mergers in the form of strategic alliances in pursuit of the bundle, have also been on the rise. As the Internet leveled the playing field of global competition and it became clear that use of information technology would be a primary driver of competitive advantage in the new millennium, even market-leading IT megabrands banded together to offer yet more robust one-stop shopping. In 1998, Hewlett-Packard essentially bundled a large portion of its company with Cisco Systems, EMC, Oracle, and SAP—respectively representing enterprise computing, networking, data storage, database applications, and software integration—to provide large customers with an enterprisewide guarantee of quantified reliability for mission-critical computing.

In many ways, Repackage is the riskiest of the 4 R's. But its rewards to marketers will increasingly justify the risk as customer stress continues to mount. So let's now examine specific substrategies that do for Repackage what Substitution and Consolidation did for Replace: make it executable.

■ Substrategies for Effective Repackaging

The *Repackage* strategy can be deployed through two stress-reducing substrategies: *Aggregation* and *Integration*. Both yield products or services that are more valuable to customers than the sum of their parts. In contrast to Consolidation (Chapter 4), which integrates complementary products (peanut butter and jelly, computer printers and scanners), value-added Aggregation brings together multiple—sometimes *many*—products or services *similar* to each other and otherwise only available from separate sources, and overlays some additional component of value available only from the aggregator. (Chapter 3 cited the example of Bloomberg L.P. aggregating financial information for professional investors with the overlay of customized computer hardware and software tailored to their needs.)

Integration goes further still, as the most holistic form of value-added one-stop shopping. Integration yields whole systems that bring together multiple related products with a single transaction and single point of contact, and also make it possible for the customer to do things that could not otherwise be done (or done as well) with separate component products alone—or without the expertise of the integrator. While Aggregation does not yield a whole system, but rather a convenient, efficient, and/or value-priced collection of similar products, Integration does create a synergistic and interdependent system of complementary products. (Consider the Microsoft Office software suite, and the interoperability and interaction between Microsoft Word, Excel, PowerPoint, Access, and Outlook programs within it.) Seamless integration of several related tasks into one integrated product or service that also improves end results for customers can be extremely powerful—so powerful that the brand providing it can dominate the category space in the customer's mind to the exclusion of competitive brands, greatly enhancing loyalty. This can be done without enjoying the extreme clout of a brand such as Microsoft. In fact, Intuit's Quicken personal finance software has always been number one in its category in spite of competing directly with Microsoft.

AGGREGATION

Aggregation provides the basic customer benefits of Consolidation, including reducing the number of decisions/purchases/transactions and the number of steps or stops (Chapter 4). But as a stress-reducing strategy, Aggregation goes further than consolidation in two important ways. One is a matter of degree: saving customers even more time and duplication of effort, because Aggregation typically repackages together a larger number of products—many, rather than the two or few that are typical of Consolidation. But the other is more strategically significant: Aggregation typically enhances the value and protects the functionality of the individual components being aggregated, rather than compromising it. (In Consolidation, arguably better results could often be achieved by customers willing to spend the time, money, and effort on separate products—for example, better results from separate shampoo and conditioner, or separate printer and scanner. But Aggregation preserves the complete functionality of its components and may even improve it.) This *preservation* aspect is key because, for customers, *compromise* can mean guilt or sacrifice or both, which in turn equal stress.

Three arenas in which to implement Aggregation to reduce customer stress include: (1) many-in-one product or service aggregation in categories with many brands and product variations, (2) digital-age information aggregation, and (3) time-saving aggregation in the distribution channel (including the Internet as a channel).

Many-in-One Aggregation in High-Choice Categories

In categories where choices are relatively limited or relatively efficient to make, Aggregation risks being perceived as adding little value. But in high-choice categories, where the options and number of brands can be overwhelming, and where choosing is relatively time-intensive, the value of Aggregation will be sought after.

Mutual funds are a prime example of many-in-one Aggregation for stress relief. (In spite of the bewildering number of funds to choose from now, the explosive growth of this category affirmed the value of Aggregation.) Consider the degree to which personal investing is a high-choice category. At the top level, whenever money becomes available to invest, the choice must be made between stocks, bonds, government securities, certificates of deposit, money market funds, commodities, annuities, real estate, precious metals, and the list goes on. Compounding the choices within each of these categories creates an incomprehensible array of options. Within just the stocks category, nearly 9,000 individual stocks are listed on the New York and NASDAQ stock exchanges alone. Each stock fund aggregates some significant number of individual stocks around a common theme that reflects the investor's desired degree of

growth/risk, company size (e.g., large-cap vs. small-cap), specific industries, or specific geographies (e.g., Latin America). Overlaying this many-
to-one aggregation is the added value of a fund manager's portfolio
management expertise, diversification of assets across the multiple holdings of the fund, and the time and money (trading commissions) saved
by aggregating the purchase (and, later on, the sale) of many stocks into a
single transaction.

Ironically, so much Aggregation occurred in the mutual funds category
that the number of aggregations (funds) eventually exceeded the number
of individual stocks. This spawned the aggregation of aggregations—
funds-of-funds. By the end of the '90s, nearly 100 such funds existed.
Although most funds-of-funds underperformed the individual funds that
invested in similar securities, they became very popular one-stop shopping solutions for diversifying and reducing volatility after a long bull
market gave way to 1998 market jitters in the face of the Asian financial
crisis. Whether there may yet be a need for funds-of-funds-of-funds
remains to be seen, but the opportunity for multitiered Aggregation is
generally something to watch for in high-choice categories where first-tier
Aggregation becomes successful, where choices continue to proliferate,
and where time/money are at the core of market emotions.

Meanwhile, specifically within the Internet sector, analysts and individual investors alike were complaining by the second half of 1999 that
there were too many Internet stocks to choose from. The resulting bewilderment and anxiety helped propel publicly traded CMGI, an "Internet
catalyst" company, to stratospheric market capitalization. By quickly and
strategically assembling, mostly through acquisition, some sixty Inter-
net-centric companies into one diverse but synergistic network, CMGI
aggregated for investors many Internet equity plays in each single share
of CMGI. The financial community loved this value-added many-in-one
aggregation, and took CMGI's share price from $15 in January 1999 to
over $150 in January 2000.

Perhaps nowhere is there more heritage of time-saving Aggregation
than in the unlikely category of entertainment. We can readily associate
the entertainment category with stress reduction, since entertainment
helps us relax. But we're less likely to associate it with *producing* stress
(except for those of us who have worked in the entertainment industry!).
Yet the process of procuring entertainment is more rife than ever with

overchoice, and can be such a time sink that it puts more stress-producing pressure on other things. Consider books and music, where two pre-digital-age ancestors of Aggregation continue to thrive: *Reader's Digest* and themed compilation music albums (such as *Romantic Jazz Ballads by Sax Legends of the '40s*).

In each issue, *Reader's Digest* has long aggregated dozens of written-word entertainment components drawn from far-flung sources to save readers time while providing variety. It has also added value by collecting, screening, and publishing stories and jokes submitted by its readers. The digital dawn left behind many traditional magazines, but *Reader's Digest* is still by some measures the most widely read magazine on earth nearly 80 years after its inaugural issue. Today, this is undoubtedly due in part to the stress relevance of the reading efficiency it offers in a time-starved world, where there's simply too much reading from which to choose.

In the late 1980s, Silicon Valley start-up Personics Corporation applied Aggregation to recorded music. Its interactive kiosk in record stores allowed consumers to pick any combination of songs from a manageable catalog to customize their own cassette tape and have it manufactured on the spot, in 5 to 10 minutes, with a laser-printed personalized cover and discography. A Personics custom cassette not only preserved the integrity of the individual songs, which were unaltered from their original form, but added value by letting music lovers thematically aggregate up to 25 of their favorite songs on one tape—saving the time and money involved in finding each of these songs on separate albums and then making a compilation recording at home. (Personics was so enthusiastically received by consumers that the record companies feared significant cannibalization of their own CD sales, so they soon cut off Personics' supply of new music and choked the company out of business.)

The Aggregation lesson from mutual funds and entertainment is the same: *Look to categories in which available choices overwhelm and in which money, time, or both are disproportionately at stake; then aggregate around themes of interest to customers in ways that make it quick and painless to buy and use.*

Digital-Age Information Aggregation

We began hearing cries of information overload even well before the digital age. And where there's overload, there's opportunity to create value through Aggregation. The exponential surge in available information, due to the rise of the Internet and the conversion of media archives from analog to digital, created its own class of Aggregation solutions. Aggregator Web sites such as Yahoo!, Netscape's Netcenter, and aol.com became known as portal sites because, as gateways to seemingly infinite information on the Web, these sites helped customers get their arms around vast quantities of information of potential interest to them through a single gateway. For their other target market—advertisers—portals aggregated something else: customer eyeballs. When CEO Tim Koogle of Yahoo!, one of the first pure Internet brands, was interviewed at the 1998 *Wall Street Journal Technology Summit*, he stated simply, "We're very clear on what we do. We aggregate."

Yahoo! has since expanded its strategy to include *demand aggregation*, developing a group buying service that aggregates the demand of the Yahoo! audience for certain products and services. Following the lead of group buying innovators Accompany.com and Mercata.com, the Yahoo! service will simplify e-commerce for sellers with one-source access to the large Yahoo! customer base while reducing price negotiation and comparison shopping stress for buyers. In fact, a whole class of online aggregators who don't actually sell products themselves has evolved on the Internet. At *mySimon.com*, "intelligent agents" trained by human shopping experts will comparison shop for the consumer's desired product at more than 2,000 online stores and provide access to more than 32,000 off-line services ranging from home-and-garden to personal finance.

Meanwhile, high-tech publishers such as IDG and Ziff-Davis replaced a lot of Internet searching with daily e-mails (by request/subscription) that reported technology news daily, gathered from many publications. Personal customization of Webcasting services added more Aggregation value still. As satellites spawn more video channels, as wireless data networks evolve, and as audio and video become more prevalent and easier to consume on the Web, there will continue to be new opportunities to aggregate digital information to save customers time, effort, thinking, and/or money.

Finally, many value-added one-stop opportunities lie in aggregating statements and invoices for multiple accounts belonging to a single customer. At this writing, a customer of Charles Schwab who has a brokerage account, two Keogh accounts, and three IRAs, could not get any aggregation of accounts on printed statements (or online, as recently as 1999). Six nearly identical envelopes arrived each month with separate transaction records and statements of holdings (and duplicate statement stuffer promotional offers). The only way to track the entire portfolio was by manually self-aggregating and then manually running asset allocation calculations. Contrast that with logging onto the Web, updating with a single mouse-click the quotes for all securities in all accounts, and instantly seeing how the total portfolio tracked against market performance—as well as monitoring shifts in aggregate asset allocation across the combined accounts. As this capability comes on stream, the time savings and customer value of doing business with Schwab improves significantly and will further enhance brand loyalty. (And the company would also save on postage, paper, and envelopes by mailing a single aggregated statement—and even save some trees along the way!)

Time-Saving Aggregation in the Distribution Channel
Aggregation in the distribution channel is as old as the channel itself; after all, what most wholesalers and retailers always did was bring together merchandise from different manufacturers for sale in an aggregated place. But back when the concept of a middleman was born, there weren't more than 35 brands and 1,600 varieties of athletic shoes—or legions of time-starved consumers. That's why in the digital age we have many-in-one retail environments like Just For Feet, which not only reduces the number of stops (like Consolidation) by preventing trips to multiple stores with smaller selections but also gives customers the added value of comparison shopping in real time (being able to try on different models—one immediately after the other—and look at them side by side). For car buying, the Auto Row in every major city attempts to do the next best thing by creating a destination neighborhood aggregating many makes and models for comparison shopping and thereby bringing a greater share of the total potential buyers into the area. Autobytel has done this on the Web, sacrificing the instant real-world test drive but offering greater selection and other value-adding elements not available on real Auto Rows.

In fact, nowhere is time-saving Aggregation more evident than in the electronic channel, where e-commerce has fostered extreme Aggregation in high-choice categories. Amazon.com became the first poster child for aggregated e-commerce by aggregating nearly 2 million books for sale in one place (more than 10 times as many as found in a typical large Barnes & Noble retail outlet). Beyond many-in-one Aggregation that preserved the integrity of the aggregated components, Amazon.com added stress-related value in several important ways—not the least of which was saving the time of physically traveling to and within real-world bookstores, offering other customers' reviews online to reduce uncertainty about the worth of a particular book, and instantly showing other titles that readers of this book have also enjoyed.

To uncover unmet needs that lend themselves to online Aggregation, two places to look are categories in which current online sellers are not adding much value beyond saving time and/or money, and categories that are buried in other online merchandising mixes. For example, gourmet coffees for sale online were typically buried among the merchandising mixes of gourmet food sites until beans.com raised the aggregation of coffee alternatives to new heights, with single-minded clarity of coffee-only merchandising and value-added information about the individual products. The beauty of Aggregation online is that it is possible to offer a broader inventory that satisfies customer needs without assaulting customers' overly cluttered psyches with aisles upon aisles of physically displayed merchandise.

INTEGRATION

The power of Integration done well can be felt at a gut level by customers like no other strategy. The marketing opportunities are enormous, largely because of a phenomenon described by Nobel physicist Arno Penzias:

> The greatest subtlety of our own human interfaces appears in the way we seamlessly integrate disparate inputs. It's the single good feeling you can get in a theater from words, music, spectacle, and someone you like sitting next to you—all at the same time. In contrast, most of our present technology tends to deal with each input . . . as a separate entity.[3]

Integration, as defined earlier in this chapter, often requires more of the Simplicity Marketer's effort and expense than does Aggregation, because even more customer stress is being absorbed as the fuel for providing the ultimate in value-added one-stop shopping. But among the substrategies for the first two R's—Replace and Repackage—it is Integration that generally yields the closest partnership and, hence, the deepest relationship between customer and brand.

In creating superior customer value (beyond economic), Integration combines the best of Consolidation and Aggregation and typically applies them to complex components. Like Consolidation, Integration bundles complementary products for synergy—and reduces the number of transactions, steps, or stops—but, like Aggregation, also preserves the integrity of the integrated components and, without compromise, produces some additional benefit beyond the sum of the parts.

Cornerstones of high-margin Integration opportunities are complex tasks, the imperative that these tasks be done, and significant possibility of error or failure. Stress-reducing approaches to true integrated bundling, enabling whole systems, and allowing the customer to do things that could not otherwise be done with separate products alone and/or without the expertise of the integrator, include: (1) integrating to save time, (2) integrating to eliminate product incompatibility, and (3) integrating for conflict resolution.

Integrating to Save Time
Nothing can potentially save customers more time than intelligent bundling of products into effective whole systems. Recurring complex tasks are fertile ground for uncovering time-saving opportunities. In Chapter 3 we discussed the consumer's act of bill paying as a regularly recurring task of multiple, often repetitive, steps. In business, this same function is even more complex by virtue of the volume of transactions as well as the firm's accounting software and payables management process.

OneCore.com has targeted small businesses with its Online Bill Payment process, a Web-based integrated solution that first reduces the number of steps (like a Consolidation, Chapter 4) but then goes further by integrating with the customer's existing accounting software and with other business banking services that OneCore.com offers. OneCore.com reduces bill payment from nine steps to four (as depicted in Table 5.1), lets the customer enter a bill into the system any time via the Web, easily download bills into their own accounting software and—by automating recurring payments—never have to see that bill again for vendors to receive an accurately processed business-style check. OneCore integrates this service with a money market account that earns money market rates while its customer keeps the float until checks are presented for payment. At the extreme, it provides its customers with one "e-Finance account" that, in addition to paying bills, integrates related functions such as payroll processing, merchant card transactions, managing the company's 401(k), and obtaining credit.

Table 5.1

Traditional Bill Payment Steps	OneCore Online Bill Payment Steps
1. Open bills and match to P.O./ invoice	1. Open bills and match to P.O./ invoice.
2. Post bills to accounting software	2. Post bills to OneCore account
3. Query accounting software to determine which bills to pay	3. Approve online from anywhere; OneCore prints and mails checks automatically
4. Print checks and remittance slips	4. Simply import file into accounting software
5. Meet with authorized check signer	
6. File appropriate paperwork	
7. Stuff checks and remittance slips in envelopes	
8. Seal envelopes and affix postage	
9. Mail checks	

Source: www.onecore.com, September 12, 1999

In the educational realm, Barnes & Noble's college bookstore division offers professors a recurring time-saver that leverages a business model pioneered by a startup called Book Tech: integrated course packs of required reading materials that are customized to the professor's specs for a given class. By integrating specified articles, excerpts of books, out-of-print material, and any other reproducible reading that a professor may prescribe, and then assessing copyright status, arranging permissions and royalty payments, and finally reproducing the materials in a bundled package for sale to students, this service is a tremendous time-saver for academics who must repeatedly face having the proper reading materials available in the campus bookstore by the beginning of each term. Adding so much value to the basic service of photocopying created a popular one-stop shopping solution that not only saves professors time but also provides students with a single time-saving transaction.

There are also increasing opportunities at the wholesale level for saving time through Integration. For example, few things are more stressful than moving one's home and, though that's a seldom-recurring event for individuals, it's a daily event for Realtors. So ServiceMaster wholesales an integrated package called MoveManager to real estate brokers such as Coldwell Banker to help ensure that their clients' moves go smoothly. MoveManager combines a moving checklist, change of address service, truck rental service, cable and satellite service connection, home repairs, and savings on home inspection services, van lines, and insurance all in one package that the Realtor can attach itself to for a comprehensive one-stop shopping solution that saves time, money, and stress.

Whether the tasks being integrated recur a few times a year (like reproduction and copyright management for college course materials) or every day (like a Realtor selling homes), *recurrence* is a pointer to time-saving integration opportunities because it multiplies customer value over and over again. Integrated services like OneCore and Move Manager not only save time but also allow substitution of *better quality time* for the time saved—since time spent on mundane, repetitive tasks can be spent on growing the business.

Integrating to Eliminate Product Incompatibility

Complex technologies interact with each other in complex ways. The result is interdependencies in which product incompatibility poses a threat to the customer that separate but interdependent products will not work together as well as they should or at all. Nowhere has the resulting anxiety created greater opportunity than in the systems integration approach to business-to-business marketing.

Systems integration brings together individual products from different vendors that must combine into a whole system. In the information technology realm, systems integrators may identify and purchase the components for resale, or may actually make one or more of the components themselves—but add value primarily through providing consulting services and customized software designed to make the component products work together seamlessly. The systems integrator provides a single transaction for the customer as well as an ongoing single point of contact for operational support and system management expertise. Since many information technology solutions must be cobbled together by combining specialized products from relatively small, young companies and core products from well-known brands, revenue growth in the systems integration category has sizzled since the mid-1990s. Vendor-independent integrators like EDS and Andersen Consulting have led the way, catering to the world's largest companies with complex multivendor solutions that require eliminating incompatibilities not just within the solution system itself, but also bridging new technologies to the customer's older legacy systems, such as long-established billing systems and customer databases.

While some of the growth in systems integration demand was driven by one-time Y2K technical concerns, most was driven by broader trends that continue to overwhelm customers with stress: Internet evolution and the rise of electronic commerce, shifting supply chains, and ever-more complex mission-critical enterprise networks. In any of these arenas—particularly the last—product incompatibilities could cause problems of ship-sinking proportions.

Representative of this value-added one-stop shopping, consider what EDS has done for gas turbine manufacturer Rolls-Royce. Using software from SAP in Germany, and more than 700 different hardware and software products from dozens of vendors, EDS integrated enterprise resource planning for all Rolls-Royce Allison manufacturing and replaced four different purchasing systems and 12 different part masters with one integrated information system that allowed data entry once and only once. For the customer, all this and the expertise to make it work came through one vendor with a single point of contact.

As systems integrators have flourished, more traditional product and service providers have made systems integration services a larger part of their own offerings—and often a major revenue stream. Professional video vendors such as Tektronix began approaching large broadcasting facilities with turnkey end-to-end solutions that involved directly competitive products as well as Tektronix' own, and integrated them into a whole system spanning the capture, editing, and broadcasting of program content. Telephone companies set up network integration subsidiaries to compete directly with the likes of EDS, Andersen, and IBM, focusing on integrating large customers' voice and data networks. The tremendous success of Lucent Technologies, which increased its market capitalization from about $17 billion to $200 billion in just the first three years since spinning off from AT&T as a separate company, did so in part by showcasing its network management services as a primary differentiator against its competition. Its NetCare Services plans, integrates, and provides ongoing management of data networks of every size. Meanwhile, in somewhat less complex markets like office equipment, there was more than sufficient complexity for Danka to take on much larger Xerox by reselling and integrating the copiers, printers, and fax machines from Kodak, Toshiba, Hewlett-Packard, Canon, Minolta, and others to compete directly with Xerox-only solutions.

In the consumer market, customers have shown their appreciation at the cash register for product-compatibility Integration in categories ranging from personal computers to home entertainment centers to retail. Back to the example of software bundled with computers: besides the obvious economic and time-saving benefit of the single transaction, the computer-plus-software bundle offers all the advantages of Aggregation plus the added value of knowing that the software will work on your new computer—without having to check each software application's system requirements, or ensure the compatibility of the particular software version, or risk problems in loading the software yourself as you would if buying the software separately.

In the home entertainment centers category, Bose introduced its Lifestyle systems to provide a seamlessly integrated world-class audio entertainment unit. Everything but the speakers fits into a sleek silvery box the size of a book, and Bose added value with the first wireless remote control that enables customers to operate it from anywhere in the home (yes, even through walls). Pushing a single button just once on the remote turns on and begins playing a CD or a favorite radio station. Integration not only ensures the compatibility of the CD player, FM/AM tuner, high-quality speakers, and wireless remote, but also is engineered to deliver performance superior to that of separately purchased best-of-breed components. For example, because the Lifestyle amplifier output is matched and contoured to its speakers, such fine-tuned Integration further simplifies by extending the life of the speakers (since it is difficult to overdrive them) and eliminating the need for the Loudness button found on most quality stereos. Lifestyle preempted the mix-and-match mentality of many stereo connoisseurs who might have otherwise carefully shopped for separate components from different manufacturers. This excerpt from the Bose Web site distilled the essence of stressless quality, under the headline, Beyond Components:

Traditionally, owning a stereo system means making room for a large stack of complicated components. . . . After all, it's the music you want in your life. Ideally, you wouldn't experience the machine at all.

Through elegant simplicity and value-added positioning, Bose now dominates the $500+ shelf system audio category, with the highest measured brand loyalty in the business.[4]

At retail, product-compatibility Integration is by no means limited to technology categories (though certainly Best Buy's success is largely due to the customers' ability to ensure—before they buy—that the PC, digital telephone, high-speed modem, and cable adaptors they just picked out will all work together). Consider the *other* kind of hardware: the low-tech, hammer-and-nails variety. The opportunity for customer failure in hardware purchases is often greater than in many other retail categories, because of the do-it-yourself wild card. Though superstores such as Home Depot have enjoyed undeniable success and do many things well, customer loyalty is especially strong at regional hardware superstores such as Eagle in the northwestern United States. With inventory that is broad and deep, but with Eagle's more accessible knowledgeable salespeople, customers can significantly reduce product-compatibility problems before they get home to work on their projects. The inventory-plus-expertise environment at Eagle helps ensure that when the customer gets home to hang wood paneling on the basement walls, the drill bit, C-clamps, wood adhesive, and caulking gun will all be the appropriate type and size for the paneling purchased at the same time. Buying these components at more than one retail outlet, or in more of a self-help environment, substantially increases the risk of either failure or having to return one or more components if compatibility problems arise. Depending on the project, a smaller hardware store might have the expertise but not the selection, and a self-help warehouse store might have the selection without the available expertise. So neither can supply product-compatibility Integration as well as the inventory-plus-expertise integrator.

Integrating for Conflict Resolution

Just as time and the frustration of product incompatibility are significant sources of stress, so are human conflict and confrontation. Notwithstanding those very aggressive individuals who thrive on confrontation as sport, in the digital age the average customer is finding it more important than ever to keep blood-pressure-raising conflicts to a minimum. Therein lies the marketing opportunity to simplify conflict resolution through Integration.

Major causes of conflict or argument related to a purchase, beyond outright dissatisfaction with a product's performance, are *postpurchase customer support* and *price negotiation.* In multivendor situations, whether it be in business or consumer marketing, buck-passing when something goes wrong after the sale can be a major headache for customers. Anyone who has done any home remodeling without the value-added Integration of a good contractor has likely experienced some variation of this: When the paint starts cracking at the corners of the new crown moulding only two months after the job is finished, the painter says it's because the carpenter who hung the moulding didn't properly putty the corner joints, and the carpenter says it's because the painter didn't put on the extra coat of paint required to put a lasting cover over the corners. Where does the customer go from there?

Opportunities for conflict-resolving Integration abound in interdependent high-tech categories. Let's say a customer is running a consulting business from home, using a PC, a digital phone line from US West, a digital modem from Motorola, and Internet service from Winstar. A client calls and says, "I just sent you an urgent e-mail. Please review it ASAP and call me back right away." But suddenly, inexplicably, the customer is unable to successfully log onto the Internet to access e-mail. Call number 1 for resolution: The customer calls Winstar, who says, "Everything's working normally on our end; it must be a US West problem with the phone line." Call number 2: US West says, "Your line tests out fine from our central office; you must be having a problem with your modem." Call number 3: Motorola says, "Let's walk through all your modem initiation programming strings (just what the customer wants to do now) to be sure the modem is dialing properly; (10 minutes later) okay, your test call just now connected with me here, so the problem's not with the modem. Sounds like a Windows 98 bug; you might want to call your PC manufacturer or Microsoft to see if something is corrupted. If that's not it, the only thing I could suggest is calling US West or Winstar to see if the problem's on their end." Of course, the average time for each of these calls was 25 minutes, including 12 minutes of hold time, so it's now nearly two hours later and the customer is nowhere. Talk about stress!

Intel saw opportunity in the frustration of conflict when it launched a subscription-based help desk called AnswerExpress. For the PC user, AnswerExpress was designed to be a place to call with a hardware or software problem and get technical help with a single phone call and no buck-passing—regardless of what brand of PC (Apple excluded) or whether the problem is with the computer itself, the operating system, or any of the software applications that AnswerExpress supports. (This service also gave the Intel brand a more direct relationship with end users of computers, since Intel's computer chips are an "ingredient brand" in PCs and the PC brands historically control end user customer relationships.)

Another source of conflict-related stress is price negotiation—as anyone who's ever bought a car knows all too well. But in multivendor situations, without Integration there may also be multiple prices to negotiate. Returning to systems integrators like EDS and Andersen, they not only provide the conflict-resolution that is only possible through a single-point of contact that eliminates buck-passing but also compress the products of multiple vendors into a single price negotiation and transaction—reducing confrontation as well as saving time.

■ How to *Repackage*

The same basic steps employed in Chapter 4 with the first R of Simplicity Marketing, adapted to the second R, can be used to develop a blueprint for implementing Repackaging. Step 1: assess the potential of your brand and products to benefit from Repackaging. Step 2: inventory ways that you could leverage the second R, using the checklists that follow for each of the Repackage substrategies, Aggregation and Integration. Step 3: ensure that the power of Repackaging is incorporated into your positioning, making stress-reduction benefits as obvious and compelling as possible.

Because Repackaging always involves bundling things together in some way, a thorough review of your options may involve scenarios that include new strategic alliances or even merging with or acquiring another company.

STEP 1: GAUGE YOUR REPACKAGE POTENTIAL

As with Replace, audit your category, brand, and products/services—including presale and postsale customer service—for opportunity assessment. (You may wish to refer back to Chapter 4, starting on page 84, for a more complete description of each of the variables below.)

1. **Assess the level of customer anxiety in the category.** This is more challenging in Integration than Aggregation. Aggregation often happens within the confines of a single product category (remember mutual funds and Just For Feet?), but Integration often involves multiple categories. So be sure to look not only at the anxiety level in each of the categories to be integrated but also at the anxiety currently produced by the ways those categories interact with each other in the customer's total experience.

2. **Qualify the product/service as an Aggregator or Integrator.** Use the checklists under Step 2 to determine if Aggregation or Integration is a good fit for your product, service, or brand. As with Replace, remember that Repackage opportunities in some categories may just as likely be found in ongoing customer care as in making the initial sale.

3. **Assess your sustainable advantage as an Aggregator or Integrator.** All other things being equal, Aggregation is easier for a competitor to emulate than is Integration. There is often less product development involved, and less complexity in packaging. Barriers to entry are relatively low, for example, for your competitor in investment services to put together a new mutual fund that has an investment theme, diversification, and risk level similar to your own—compared to, say, how high barriers to entry are for a competitor in the broader category of financial services to offer a meaningful package of integrated banking and investment services.

4. **Assess the likely perceived economic value of stress reduction.** The cost associated with acquiring the ingredients for Aggregation or Integration may result in a business model incapable of producing a selling price that the customer is willing to pay. Whether driving up your costs by acquiring intellectual property for repackaging and resale (*Reader's*

Digest and Personics), or wholesale purchasing of software (systems integrators), ensure that you can protect minimum acceptable margins within your customers' price elasticity threshold.

5. Assess your opportunity to differentiate an aggregated or integrated package. In Repackaging, differentiation versus other aggregators or integrators may occur on three levels beyond price and distribution: (1) within individual components of the package/bundle, (2) in the composition of the bundle (that is, what components are present at all), and (3) in the way that the bundle is presented to leverage its simplicity and stress-reducing capability. The most powerful differentiation opportunities leverage all three of these dimensions just as Bose Lifestyle has.

Reminder: Numbers 1, 2, 4, and 5 above may require customer research.

STEP 2: INVENTORY YOUR AGGREGATION/INTEGRATION PROOF POINTS

Whether Aggregating or Integrating, the Simplicity Marketing message will be built on proof points, as discussed in Chapter 4, that give customers reasons to believe the promise of stress reduction. Use the following checklists to answer questions about your product or service that will help identify relevant proof points.

Aggregation Checklist

1. What components does this aggregate? (If five or less, be sure this is not more appropriate for a Consolidation strategy than for aggregation.)

2. Does it preserve the integrity of the individual components being aggregated? (If the individual components are significantly compromised versus how they behave as stand-alones, this may also signal Consolidation rather than Aggregation.)

[continued]

3. What added value does this overlay on top of pulling together the aggregated components into one product or service?

4. Does this significantly reduce customer stress? Specifically, how does it save time, thinking, effort, or headaches?

5. To what degree and how does this fulfill the promise of one or more types of Aggregation: many-in-one aggregation in a high-choice category, aggregation of digital-age information, and aggregation in the distribution channel to save the customer time?

6. Is there significant current dissatisfaction level with the unaggregated components and/or with other aggregators? How does this Aggregation address that dissatisfaction?

Integration Checklist

1. What components does this integrate?

2. Does it preserve the integrity of the individual components being integrated?

3. Does it create a whole system that provides customer value beyond the sum of its parts?

[continued]

4. How does that value significantly reduce customer stress?

5. How does this save the customer significant time? If business-to-business, does it also save the customer significant time to market with products and services for their end user customers?

6. How does this eliminate or significantly reduce product incompatibilities that would otherwise exist between the separate components of the bundle/package?

7. How does this significantly reduce the potential for stress-producing conflict or confrontation after/before the sale?

8. Does this Repackaging incorporate components that will likely be perceived as too far removed from the core identity of your brand? (See the next section, "When Repackaging is a Bad Idea.")

9. Will this Integration require a significant strategic alliance with another brand, or perhaps even its acquisition, to effectively provide the proposed bundle and sufficiently service the customer after the sale?

STEP 3: INCORPORATE REPACKAGE IN POSITIONING

The following final checkpoints clarify positioning issues, as demonstrated in "Anatomy of a Repackaging: Integrion Financial Network" which follows the next section. As explained in Chapter 4 for use with Substitution and Consolidation, these questions are just as relevant for ensuring effective Aggregation or Integration:

1. Is stress reduction built into the positioning?

2. What are the stress-related reasons to believe?

3. How does stress reduction impact perceptions on key drivers of brand choice?

4. To what degree can you own stress reduction in the category?

■ When Repackaging Is a Bad Idea

In the past decade's rush to bundle, marketers have often underestimated the risks. Those risks are largely about *degree*, as overzealousness can result in bundling *past* the point of diminishing returns—and losing sight of *optimum* choice versus maximum choice (Chapter 2). Misreading the risks of "overbundling" has already cost some companies not just millions, but *billions* of dollars. So let's confront and review the perils of going too far, in hopes of avoiding them.

A strategic checklist of Repackaging risks includes underestimating any or all of the following: (1) diversity of individual customer needs; (2) the customer's need or desire to create their own "best-of-breed" bundle; (3) apathy about one or more components of the bundle; (4) the burden of customer care and systems support; (5) vulnerability to niche specialists and strategic marketing alliances; (6) consequences of problems with any single product in the bundle; (7) customer resistance to how far your brand can be stretched; (8) leaving money on the table by unnecessarily sacrificing margin. Because the bundling frenzy has been so intense in the telecommunications category, and because this category is so pervasive and the dollar stakes so high, we will use examples from it to illustrate each risk.

DIVERSITY OF INDIVIDUAL CUSTOMER NEEDS

As choices proliferate and mass customization increases, customer savvy and expectations can translate to a greater diversity of needs from one customer to the next. With more heterogeneity in needs, the more robust the bundle, the more likely that larger numbers of customers will perceive only part of the bundle as relevant. And the more of the bundle perceived irrelevant, the more irrelevant your brand.

Several years ago, MCI introduced a new bundle of residential telecom services that included a home security system (given its use of the telephone for monitoring the alarm), along with services like long distance and Internet access. But did home security really make the MCI brand more relevant to the communications customer, or did it dilute the clarity of MCI's perceived core competencies? The answer is implied in the fact that, as MCI has continued to refine its bundling, home security is absent from today's residential bundles.

CUSTOMERS' NEED TO CREATE THEIR OWN BEST-OF-BREED BUNDLES

Customers' savviness may also translate to a preference for creating their own best-of-breed bundles involving more than one brand. By 1995, even before the Telecom Reform Act of 1996 sought to allow long distance and local phone companies to compete in each other's core businesses, most leading telecommunications brands were positioning themselves as one-stop shopping sources across a range of products and services—especially in high-value market segments such as home-based businesses and technology-intensive vertical markets. Yet, even as major brands touted promises of imminent full-service one-stop shopping and spent billions on the infrastructure to deliver it, a Mercer Management Consulting study reported that only 6% of all customers would seriously consider buying all of their communications services from one company.

Some customers believed that they could get better individual best-of-breed services from multiple vendors, while others (in spite of time constraints) thought they could save money by piecing together their own quilt of services and shopping aggressively for the best value in each one. Still other customers—notably IT managers in larger companies—prided themselves on their expertise in identifying the components of best-of-breed bundles and then managing implementation, so one-stop shopping was perceived as a threat to their job security.

APATHY TOWARD ONE OR MORE BUNDLE COMPONENTS

Sometimes the bundling opportunity tempts marketers to reach for the newest, hottest innovation as a key component of a package—to add excitement, breadth, or both. But often what is newest and hottest either doesn't have the product kinks worked out yet or will appeal only to bleeding-edge early adopters. This drags down the rest of the bundle with the mainstream market.

While the World Wide Web was just being born, the Baby Bells, Time Warner, and other communications giants were investing aggressively in the development of interactive television and so-called full-service networks. The exception was Southwestern Bell, which was roundly criticized as a laggard in pursuing the vision of offering video-on-demand and other interactive broadband services in a package with telephony, Internet services, and traditional one-way cable TV. With 20/20 hindsight, we now know what happened beyond the technical issues that thwarted full-service network deployment: customers preferred their interactive services via computer rather than television, and the Web trumped interactive TV and essentially rendered it irrelevant for the remainder of the twentieth century. Fiscally, Southwestern Bell had the last laugh when its competitors—the presumed leaders in pursuing the broadband bundle—had *each* spent hundreds of millions or even billions of dollars on infrastructure to deliver bundle parts that customers were largely apathetic toward (especially as the Web began to satisfy more of the customers' needs for interactive information and entertainment).

BURDEN OF CUSTOMER CARE AND SYSTEMS SUPPORT

In some cases, the requirements for postsale customer care increase exponentially when a bundle gets too robust. Complex bundles can place complex demands both on the marketer's human resources and internal systems. Such demands may include training single-point-of-contact service representatives on multiple components of the bundle, integrating the customer databases of different business units, integrating previously separate extranets and/or separate Web sites of different business units, and getting billing systems in place to provide the customer with a single integrated bill for multiple services.

Billing for bundles is no trivial matter. The software reengineering required to support integrated billing for previously separate products and services can cost millions if not tens of millions of dollars for large companies. This complexity is also often a key driver of time to market. As the Baby Bells scrambled to compete with major long distance brands on services beyond local phone service, product managers would identify compelling concepts for products/services bundles—only to find out that there was no way to bill for such bundled services and that integrated billing capability would take much longer to develop than developing specifications for the bundle itself, ensuring the interoperability of bundle components, and pricing and packaging them for sale together.

And even when done, aggregated billing may not be enthusiastically received by customers if the format of the bill itself is confusing or hard to digest. By 1998 Ameritech was among the first to have bundled local and long distance phone service, cellular service, Internet service, security monitoring services, and cable TV service on a single bill—yet it initially met resistance because the bill was difficult for customers to understand. Ensure that you have a billing strategy before investing in bundled product development.

VULNERABILITY TO NICHE SPECIALISTS AND STRATEGIC MARKETING ALLIANCES

The allure of one-stop shopping and "share of wallet" can compel marketers to try to be all things to all people. But when a brand spreads its bundle beyond its perceived core competencies, vulnerability to competition from niche specialists or strategic marketing alliances can increase dramatically.

Niche competition may manifest in two forms: smaller, "pure-play" competitors who specialize in one of the products within your bundle, and big brands from another related category that muscle into a niche with a relatively narrow and tightly targeted product offering. Pure-play competition against the titans of telecom was most evident in the Internet services arena. Regional ISPs (Internet service providers) were initially perceived as better equipped to provide Internet access service than, say, a Baby Bell, because pure-play ISPs specialized exclusively in the Internet and had to do a better job than a large corporation whose perceived core competencies and primary revenue streams were in voice telephony rather than digital data.

Meanwhile, vendors such as Cisco and 3Com that supplied big telecom brands with networking equipment saw another big brand that had not previously been a competitor—Intel—start muscling in on a tightly defined but very profitable niche in networking, while being careful not to compete with Cisco's core products in Cisco's primary target markets. Suddenly Intel, long perceived as just a chip manufacturer, was offering its first networking products that competed with Cisco and 3Com's bundles of connectivity products for small business.

Strategic marketing alliances can also threaten bundling success, even more so than niche specialists in cases where powerful brands are involved. With the proliferation of digital-age *keiretsu*, even AT&T's bundles were being effectively attacked by multivendor bundles in which at least one of the bundle component providers was perceived to have superior products to AT&T and reasonably comparable overall brand reliability.

PROBLEMS WITH ANY SINGLE PRODUCT IN THE BUNDLE

Like any system, the bundle is only as strong as its weakest link. Perceived or actual weaknesses of any single bundle component can lose customers for all the product lines involved. Such weaknesses may be in perceived product performance or actual product failure/under-delivery, or in either actual or anticipated product-specific postsale customer care.

If, for example, for the business market in the '90s, a Baby Bell bundled voice mail, local and toll calling plans, and an 800-number service that was inferior to AT&T's, some business customers shunned the Bell's bundle that included 800 service—sometimes because the 800 component wouldn't meet their needs, and other times because it raised perceptual issues: "If their 800 service isn't competitive, I wonder how good their business voice mail product is." It wasn't long before that customer was buying an AT&T bundle which, among other things, packaged toll calls with 800 service. Suddenly the Bell company had lost an existing customer of its highly margined toll call product.

CUSTOMER RESISTANCE TO BRAND EXTENSION

Brand extension can confuse customers when the value promise is unclear. The perils of overbundling often boil down to a customer thinking "What does Brand X, which is known for *that*, know about *this*?

In the pre-Web rush to bundle telecom and cable TV services, cable companies began making huge investments in trying to upgrade their networks just as telcos had invested in broadband infrastructure. But in essence, many customers said, "I'm not sure my cable company is reliable enough to provide reliable phone service—and, by the way, what does my phone company really know about television and entertainment?" Especially at that time, both the telco and cable brands were reaching too far beyond their core brand equities, and risked tarnishing perceptions of core products bundled with products best left to each other's existing businesses. Fortunately for all concerned, the rise of the Internet ensured that this kind of convergence battle didn't proceed far enough back then to "blow the whole bundle" and cost either side too many of its customers.

Leaving Money on the Table

If you are already the leader in each product line that is bundled together, you will have to weigh the trade-off between the incremental loyalty created by successful bundling and the risk of reducing margins (vs. margins on separate sale of the bundled components). Margins may be impacted by customer expectations of paying less for a package, though there are surely cases where the package justifies a premium instead. Margins may also be very significantly impacted by the increased cost of customer care, systems support, and product interoperability requirements as discussed above.

But when in doubt, if you don't lead the way in bundling, a competitor likely will—especially as customers' perceived value increasingly rests on stress relief.

To Repackage or Not to Repackage: Prudence versus Pessimism

It's not that difficult to generalize from these telecommunications examples. Some would argue, for instance, that the rise of post-PC era information appliances is a testament to the fact that desktop computers overbundled all along by doing too many jobs not particularly well—which the individual, dedicated-task appliance is designed to do better. It remains to be seen to what degree the limitations of the PC will be sufficient to fuel a revolutionary fragmentation of the personal computer market that runs counter to integration and one-stop shopping.

Regardless, this formidable list of potholes in the yellow brick road to bundling is not intended to scare you away from Repackaging. If you have asked and answered the questions posed by the considerations above, your chances for success—and for optimal scaling of the bundle to reduce customer stress—will be far greater.

Anatomy of a Repackaging: Integrion

SIMPLICITY MARKETER:	**Integrion Financial Network LLC**
PRODUCT:	**Integrion Interactive Financial Services**
LAUNCH:	**1997**
PRIMARY SUBSTRATEGY:	**Integration**

When the Internet turned the business world on its ear in the '90s, the banking industry realized that it could dramatically cut costs by bringing transactions and customer care online. But actually executing was formidable. Some banks tried to tackle electronic commerce by building their own systems and cobbling together network upgrades and software from multiple vendors, and a very few even succeeded—mistakes and expense notwithstanding. But most waited, hoping for a savior. In 1996, that savior was born when IBM and 16 banks invested in a new independent company to be called Integrion.

Integrion's sole focus would be to provide financial institutions with integrated solutions and a shared infrastructure for interactive banking and e-commerce services, selling these services not only to its owner banks but also to their competitors. Created to make complex e-commerce technology and integration simple, Integrion set out to be the banking CIO's best friend with the promise of stress reduction. And plenty of stress there was, as banks worldwide raced to leverage the Internet to improve customer service, reduce operating costs, and gain competitive advantage—with great uncertainty, and with many billions of dollars at stake.

In contrast to Chapter 4's consumer product case (Apple's iMac), Integrion is a broad-shouldered business-to-business application of Simplicity Marketing. The following profiles Integrion's strategy in the context of Simplicity Marketing's 4th R, Repackage, and specifically its Integration substrategy.[5]

PRODUCT

Integrion's initial product offering was a bundle of bundles—three integrated packages in one that would allow banks to offer their own customers a full range of online banking services and support. These packages ran on an IBM-built-and-managed network (subsequently acquired by AT&T), a proprietary Interactive Financial Services (IFS) platform, and software from multiple vendors integrated to work together seamlessly while still allowing individual banks to customize their own front ends (the look and feel of what the bank's customers see online at the bank's Web site).

Integrion's initial three online banking packages were Core Banking, Bill Payment and Presentment, and Consolidated Customer Care. Core Banking included checking and savings accounts, credit cards, certificates of deposit, mortgage loans, installment loans, and lines of credit. Bill Payment and Presentment, for which Integrion integrated the services of CheckFree Corporation, enabled electronic delivery of bills, one-click payment approval, remittances for electronic payment of one-time and recurring bills, payee management, and storage of bills. Consolidated Customer Care allowed banks to electronically handle customer inquiries, statements, payment status, claims tracking and resolution, check requests, management of incoming message queues, technical support, and communicating with customers online both through e-mail and broadcast messages.

INTEGRATION CHECKLIST

What components does Integrion integrate?
Twenty or so functional components itemized above, plus several ancillary product components, and hundreds of behind-the-scenes, invisible technical pieces that comprised a whole, synergistic system. Somewhat in the vein of "mutual funds of mutual funds" (but much more complex), one aspect that made Integrion such a powerful package is that it not only integrated multiple components into three focused bundles but also added an additional layer of integration by integrating the bundles into a full-service portfolio of solutions—while still offering the flexibility of allowing banks to buy any one of the bundles individually or all together. (For example, some banks that had already invested in their own electronic bill payment and presentment systems wanted to keep what they had, but still needed lots of help on core banking and customer care.)

Does Integrion preserve the integrity of the individual components being integrated?
Yes. With the possible exception of special nuances that "build-your-own" banks, such as Wells Fargo, may have built into their own internal systems to address a special need, each Integrion component was at least as functional, robust, and secure as the equivalent component purchased separately from a niche vendor (and had the advantage of being integrated with the rest of the Integrion system).

Does Integrion create a whole system that provides customer value beyond the sum of its parts?

Absolutely. Many online banking functions and services are highly interdependent (such as paying bills and managing a checking account), so most of Integrion's value was in the "connective tissue" it provided—the way that the system components work together—rather than in the value of the components themselves. Beyond the technical value, there was very significant economic value. As a contrasting reference point, when banks deployed ATMs, each had to build their own ATM technical infrastructure. Integrion took such inefficiencies out of the system for e-commerce, so that Integrion's customers didn't have to build the system, maintain it, upgrade it, or hire and support the expensive, hard-to-find technical people that it required to be effective and reliable.

How does that value significantly reduce customer stress?

As the Internet mainstreamed, both the management and technical personnel of major banks were under tremendous pressure to demonstrate leadership in online banking services. There was investor pressure to reduce costs and strengthen competitive advantage, for which online transactions and service held great promise. There was customer pressure as well, as time-starved consumers increasingly turned to the Internet as a replacement for trips and calls to the bank. So Integrion came on stream at the very time that banks needed more robust online services to succeed in retaining their customers. The considerable cost advantage also reduced budgetary stress and freed up bank CIO's financial resources for other stress-reducing activities. Integrion consolidated tremendous volume from multiple large banks to make online banking a mega-scale business—driving the cost per transaction below what even the biggest banks could do on their own. By functioning as a "buying club" on behalf of its customer banks, Integrion exercised tremendous leverage when weighing in on pricing discussions with suppliers of the required technical and processing pieces.

How does Integrion save the customer significant time? If business-to-business, does it also save the customer significant time to market with products and services for their end user customers?

Integrion saved banks both time and time to market. From a bank CIO's perspective, it would likely have been necessary to work with *dozens* of individual vendors to emulate Integrion's integrated services, so there was tremendous time savings among CIO organization managers just in dealing with vendors alone—

savings which was additive to the time saved day to day by having Integrion maintain and upgrade infrastructure and software. From a time-to-market standpoint, working with a single vendor not only saved staff time but especially compressed the development time required to make all components work together (as discussed next under product incompatibilities). Integrion customer Washington Mutual estimates that—given the other business initiatives the company was pursuing at the time—its online core banking services came to market at least a year sooner by virtue of Integrion's services than if the bank had built its own system, and at least six months sooner than if the bank had gone to an Integrion competitor (which typically offered the additional service of front-end design, but offered less robust, less well-integrated middleware— the guts of the transaction and inquiry management systems).

How does Integrion eliminate or significantly reduce product incompatibilities that would otherwise exist between the separate components of the bundle/package?

Without Integrion, banks had tremendous challenges in integrating server technology, software, network technology, Web browsers, and transaction processing methodologies such as CheckFree's. In building the Integrion network, IBM used tools and software from more than 30 different vendors and produced programming solutions to make them all work together seamlessly. Very few of these components worked together in the required way without some sort of customized technical integration. (Incompatibilities were not just limited to products; they extended to the cultures of the different vendors required to cooperate on product development. For example, Integrion not only had to make the products of IBM and CheckFree work together, but also had to manage getting the cultures of these two vendors—IBM's deep-rooted, process-oriented culture, and CheckFree's more nimble and entrepreneurial but less process-oriented culture—to work together, which was not a trivial management integration challenge that Integrion's bank customers were spared.)

How does this significantly reduce the potential for stress-producing conflict or confrontation after/before the sale?

Integrion reduced the potential for conflict on three dimensions: price negotiations, postsale customer support, and network security. While build-your-own banks individually negotiated pricing with multiple vendors occurring at frequent intervals as each component was needed, Integrion reduced this process for its customers to a single negotiation that was locked into a multiyear services contract. For operational support, maintenance, and upgrades, these contracts spelled out performance standards and penalties if Integrion failed to meet those standards. Security was another key flashpoint for stress, as no bank CIO wanted to ever be in the position of explaining to the CEO how private customer accounts or transactions were violated by computer hackers. So banks could put the onus on Integrion and a network built by IBM, the world leader in developing secure systems. For all these areas of potential conflict and confrontation, Integrion stood as one vendor, one phone call, with no buck-passing if and when problems occurred.

Does this Repackaging incorporate components that will likely be perceived as too far removed from the core identity of the Integrion brand?

Every service bundled by Integrion was part of the vision that created the company, and all were integral to online banking and customer care. Though Integrion was a young brand with minimal brand equity initially, having been created in 1996 and not aggressively marketed before 1999, early brand/corporate identity research found that "Integrion Financial Network" perceptually telegraphed industrial-strength *integrated* services as well as "integrity" (another stress-reliever), and "network" at least implied online as part of the identity. To keep products close to this core identity, Integrion set boundaries and resisted early temptations to stretch the brand too far. For example, it declined to get into the front-end business, deciding that designing customized end user Web sites for banks was better left to either the multitude of Web designers who had no middleware or systems expertise, or to competitors like Security First (which offered a range of services similar to some of Integrion's but specialized in world-class front-end design). In fact, *not* offering front ends helped Integrion differentiate against Security First by emphasizing core competency in middleware, systems, infrastructure, and ability to handle heavy volumes—all of which were harder to develop than front ends and maximized Integrion's credibility in the areas that bank CIOs would likely perceive as most formidable (and, therefore, most anxiety-producing).

Will this Integration require a significant strategic alliance with another brand, or perhaps even its acquisition, to effectively provide the proposed bundle and sufficiently service the customer after the sale?

Integrion was unusual from the start by virtue of having been created by a consortium, which was a considerable alliance from day one. But there was recognition from the beginning that strategic partnerships with two brands—IBM and CheckFree—would be critical in getting Integrion services to market in a timely, reliable manner. So Integrion not only worked with each of these partners extremely closely, but spent considerable time and energy to get them to work with each other (as noted in the culture comment above). While product development was one key driver of this strategy, certainly the other was the brand equity and credibility that IBM and CheckFree had already established in their respective areas of expertise. Without such credibility, it is extremely difficult for a new company to be taken seriously as an "enterprise-level" information technology vendor (as demonstrated by the fate of Netscape Communications when it tried to reposition itself from a Web browser company to an enterprise software and consulting company before finally being acquired by America Online).

POSITIONING LEVERAGE

Is stress reduction built into the positioning?

First, Integrion built stress reduction into its very identity by developing a preemptive corporate brand that said, first and foremost, integration—a loaded word laden with heavy overtones of stress for bank CIOs faced with integrating a complex array of products, processes, functions, technologies, and vendors. Integrion as a brand name was a strategic bullseye in encompassing a relevant, robust promise within. This was augmented by Integrion's positioning as a "buying club" that potentially represented 60% of all the demand deposits in the United States, signifying clout with vendors and the absorption of stress that banks would otherwise experience in dealing with these vendors on their own without an ally. Though Integrion's advertising was minimal (since the company initially targeted only the top 50 banks and therefore was able to communicate with them by more cost-effective means), its early Web presence and collateral material emphasized its simplicity payoff by positioning The Integrion Solution as a "single point of connectivity" for end-to-end services integrating best-in-class applications with the bank's host systems, the Internet, and the telephone.

What are the stress-related reasons to believe?

Stress-related reasons to believe the Integrion brand promise included the presence of IBM and CheckFree "ingredients," and the fact that 16 of the best-known banks in the United States were investors and customers. All that this implied allowed the Integrion target audience to take a shortcut to feeling more comfortable and believing that reliable help was on the way even before taking the time to fully investigate Integrion products, service, and cost. Integrion's obvious understanding of their customer's business was also a key reason to believe. Integrion made this apparent with specific, empathetic messages about freeing up its bank customers to focus less on technology deployment and more on strategic business intitiatives. In essence, it said, "We'll worry about system scalability while you focus on growing your customer base; we'll worry about data storage while you focus on data mining; we'll worry about managing the channel while you focus on managing your market segments; we'll worry about disaster recovery while you focus on customer retention; we'll worry about supplier management while you focus on customer service; we'll worry about security while you focus on providing trusted services; we'll worry about system conversions when you are focused on mergers or acquisitions."

How does stress-reduction impact perceptions on key drivers of brand choice?

Key brand choice drivers in this market, beyond cost, were nearly perfectly aligned with the cornerstones of integration as set forth in this book: component/product compatibility, ability to improve time to market, operational support, and security (a price of entry in banking services, as is "taste/flavor" in food products and "reliability" in high-tech categories like data storage or telephone networks). Each of these drivers was closely related in the bank CIO's mind to pressure and anxiety and, in some cases, even to job security. So Integrion's positioning—and demonstrable ability to relieve stress on these choice dimensions—immediately began to build strong brand equity ties between stress, Integrion brand perceptions, and key drivers of brand choice.

To what degree can Integrion own stress reduction in the category?

Being early to market (and with a strategic, simplicity-focused proprietary brand), Integrion had high opportunity to differentiate on stress reduction and, in fact, become synonymous with it. Competitors were generally more focused on providing templates and interfaces than on infrastructure, and had arguably less credibility in the most challenging, broad-shouldered aspects of providing core services. Had Integrion been competing with highly trusted, established megabrands, stress reduction ownership would have certainly been less attainable and barriers to emulation would have been lower.

RESULTS

Integrion measured its overall marketing results in two ways beyond revenue and retention: penetration of its platform among the top 50 banks, and the number of consumers using Integrion-enabled services of the banks Integrion serves. At this writing in 1999, Integrion is tracking ahead of its ambitious objectives by having sold online banking solutions to 16 of the top 25 banks during its first two years of marketing. Integrion was adding more than 2,000 new end-user customers a day to most likely surpass its year-end 1999 objective of 1 million by a considerable margin.

■ Summary

Stress-relieving strategies covered in this chapter are summarized in Figure 5.1, showing that the second R of Simplicity Marketing—*Repackage*—can be executed as either of two substrategies: *Aggregation* or *Inte-*

Figure 5.1

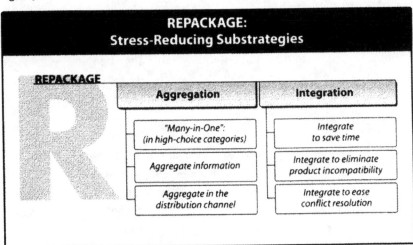

gration. For each substrategy, this chart recaps the key building blocks on which Simplicity Marketing effectiveness can be built. We identified in this chapter examples of Repackaging in action, and then provided checklists for each substrategy to help you gauge your product's/brand's potential to reduce customer stress through Aggregation or Integration. We looked at the risks of Repackaging and pitfalls to avoid in reaping its rewards. Finally, we looked in depth at how Integrion Financial Network leveraged the second R by integrating complexity into a value-added one-stop solution for online banking services.

Summary Postscript: The Substitution-to-Integration Continuum

Before we move on, let's now pull together all the strategies from Chapter 4 and 5 to see how they relate to each other. Substrategies of the first two R's of Simplicity Marketing can be viewed as a value continuum (Figure 5.2), beginning with Substitution and progressing to Integration. For example, Integration tends to be more complex to execute and tends to provide more stress-reducing value than Substitution or Consolidation. Certainly there are exceptions, but this represents a generalized way to think about the strategies covered thus far in rela-

Figure 5.2

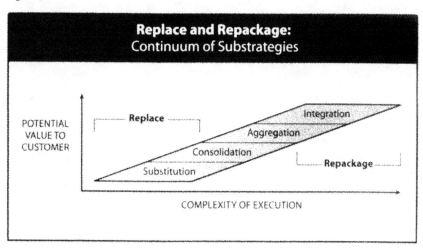

tion to each other. This inverse relationship between simplicity for the customer and complexity for the marketer stands to reason, since the marketer is essentially providing value by absorbing customer-level complexity. This doesn't mean, however, that Simplicity Marketing can't also simplify things for marketers as well, as we will dramatically see later in Chapter 10.

Chapter 6

REPOSITION

Simplifying the Customer's Brandscape

> There really are two ways to win: Do something better or do something extra or different. With a mature product, it is more feasible to do something extra or different than better. —David A. Aaker, *Managing Brand Equity,* The Free Press

> It is extremely difficult to kill an established brand but relatively easy to weaken it. The principal reason this occurs is the brand is allowed to mature, its brand essence is not supported or its performance standards are allowed to decline.
> —Michael Beindorff, Chief Executive Officer, PlanetRx.com

G REAT BRANDS DO not die normal deaths nor do they have predictable lifespans. Brands can in fact remain vibrant and youthful and span decades enjoying positions of market leadership. Alternatively, brands can fade and decline and many suffer exactly that fate. What causes the decline and early death of a brand? Simply stated, brands decline and die because they are allowed to mature and cease to have a compelling reason for being in a constantly evolving environment. What can the marketer do to avoid mistakes causing decay and loss of market position? What can the marketer do to ensure continuing brand vitality and freshness?

In this chapter, Repositioning as a means of ensuring an extended brand life span will be examined. And by Repositioning, we will examine the task of simplifying the customer's brandscape, simplifying what the brand represents, simplifying the brand's core promise to the customer, simplifying the brand's role in the customer's whole life experience.

There are three primary means of brand expression the sum of which define and place the brand in the consumer's mind. First and most important is the brand's *positioning*—the core promise of what the brand will deliver to the customer. Second, there is the brand's *personality*—why the customers should like the brand. Finally, there is the brand's *attitude*—what customers feel the brand thinks about them.

The most fundamental and basic of this triad is the brand's positioning. This is the essence of the brand and represents the reason why a customer should consider buying the product or service. Since both the environment in which the brand competes and the characteristics of the brand's customers change over time, the astute marketer periodically reexamines and reevaluates the brand's historical positioning, that is, considers *Repositioning* the brand's core promise to the customer. That is the subject of this chapter. (We leave to other marketing texts exploring the related but less central aspects of brand personality and attitude.)

Brands that choose the correct positioning can enjoy extended lifespans with some brands spanning 50, 75, or even 100 years of sustained market leadership. The Simplicity Marketer, however, must be alert to threats that can erode the brand's central promise and jeopardize its market position. The marketer must be prepared to act decisively to protect the brand's franchise and that might encompass a Repositioning strategy.

Assume for the moment that you are the marketer of a food product that is used in meal preparation in the mid-1950s. As a marketer, you understand that the average American household spent a total of 131 minutes per day preparing food at home in the 1950s. Then contemplate that by the mid-1990s, the time spent preparing food in the average household had declined to 17 minutes. Do you suppose the core promise and performance of your brand is impacted by this change? Surely it would be. Repositioning can be the salvation of a brand in an evolving environment.

Proliferation and brand clutter were a natural evolution of the consumer package goods industry beginning in the late 1940s. Before World War II, we shopped for our groceries and household items in individual shops. We had the small drugstore, the baker, the butcher, the green grocer, and the hardware store. We did not have today's large refrigerators or freezers so we shopped for many of our perishable items on a daily basis. More importantly, we received individual attention from a salesperson. In many cases, others made the selection for us and presented us with the grocery item.

Now consider the revolution that came after the war. Thousands of returning servicemen and women took advantage of inexpensive veteran's loan programs to populate burgeoning suburbs. Levittown, New York, became the symbol of a new generation of home ownership. Merchants followed the population from the city and town center to these new enclaves of consumers. New on the scene were the first of the large, self-service supermarkets with aisle after aisle of choices.

Many of these newly formed households started families and the baby boom generation was born. Separated from the close nuclear family of past generations, these families had to go about the care and feeding of children without the advice available in the extended family. In this environment, the large grocery, drug, and household product marketers had to create awareness and interest in their products and brands. There was no helpful sales clerk available in the supermarket to answer a new mother's questions about what to feed the baby.

Fortuitously, the very rapid adoption of television as the entertainment medium of choice gave the marketers an ideal platform to create awareness and demand for their brands. We must remember that in the halcyon days, 90% of Americans sat down at 7:00 P.M. and watched three or four hours of television on one of three networks. Marketers had the luxury of a full 60 seconds to develop an advertising message. This was the beginning of the problem/solution television commercial and Rosser Reeves' "Unique Selling Proposition" forms of advertising.

Adding to this, these families were in households where only one parent, usually the father, worked outside the home. This meant millions of women were at home and available to watch daytime television. Astute marketers such as Procter & Gamble transported the successful soap opera radio format to the television screen. This was such a critical component of P&G's marketing effort that the company actually owned and produced several of these shows such as "Search for Tomorrow" and "As the World Turns." Naturally these programs featured P&G commercials for Crisco, Tide, and Ivory Soap.

This was the environment that bred brand proliferation and extensive segmentation. This was the petri dish that cultivated the virus of complexity resulting in a supermarket with 35 to 40 thousand stockkeeping units. Brand, size, and item proliferation was guaranteed to flourish by the simple laws of economics.

BRAND COMPLEXITY RUN AMOK

Fast-forward to 2000 and look at a day in the life of our inveterate shopper, John Braxton from Chapter 1. John has decided to purchase a new car. Concerned about the survival of the U.S. automotive industry, John has decided to look specifically at General Motors (GM) vehicles. What we will see as we shop with John is unnecessary brand proliferation and complexity. Let's begin by taking a look at General Motors at its inception.

Had it been 50 years earlier, John would have found a masterful General Motors. Under the visionary leadership of Alfred P. Sloan, the General Motors Corporation was conceived on a seminal marketing premise: five separate and distinct automotive divisions or master brands tiered upward in an increasing order of price, quality, and perceived prestige: Chevrolet, Pontiac, Oldsmobile, Buick, and Cadillac. The divisions were king; there were models within each division but primarily the branding remained at the division level. Each division had two or three models such as Oldsmobile 88 or 98.

Sloan's construct had these brands beginning in price at the lower end with Chevrolet and working up the hierarchy to the Cadillac division at the top. In the world according to Sloan, one began his automotive life with a Chevrolet and, with age and increasing spending power, worked one's way up to the penultimate Buick and finally to a Cadillac. With a Cadillac, one was prepared to depart the earth and meet his maker for the ultimate automotive pinnacle had been achieved. Five divisions with five gradations designed to span an automotive lifetime—it was simple and understandable, and it worked for 50 years.

But this is not at all John's experience. Instead of the original five domestic divisions, General Motors now has seven domestic divisions or master brands given the addition of Saturn and GMC. More importantly, the discrete price separation between divisions has been blurred and merged to become almost meaningless. A GM buyer can spend more on a Chevrolet product model than on a Cadillac. The fundamental price ladder constructed by Sloan has been eroded, if not destroyed, taking with it the very rationale for the five divisions. Of greater consequence, however, has been GM's tendency to sub-brand models within the divisions with the result of de-emphasizing and diluting the divisional brand.

John begins his foray into General Motors by going to Autoweb.com, a Web site of one of the automotive shopping services. He pulls up the GM database and what he finds appears in the accompanying table.

Astro	Blazer	C1500	C2500
Bonneville	Achieva	Century	Trans Sport
C3500	Camero	Cargo Van	Cavalier
Eldorado	Alero	Escalade	Eighty Eight
Firebird	Cutlass	Montana	LaSabre
Catera	Envoy	Aurora	DeVille
Corvette	Express	K1500	K2500
Grand Am	Jimmy	Sunfire	Bravada
Savana	Seville	Sierra	Suburban
K3500	Lumina	Malibu	Metro
Regal	Intrigue	Safari	Sonoma
LSS	Yukon	SC1	Regency
Monte Carlo	Prizm	S-10	Silverado
Silhouette	SL1	Park Avenue	SC2
SL	SL2	SW1	Riviera
Suburban	Tahoe	Tracker	Venture
SW2	EV1		

From Alfred Sloan's simplicity, John now finds 66 sub-brands (if we count the Suburban's dual appearance in both the Chevrolet and GMC divisions, which in itself reaches a new high of branding complexity).

(By the way, take a test and see how many of these brands you can link to their parent division. Rare would be even the automotive buff scoring a 50% accuracy rate in linking divisional brand to the model sub-brand.)

To add to this complexity, we find GM has the largest advertising budget of any American corporation. We can expect our confusion to be fully compounded by aggressive exposure to these many sub-brands. As a final tribute to complexity, GM adopted a brand management organizational structure in the late 1990s seizing the model that was created by the Procter & Gamble Company for consumer package goods. Each of GM's sub-brands now has a brand manager devoted to crafting a distinctive positioning, personality, and attitude for it. Is there anyone who believes there is room for 66 such branding possibilities in a firm that itself enjoys about 30% of the U.S. automotive market? Certainly not John. He is overwhelmed and confused.

John now requests the BMW and Audi databases, and here is what he finds: With clarity and simplicity, he can buy a BMW in the following sub-brands: 318, 323, 328, 528, 540, 740, 750, 840, and 850.[1] There are the 3 series, the 5 series, the 7 series, and the 8 series. John can easily understand that the BMW 318 has a 1.8 liter engine and the BMW 850 has a 5 liter engine. A simple premise is used: the three digit numerical identifier uses the first digit to identify the vehicle size and price, from the 3 series to the 8 series, and the second two digits denote the approximate displacement of the engine in liters.

Even more direct and functional is the model line up of Audi: A4, A6, and A8. Each model is successively larger and the numerical designation identifies the number of engine cylinders. Cost, performance, and size are all conveyed with simplicity and clarity. Simplicity Marketing and Brand Streamlining are alive and well at BMW and at Audi but are not yet on the horizon at the world's largest automotive manufacturer. John decides that he will visit both the BMW and Audi dealerships nearby for a test drive. As for GM, he decides that the landscape is just too confusing.

What should GM have done to attract John to its products? How should GM have given order and rationale to 67 brand names, lacking any organizational framework? How should GM have created a hierarchy that denotes car or engine size? How should GM have signaled relative pricing levels within its divisional models? What used to be a clear steppingstone, Chevrolet to Cadillac, has become blurred and indistinct.

What GM needs to do is to move its five automotive divisions with their numerous sub-brands from the passive to the active brandscape (we define passive and active brandscapes in the next section). This should be done in two steps: First, GM needs to acknowledge that there is no justification for five automotive divisions. At most, there should be three. Second, within each division, GM needs to establish a nomenclature and branding approach that signals price, size, and performance with ease. If GM had done this, John might have been able to determine where he belongs in the GM hierarchy and he might have been interested in taking a GM car for a test drive.

In this chapter, we will examine Repositioning, that is, the task of simplifying, clarifying, or modernizing what the brand stands for. We will see that in contrast to *Replacing* (Chapter 4), where we substituted one product for another or consolidated complementary products, and *Repackaging* (Chapter 5), where we aggregated and integrated products, *Repositioning* goes to the core of the brand itself.

BRANDSCAPE

Central to an understanding of Repositioning is the space in which brands live and exist, the "brandscape." Like the word from which it is derived, brandscape is much like the landscape for a traveler in the marketplace—a distant view that shows in broad relief a horizon of brand options. The context for defining brandscape is the totality of brands across the sum of all categories carried in a customer's mind. This brandscape can be further divided into two parts:

> *Passive brandscape*—the landscape of all brands of which the customer is aware.

> *Active brandscape*—the landscape of *relevant* brands in appropriate categories; that is, brands with the potential to be in the customer's purchase consideration set, now or in the future, due to currently existing customer perceptions.

A passive landscape is one where a consumer has a general awareness of a sub-brand, but lacks a schema or cue to organize a disparate nomenclature. For example, General Motors' problem is that its 66 brand names exist in John's passive landscape. John generally understands that Buick is an automotive division higher in the hierarchy within GM than Pontiac or Oldsmobile. Beyond that he is confused.

With this as background, we identify three substrategies of Repositioning, and each substrategy has three variations. Each of these substrategies has a positive benefit on the customer's brandscape.

BRAND STREAMLINING

Clarifying the brand's reason for being involves

Simplifying brand architecture

Eliminating sub-brands

Using descriptive branding

With Brand Streamlining, the number of brands in the customer's active brandscape is reduced and thus the environment is de-cluttered and made more manageable. Making the brand architecture leaner and more logical allows the customer to store and recall the brand promise more easily. Using descriptors and nomenclature that clearly telegraph the brand's function and purpose makes understanding by the customer both easier and quicker. Brand Streamlining makes the consumer's whole life context just a bit more manageable and understandable.

Simplifying the Brand Architecture. *Brand Streamlining* can be executed at the brand level for the purpose of simplifying the ways in which a customer sees the brand, and most important, reducing the number of brands a customer must deal with. Brand Streamlining can become, like zero defects and continuous quality improvement, an essential requirement for today's marketer.

Simplification can take place at the master brand level or below that by the elimination or consolidation of sub-brands. The benefits of Brand Streamlining come into play at three levels: for the marketer, for the channel partners, and for customers.

Before attempting Brand Streamlining, it is important to identify an unexpected impediment to streamlining: internal resistance *within* the firm, principally from within the marketing and sales departments. The resistance from within is illustrated in a 1975 article by Steven Kerr entitled: "On the Folly of Rewarding A, While Hoping for B."[2] Kerr's article addresses the following conundrum: "Supposedly, we reward people for doing what we want them to and don't reward them when they do something else. While it sounds very simple and straightforward, . . . it isn't that way at all . . . all too often organizations create motivational forces which lead to unwanted and unintended consequences by rewarding behaviors that are not desired and by discouraging behaviors that are desired."

Kerr's theory represents one of Brand Streamlining's greatest obstacles. Contrary to what might be expected, the firm's marketing department, advertising agency, sales promotional suppliers, market research department, and sales organization are actually rewarded by complexity and punished by streamlining. Most firms would state that they seek to eliminate unnecessary products, adhere to principles of lean staffing, and minimize costs. This is Kerr's theory A. However, complexity itself requires more people so managers will often seek greater staffing in their departments to enhance their job function. Complexity generally requires larger budgets and managers usually seek greater funding of their activities.

With these negatives, is there any rational reason for increasing complexity? The answer is as seductive as it is pernicious: *Complexity often results in short-term gains in volume and market share as the pipeline is filled and as sampling and introductory pricing give temporary gains while pushing incremental costs downstream.* Add a new stockkeeping unit, another SKU. Identify a new service to be offered. Create a new menu item for a quick service restaurant. Add a new billing plan for a cellular service. These are tangible and the short-term positive results can be seen while the longer-term consequences are often hidden and delayed.

The danger is that marketing and sales organizations will respond as Kerr anticipates: They will take the core brand and make it more complex and segmented because it rewards them with a larger budget and increased staffing even if these results are only short term. Managers will respond to "expect A and reward B" by doing B.

While GM might be given some latitude because its divisional structure made sense at one point in time, such is not the case with one of the world's largest mergers and the resulting branding strategy. The December 1998 announcement of the Exxon/Mobil merger represented the formation of an enormous industrial corporation and the linking of two legendary brands. This merger represented two parallel enterprises with little real product differentiation. Exxon has 8,500 gas stations and Mobil had almost 7,500. The combined entity will have substantial market concentration representing 26% of the stations in New Jersey, 22% in Connecticut and New York.[3]

This merger offered an ideal opportunity for Brand Streamlining into a single focused entity. The strong surviving brand would have enormous economies of marketing scale. With its larger international presence, the Exxon brand seemed the logical surviving trademark. However, the merged company chose differently. In a statement on December 2, 1998, a company spokesperson said: "Both the Exxon brand and the Mobil brand have global recognition and are known for quality. While we have no intention to spend money on any major rebrandings, we expect that over time brands may be used on a differentiated basis by market, by product and/or by offering."[4]

How will Mobil and Exxon differ? Will their products have real differences? Will Mobil's 87 octane gasoline really be different in formulation than Exxon's 87 octane? Will they compete at different price points? These questions should have clear and compelling answers before the costs and complexity of maintaining two brands is contemplated. The core lesson is this: Unless there are distinct and commanding reasons to do otherwise, simplifying the brand's architecture and nomenclature is always preferable to segmentation and complexity.

Eliminate Sub-Brands. In contrast to Mobil/Exxon strategy, consider DaimlerChrysler's decision in late 1999 to phase out the legendary Plymouth brand. DaimlerChrysler's U.S. management decided the Plymouth brand simply had no reason for being from a dealer or consumer standpoint. The brand had outlived its usefulness and meaning. The various models Plymouth marketed, including minivans and the Neon subcompact, were sold in virtually identical versions by the stronger Dodge division. With this simplification, DaimlerChrysler has four strong and distinct sub-brands under the corporate brand: Jeep, Dodge, Chrysler, and Mercedes-Benz.

Use Descriptive Branding. Finally, Brand Streamlining can be accomplished simply by the way we describe the brand. The careful use of descriptive branding can be a way to effectively streamline a brand's presence and simplify communications to the customer. No one has been better than the leading household products marketers in effective and skillful use of descriptive branding. Consider as evidence these products:

Easy Off Oven Cleaner

Liquid Plumr Drain Cleaner

Off! Insect Repellant

Comet Multi-Room Cleanser

Woolite One-Step Carpet Cleaner

Windex Outdoor Glass Cleaner

Blue Coral Dri-Clean Upholstery Cleaner

The descriptive branding nomenclature itself almost replaces the need for advertising to explain the product's benefits. "One-Step," "Easy Off," and "Dri-Clean" all telegraph the product's core promise and benefit.

Descriptive branding can be used in other sectors as well. When a traveler sees the brand United Airlines, the connotation is a full service, major air carrier flying full-size aircraft. When the same traveler sees Shuttle by United, the connotation is one of shorter routes, smaller planes, and less service. When the same traveler sees United Express, this signals even smaller aircraft flying into regional airports with no on-board food or beverage service. In each case, descriptive branding signals a benefit or functionality that is embedded within the brand itself. The brand, its purpose, and why the customer should buy it are all rolled into the brand's overall identity. The use of descriptive branding might appear pedestrian but its impact can be substantial in reducing customer confusion and simplifying the brandscape.

VERTICAL EXTENSION

Extending the brand's reach allows the marketer to lengthen and extend the brand's relationship with the customer in logical and consistent ways. It is as if an old friend can suddenly do more for you and allow you to be concerned with one less thing. Vertical extensions are simply a way of doing more of what the customer desires and this can be based on one or more of three variations:

Technology-driven extensions

New feature sets

Channel-based extensions

Against the tide of niche marketing and customization, repositioning a brand to make it more accessible to a broader number of customers can, under the right circumstances, pay off in the era of replacement marketing. The following example from the automotive industry illustrates this point.

Technology-Driven Extensions. Advances in technology can permit the marketer to change the very nature of brand competition. Technology can offer opportunities to add new features, new capabilities, or even reduce costs to a point unattainable before.

For many car buyers who are not among the idle rich, two "brand sets" are carried in the psyche. One is the ideal ("someday I'll own a Mercedes or a BMW") and the other is the here-and-now ("I need a new car this year; I think I'll test-drive a Taurus and a Camry"). Repositioning a brand to make it more accessible can replace those two brand sets with one brand that gives the consumer a "migration path" from present to future without ever leaving the one brand. (This is the modern equivalent of General Motors' old five distinct divisions strategy.) This partially explains the recent rebound of the Mercedes brand.

Until 1986 Mercedes-Benz reigned supreme at the top of the luxury import hierarchy. Price was almost immaterial. Engineering-driven innovation and performance standards meant that, even though the Mercedes powerful V-8 328-horsepower engine was more than enough for all but a handful of power-hungry enthusiasts, a greater horsepower V-12 was built. Twin automated antennas would pop out of rear fenders upon putting a Mercedes in reverse. This feature was added to make clear the rear limits of the vehicle were protected against scraping or bumping. Mercedes advertising was imposing and austere, and pricing was astronomical.

Mercedes practiced what Peter Drucker calls "cost-based pricing:" take whatever it costs to produce a product, add a handsome profit margin, and—voila—you have the selling price. But Toyota's Lexus changed the rules of the game in 1986 with what Drucker terms "price-based costing." Customer research identified a burgeoning demand for Mercedes-type luxury at a price point below $40,000, so the need to price the Lexus 400LS sedan at $38,000 drove product development. The resulting combination of luxury and value sent shock waves through the market, as it became savvy to buy a Lexus instead of a more expensive, over-engineered Mercedes.

After five years of declining market share, in 1991–92 Mercedes adopted technology, enabled cost control, and targeted list prices that made Mercedes more accessible. (This was based in no small part on Mercedes' study of Japanese design, manufacturing, and logistical practices.) Mercedes repositioned the brand from "The Best-Engineered Car in the World" to the car that makes you "Sacrifice Nothing" (suggesting you can still have the Mercedes dream without spending what a Mercedes used to cost).

By 1994, when Mercedes pushed its "C class" prices down to $31,000, sales increased 60% in one year as buyers who were previously excluded allowed their future brand of choice to also become their present brand of choice. This repricing-enabled Repositioning, implemented through a new advertising style that made the brand more approachable and less ivory-tower, allowed more (and especially younger) consumers to consolidate, or simplify, their brand relationship in this important category. It allowed them to become a customer of a brand that they need never outgrow as they continue to trade up in automobiles over the years. This concept was taken a step further with the introduction of the Mercedes ML320 sport utility vehicle, manufactured in a state-of-the-art plant in Alabama to reduce assembly costs. Now, a Mercedes buyer could not only migrate upward within the passenger car migration path but also not leave the franchise if an off-road vehicle was desired. In the process of this Repositioning rebound, Mercedes has expanded its customer base to younger consumers with greater long-term value given the remaining number of cars they will buy during their lifetimes.

United Parcel Service has launched another example of a technology driven vertical extension. UPS, the world's largest package delivery service, has made an enviable reputation for the delivery of packages and letters/documents since its founding in the Pacific Northwest in 1907. Physical packages or documents can be delivered by UPS in the United States and worldwide in an array of delivery times: same day, next day early AM, next day, second day, and so on. With UPS, the shipper picks the time in transit and UPS does the rest.

Enter into this mix of physical delivery options the emergence of electronic delivery of letters and documents via the Internet. One might quickly assume that this leaves UPS without a business strategy. With a technology driven vertical extension, this proved not to be the case. In 1998, UPS introduced a new delivery service: UPS Document Exchange. With Document Exchange, UPS customers can affect electronic delivery of letters and documents with these benefits:

- Electronic delivery is speedy and secure.
- A detailed audit trail and point-to-point tracking feature is included in the service.
- Insurance against business losses from tampering with a transmission or receipt is offered to the customer.

UPS is positioned to benefit from any transition to electronic delivery of letters and documents from the traditional shipment of hard copies. In addition, the UPS brand is further enhanced and enriched by this vertical extension. Vertical extensions do not just apply to big-ticket items such as automobiles.

New Feature Sets. As the epitome of a franchise for babies, Gerber faces the inevitability of its consumers growing up and migrating away from the high chair and the brand's franchise. Enter a Repositioning in the form of a vertical extension; Gerber Graduates made this promise: "Being on the go doesn't mean sacrificing nutrition for convenience. With Gerber Graduates Finger Foods you get both." Taking the traditional Gerber formulas into finger food brought a whole new feature set to the product and opens a new market.

New feature sets can also be implemented by reducing or narrowing the previous offerings of the brand. A case in point is Tricon's Pizza Hut chain of restaurants. Wherever locations are not conducive to a full Pizza Hut restaurant, this chain now has the option of opening a Pizza Hut Express unit with a limited food and beverage menu, and no table service. The smaller building reduces construction costs.

Channel-Based Extension. Vertical extensions can be effected with a channel-based strategy as well. For example, Wal-Mart is the largest retailer in the world with annual sales volume having long soared past $100 billion. Just-in-time delivery, elimination of middlemen, and extensive use of information technology are some of the techniques Wal-Mart used to gain a position of industry leadership. But just as Wal-Mart has blanketed the country with giant discount outlets, this savvy marketer is looking beyond this dominant position.

Wal-Mart announced plans to open smaller outlets of 40,000 square feet to compete with convenience stores and traditional supermarkets. These stores would be less than half the size of the average Wal-Mart store. These outlets would sell a limited selection of groceries and general merchandise and operate drive-through pharmacies. The move to smaller stores underscores Wal-Mart's concern that the larger format stores are not convenient for certain types of shoppers or shopping trips. "We lose a lot of customers because the supercenter is too busy and not convenient," said Wal-Mart Senior Vice President Jay Fitzsimmons.[5]

The core conclusion is that vertical extensions, properly conceived and executed, can extend the brand's usefulness and customer base. This is a central advantage to the marketer. More important, this same step can simplify the active brandscape for the customer which is the strategy's greatest contribution. Overall, this is a powerful tool in the marketer's arsenal.

DISCONTINUOUS REPOSITIONING

Changing the brand's core promise to the customer permits the brand marketer to fundamentally broaden the relationship the consumer can have with the brand by identifying a hidden benefit of the brand. Frequently, this new functionality so extends the brand's performance envelope that consumers can eliminate an entire brand from their active brandscape. Discontinuous Repositioning can take three forms:

New uses

New functionality

New occasions

The most adventuresome and potentially risky variant of Repositioning is Discontinuous Repositioning; that is, a clean break with the past. This is not evolution but revolution. This is a discontinuity with what the brand had previously stood for. Indeed, this is the branding equivalent of immigrating to a new country where the language, the competitors, and the business conditions are entirely different and new. With all the inherent risk, Discontinuous Repositioning can be very rewarding because it offers an entirely new life for a brand.

New Uses. The venerable Arm & Hammer Baking Soda brand is a case study in Discontinuous Repositioning. Baking soda is an essential ingredient for home baking and Arm & Hammer has long been the market leader. Therein lies the problem. The amount of baking soda necessary to prepare eight dozen 2-inch cookies is approximately one teaspoon. By that measure, a typical one pound box of Arm & Hammer Baking Soda contains 908 individual preparations of baking soda. It doesn't take a great leap to conclude that the in home consumption of baking soda will result in a single box lasting a long time.

Enter Discontinuous Repositioning. Church & Dwight, the marketers at Arm & Hammer, understood that an additional attribute of baking soda was its ability to absorb odors. Seeing a new opportunity, a new advertising campaign suggested placing the current box of Arm & Hammer in the refrigerator to absorb odors and buying a replacement box for baking. This opened up an entirely new market for this product. The replacement cycle for repurchase was potentially shortened based on this new positioning as a deodorizer. Seizing on this trend, Arm & Hammer put on the side panel of the box a recommendation to "Replace with a fresh box every 3 months" along with a handy calendar to mark the replacement date. This was then augmented with a special container with "spill proof vents" marketed as the Fridge-Freezer Pack.

To further extend the use of the product and with another discontinuous repositioning, a side panel was added to the baking soda box promoting antacid use: "Arm & Hammer Baking Soda is effective as an antacid to alleviate heartburn, sour stomach and/or acid indigestion." With three simple propositions, baking soda, deodorizer, and antacid, this savvy marketer extended the scope and usefulness of a simple product in an effective and coherent manner. If you go into a supermarket today, you will probably find Arm & Hammer brand as toothpaste, liquid laundry soap, cat litter, dental care gum, and a deodorant/antiperspirant. Arm & Hammer marketers adroitly repositioned and extended a single brand to encompass new functionalities and a broader customer base.

New Functionality. As with baking soda, another product from the nineteenth century found new life in Discontinuous Repositioning: Bayer Aspirin. One attribute of aspirin is the drug's ability to thin the blood. Long considered a negative, this became a feature to market when studies showed that patients at risk for a heart attack or stroke benefited by taking a single tablet of aspirin per day. Clinical studies indicated a beneficial effect in reducing heart attack and stroke if daily aspirin use was undertaken. By marketing this benefit, Bayer encouraged consumers to begin to consume aspirin regularly and on a permanent basis opening up new opportunities for this venerable brand.

Taking advantage of this new functionality, Bayer took the additional step of introducing Aspirin Regimen Bayer, a coated and time-released product designed for daily use. Promotional literature for the product suggests: "Doctor recommended for regular use. Specially designed for people on a regimen of aspirin, or as directed by your doctor."

Another example of Discontinuous Repositioning from the medicine cabinet is Tums antacid. While Arm & Hammer repositioned a baking product as an antacid, Tums, an antacid, was repositioned as a source of dietary calcium. This nutritional benefit was highlighted for women who are at greater risk of osteoporosis.

While Arm & Hammer, Bayer, and Tums all repositioned themselves in a fundamentally new way, Coca-Cola was able to accomplish a Repositioning based on an equally valid premise—the occasions when the product is used.

New Occasions. Market research studies showed Coca-Cola was consumed at all times of the day with the exception of the breakfast meal. For this one occasion. consumers simply did not consider or put Coca-Cola into their set of beverage alternatives. As a result, Coke saw an opportunity.

First, Coke correctly targeted coffee as the competitor. Coca-Cola correctly saw coffee as a dark, caffeine containing, sugared *hot* beverage while Coke was a dark, caffeine containing, sugared *cold* beverage. Why not position Coke as an alternative to coffee was the unconventional question. All the ingredients, literally, were in place. With the cooperation of a major fast-food restaurant chain, Coke began airing commercials that suggested having the chain's well-known breakfast sandwich with Coke instead of coffee. The campaign was successful and now Coke is making inroads into what was once a market void.

A Repositioning tour de force was introduced by the cellular telephone company QualComm in the form of the pdQ unit. This Discontinuous Repositioning was a double play involving both new functionality and new use occasions into one combined package. This new wireless phone entry combines a traditional cell phone with the phenomenally successful Palm Pilot personal digital assistant. According to QualComm, the core of the pdQ is a pure Palm with 2 MB of RAM and most current Palm operating system. With the pdQ, the user simply brings up the Palm's address book feature, taps a name with the stylus and the dialing is initiated. Even the traditional Palm Pilot cradle serves its normal purpose as a docking station but it also is enhanced to recharge the batteries. With the pdQ, QualComm has added new functionality and extended the use occasions by simplifying and enhancing the phone's usefulness. Befitting such an advance, the price of the pdQ is upwards of $1,000, generating what should be a nice margin for the manufacturer over the rock-bottom prices of many traditional cellular phones.

Taking the QualComm approach one step farther, the cofounders of the Palm computing platform, Donna Dubinsky and Jeff Hawkins, create a new company in 1999 called Handspring. This new firm licensed the Palm operating system and developed the Visor handheld device that performed all of the essential functions of the Palm but with a twist: the addition of an expansion slot that permitted the Visor user to add completely new components such as:

- MP3 music player
- Ground Positioning Satellite
- Cellular phone
- Pager
- Video games
- Image Capture Module
- Radio Module
- Modem
- Universal Remote

These entrepreneurs are using third parties to develop these add-on modules and given the very aggressive pricing of the Visor, from $149 to $249, there should be a continuing flow of such enhancements. Finally, taking a cue from the phenomenal success of the Apple Computer iMac, the higher end Visors will come in five designer colors: blue, green, orange, graphite, and ice.

When we take all three basic substrategies covered in this chapter together—Brand Streamlining, Vertical Extension, and Discontinuous Repositioning—the cumulative effect can be dramatic. The customer's active brandscape can have significantly fewer brand entrants. The need of the customer to keep informed and updated on multiple brands can instead often be focused on a single brand. The element of customer trust and comfort with the brand can be increased. In total, the customer has less stress and the marketer has a greater total share of market.

TO REPOSITION OR NOT TO REPOSITION?

Repositioning can be the most extreme and risky of the 4 R's but at the same time it can be the most rewarding. At the least, today's marketer must go through the brand portfolio and ask the pertinent questions:

Can we benefit from simplifying the brand's architecture?
Complexity creeps into the brandscape over time and the task of simplification takes a concerted and concentrated effort. Has the brand's architecture and structure become convoluted and obscure over time? Have our sub-brands become obsolete and do they need to be eliminated? Are we using descriptive branding to the best advantage in our advertising, packaging, and point-of-sale materials? Simplification is like spring cleaning for the house or organizing the office. It can only be put off so long or the results are truly negative. To get it done takes concerted effort.

Are there vertical extensions of the brand that are ripe for exploitation?
What new technologies have come onto the market that could be useful to the brand? Could new feature sets be added to the brand that would enhance or broaden its appeal? What new distribution channels have come into play that could extend the reach of the brand?

Should Discontinuous Repositioning be considered?
Has the brand matured to the point that something radical is needed to reenergize it? Are there fundamentally new uses or reasons why the brand should be purchased? Could totally new functionality be introduced beyond what the brand has stood for historically? Are there completely fresh occasions for the brand to be used or consumers that have not been previously targeted?

Discontinuous Repositioning is risky because it takes the brand on a leap into totally new territory and this can be a failure. Once Cadillac tried to introduce a small car, the Cimmaron, and this proved to be an abysmal failure. Ditto for the Apple Newton, the IBM PC Jr., New Coke, Premiere Smokeless Cigarettes, and AT&T Picture Phones. Tread lightly here for the risks are high but so are the rewards of success.

Anatomy of a Repositioning: Porsche

SIMPLICITY MARKETER:	**Porsche Cars of North America**
PRODUCT:	**Porsche Boxster**
LAUNCH:	**1998**
PRIMARY SUBSTRATEGY:	**Vertical Extension**

The first Porsche was inauspiciously born in 1948 in the small Austrian town of Gmünd. Raising from the devastation of World War II, the automotive legend Dr. Ferdinand Porsche designed and built a small, mid-engined roadster powered by a flat, air-cooled engine. He designated this model as the 356/1. The car was an under-powered, largely hand-built prototype constructed using machinery and parts left over from the war's devastation. It was powered by a modified Volkswagen engine. About 50 more of this model were produced over the next 18 months before Porsche moved to its permanent home in Stuttgart in 1951.

Few could have foreseen that this modest beginning in Austria would initiate one of the great automotive legacies of all time.

Fifty years after the 356/1, Porsche introduced another new model: the Boxster. This was another small, mid-engined roadster powered by a flat, water-cooled engine. The Boxster was an immediate, international success and customer demand was unprecedented. Customers hurriedly placed deposits and the waiting time for delivery exceeded one year in some markets. Buyers paid full list price and some offered premiums to dealers to move higher on the waiting list. Demand was so great Porsche contracted with a specialty automotive company in Finland, Valmet, to assemble 7,000 additional cars per year destined for North America to meet this unprecedented demand.

This dramatic and heralded success with the Boxster was something unusual for Porsche. Prior to the Boxster, the first half-century of Porsche's new model introductions, other than the defining 911 series introduced in the early 1960s, presented a case study of not leveraging and extending a legendary automotive brand. In contrast, Porsche demonstrated with the Boxster how to vertically extend this great marquee in a manner consistent with the brand's heritage. Using the principles of Simplicity Marketing, Porsche adroitly allowed an entirely new buyer profile to emerge by pricing the Boxster more than $22,000 below the lowest-priced 911 model, $41,000 versus $63,750. With the Boxster, Porsche allowed younger buyers to enter the buyer pool and grow up with the brand.

The Brand

Porsche is not a logical automotive product. Nor are its buyers acting in what could be seen as a rational manner. In fact, Porsche is an evolving contradiction.

Consider the cars themselves. Porsche's most successful model, the legendary 911 series, defies most automotive logic.

- The car's engine is flat and the cylinders are not vertical or in the V shape used by most manufacturers. A flat engine is simply more difficult to configure into an automobile than a conventional engine.

- Through most of its history, Porsche engineers used air to cool the engine and not water. Automotive engineers know it is more difficult to dissipate heat with air than with water. (Think of blowing on a hot cooking pan as contrasted to running cold water over its surface for cooling.)

- Next, in a taunt to the laws of physics, the 911's engine was put in the rear of the car at the extreme: hanging behind the rear axle. One does not have to enter Newtonian physics very deeply to quickly understand that turning or stopping a moving object where the weight is rearward creates a strong tendency for the object's rear end to swap places very suddenly with the front end. This is generally acknowledged as not being a good attribute for an automobile. Indeed, this is why most cars have the engines in front.

- Finally, Porsche cars were expensive. Priced in the automotive stratosphere, a Porsche owner paid dearly to drive this marquee but the price was deemed justified by a loyal following of enthusiasts.

Porsche's success and legacy, however, developed around the 356 and, its successor, the 911 series. Through what can only be described as examples of engineering genius, Porsche perfected this quirky design and tamed its most undesirable attributes. In doing so, it created an automotive legend and a cult following.

Unsuccessful Attempts at Vertical Extensions

During its half-century existence, Porsche attempted several times to extend the brand beyond the expensive 911 series. Most of the attempts were for models priced under the 911 and all were failures or at best, not successes. None survived as enduring models.

914 SERIES

The 914 series was an attempt at a lower priced, air-cooled mid-engined model. The essential failure was the use of a modified Volkswagen engine. This was inconsistent branding and was greeted with the same enthusiasm as putting vin ordinaire into a Chateau Margaux bottle. Moreover, this model was manufactured by Karmann at its factory in Osnabruck.

924/944/968 SERIES

Porsche's second attempt at vertical extension was the water cooled, front engined 924/944/968 series. Again priced below the 911, these models violated the Porsche brand heritage by putting the engine in the front of the car. Porsche loyalists rejected a deviation from brand heritage and the series was eventually discontinued.

928 SERIES

Undaunted, Porsche next attempted a model price at or above the 911 series and powered by a front mounted, water-cooled V-8 power plant. Porsche loyalists again rejected this deviation from the norm and this series also met its demise.

Reclaiming the Brand

After the lessons of the 914, the 924, and the 928, Porsche finally succumbed to the obvious and announced that the successor to the fabled 911 would be a variation on the 911 design; albeit with a water-cooled engine necessary to meet increasingly stringent emission standards.

However, the rest of the Porsche heritage was maintained intact: the new 911 looked like an updated previous generation 911 with its familiar flowing shape. The engine would be in the rear where a Porsche engine was deemed to be by almost a biblical edict. After a 30-year production run, one of the longest in automotive history, the original 911 at last had an heir. Unfortunately, another carryover from the previous 911 series would be the very high price: $65,030 to $74,460 list prices at introduction.

Porsche announced this return to its roots well in advance of the arrival of the new generation of 911s. The Porsche loyalists could now breathe easy; the 911 would continue on into the twenty-first century as a true Porsche.

Enter Simplicity Marketing

At this juncture, Porsche again faced the company's continuing conundrum: the elevated prices of the 911 series. With the new 911 beginning with a list price of more than $65,000, Porsche was restricting itself to an increasingly narrower and wealthier buyer pool. What could it do about the recurring need for an entry-level model to bring younger owners into the buyer pool and establish a migration path upward to the 911 series? How could it avoid the missteps of the earlier attempts with the 914, 924, and 944?

This time Porsche had the same objective but, unlike previous attempts, executed flawlessly with the Boxster series. At its core, the Boxster journeyed back to the very first Porsche for its inspiration: this car was to be a small, mid-engined roadster powered by a flat six-cylinder engine. The exact same configuration as the 356/1 enjoyed. For styling cues, Porsche returned to a limited production model from the mid-1950s: the legendary 550 A Spyder roadster. This ultralight racing model gained infamy on September 30, 1955, when the actor James Dean was killed while driving his Spyder from Los Angeles to the races at Leguna Seca in Monterey. The engine for the new Boxster was also to be pure Porsche. The power plant was essentially a smaller displacement version of the engine being built for the new 911 series. This was exactly what Porsche loyalists wanted.

Finally, to ensure linkage, the Boxster was almost the same car as the new 911 series from the doors forward to the front bumper. In addition to building family resemblance, this was actually a clever way to capture significant cost savings by sharing many common parts with the new 911.[6] The Boxster is a textbook case study of using the precepts of Simplicity Marketing to vertically extend a brand, simplify the brandscape for the buyer, and extend the reach of ownership significantly. With the Boxster in the product array, Porsche sold approximately 20,000 cars in the United States in 1999; up from only 3,700 cars sold in 1996.

Reposition Checklist

The Porsche Boxster is, at its core, an effective vertical extension of the brand. In addition, this introduction incorporates effective use of Brand Streamlining.

Does the Boxster effectively move Porsche from the Passive Brandscape to the Active Brandscape? How?

The introduction of the Boxster, priced one-third lower than the 911 model, effectively moves the brand into the active consideration set of an entirely new generation of younger, less wealthy buyers. In a single move, Porsche allows a younger buyer to consider a Porsche as much as a decade sooner than would be the case at the higher 911 price. This permits a much longer migration path for the buyer to be included within the Porsche franchise.

Does this product use the principles of Brand Streamlining?

There are two elements of Brand Streamlining employed by the Boxster. The first part of the brand name, *Box*, is a partial use of boxer, which is the term used to describe a flat, horizontally opposed engine configuration. Second, the model name also designates this as a *roadster* which is the term used to describe an open top two-seat car. The resulting Boxster name quickly communicates this as an open, two-seat roadster powered by a flat, horizontally opposed engine. The model name thus simplifies and describes. The additional brand was justified (versus just a model number) because the Boxster was such a radical departure from the 911 both in design and price.

Is the product an effective vertical extension of the master brand?

First, the Boxster should be recognized as a highly refined and effective vertical extension. By recapturing the engine and body style of the very first Porsche built in 1948, this car is on solid design ground among knowledgeable Porsche buffs. Second, by modernizing the classic 1955 Porsche 550 Spyder body style,

Porsche captures a trend toward retro design evidenced in the phenomenal success of the new Volkswagen Beetle.[7] From a technology and design standpoint, the Boxster is a highly effective vertical extension.

Is stress reduction built into the positioning?

The Boxster buyer can find assurances of stress reduction in choosing this model. First, the Boxster's predecessor, the 911 series, had a production life of over 30 years. Rapid obsolescence is not a worry with this model. The Boxster owner, while probably not expecting a three decade production run, can nonetheless anticipate the same basic model lasting well beyond a decade of active production. First, this anticipation should remove the stress of having a luxury car outmoded in three or four years. Second, Porsches have had unusually low rates of depreciation. The Boxster owner can anticipate similar patterns so the erosion of one's financial investment is minimized. Long model life and minimal depreciation removes a key stress point of ownership.

What are the stress-related reasons to believe?

For 50 years, Porsche has made one essential brand promise—this is a performance car for the serious driver. After the new model was first introduced, slightly used Boxsters were selling at substantial premiums over the manufactured suggested list price of a new car. When prospective buyers inquire about service intervals on a Boxster, they are informed the car does not require its first service for 15,000 miles after being driven off the showroom floor. Consistency, focus, and reliability are key reasons to believe that the Boxster relieves stress for those willing to pay the price.

Final note: the Boxster has met with such strong market acceptance that Porsche has delayed the introduction of the Boxster "S" model with a larger 3.2-liter engine. Porsche management must have correctly concluded that the brandscape need not be cluttered with a variation when success was so forthcoming with a single Boxster model.

■ Summary

Simplicity Marketing's third R—*Repositioning*—can be a vital means of simplifying the consumer's brandscape, reducing stress, and extending

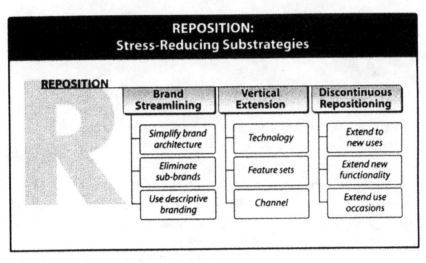

Figure 6.1

the life of brands (see Figure 6.1). The three main substrategies offered give the brand marketer key means of contending with a constantly changing marketplace. The astute marketer will use all these tools in gaining maximum profits from a brand franchise.

Chapter 7

REPLENISH

Continuous Supply, Zero Defects, and Competitive Price

> You're about to pour the last ounce of milk into your late-night bowl of cereal. Oops—looks like there'll be none left for your morning coffee! All the stores are closed. What's a hungry night owl to do? Pour away. By 6 A.M., a new gallon will be on your doorstep, thanks to a microchip sensor embedded in the milk carton and transmitted to an Internet device on your kitchen counter.
>
> —"Battle for the Fridge," *Computer World*, April 5, 1999

IN THE PREVIOUS CHAPTER, we saw how the third R, Repositioning, simplifies the brandscape, relieves stress, and makes the purchasing decision and task easier within the context of the current model of retailing. But what if we do not accept the limitations of the present model of distribution and retailing? Is there a way to move to a new model that will simplify our lives and reduce stress?

In Chapter 1, we saw much evidence of how our lives are increasingly time constrained and why a new approach is needed. Think about the extraordinary amount of time consumed by the *repetitive tasks* involved in shopping for the same things over and over again. Replenishing the supply of products needed to run a household or even a factory not only is a huge time sink but also among the least rewarding activities in life. Consider this view of the act of routine shopping as a source of stress; it is from the Automatic Product Replenishment Services Web site:

> What do you like about grocery shopping? Getting the kids ready to go? Driving to the supermarket in rain or snow? Maybe you like going up and down the aisles loading a buggy with a bunch of stuff much of which you didn't intend to buy? And, you like the surprises at the cash register, you know . . . finding the wrappers for the things your kids

already ate; or, the items they loaded into the buggy? You really like emptying the buggy you just loaded up, so the cashier can tally them, so that you can put them back in the buggy you just emptied. Then, of course, you love navigating the top-heavy cart through the pothole-riddled parking lot just so you can empty the thing, yet again, into your car. Now, you can fight the traffic to get home again, so that you can remove the groceries from the car and carry them to the front door, fumble with the door key, trip over the dog and, finally, get the stuff into the kitchen.

Automatic Product Replenishment Services Web Site, May 1999

With this background, we can now explore the final R of Simplicity Marketing and see if there is in fact a fundamentally better marketing approach to satisfying today's consumer and converting that satisfaction to loyalty.

The 4th R—*Replenish*—was defined in Chapter 3 as providing a readily available continuous supply of zero-defect products or service at acceptable price points, resulting in the customer only having to make the purchase decision (and the shopping effort) once. We can illustrate the potential of the Replenish strategy by dividing our universe of purchases into two broad categories:

- Standardized goods and services.
- Situationally dependent and/or nonstandardized goods and services.

Standardized goods and services are products and services with little or no variation as to quality, or suitability for use. Such products or services do not vary in appearance, quality, or price from one purchase occasion to another. Our need for these products does not change from one use occasion to another. In addition, we use these products and services at a predictable rate of consumption. These products inhabit both the consumer and business worlds, from household staple goods to the myriad of industrial component parts, materials, and substances used in manufacturing processes.

Such products and services tend to be the routine components of our day-to-day lives. They are our "friends" in fulfilling our daily needs.

Often, we have used these brands for years, we are comfortable with them and we have no interest in changing our buying patterns without a major reason. We purchase these products without analysis or thought. Most of us could name many personal contenders for this category. We have a definite preference among beverages and have long ago made our basic brand choice. We have a favorite brand and size of toothpaste. We routinely take the family car to a neighborhood automotive quick-change oil center. The list is extensive and each of us could name a dozen or more such candidates. But for illustrative purposes let's consider one contender: Tide laundry detergent.

Introduced by Procter & Gamble shortly after World War II, Tide represented a major breakthrough in cleaning efficacy over soap powders of the day. Tide quickly became the leading brand in its category and remains the dominant brand today. We can therefore assume that Tide enjoys a broad base of users who have grown comfortable with the brand. Over its half-century of existence, Tide has undergone various product and formulation improvements; for example, condensed powder form, liquid form, powder with bleach, and so on. We can assume that Tide's users have accepted these variations and chosen the ones they prefer.

As such, Tide is not in a category of products with a high information content or rapid changes as we might find in personal computers. The detergent category is slowly evolving at best, and we simply are not required to think very much about our purchase.

Tide is a classic example of a standardized product with long standing brand loyalties. In such cases, consumers often make a more or less permanent buying decision for a particular brand that might span years if not decades. Perhaps a P&G competitor has made a minor improvement in laundry detergent, but in the broad scope of today's hectic life, these decisions are simply not critical for us to analyze. We assume Procter & Gamble will continue to improve Tide as new technologies evolve. The brand decision therefore has been made so the only remaining issue besides pricing is maintaining adequate supply. Tide becomes a classic candidate for the Replenish strategy.

A second category of goods and services is typically purchased on a less frequent basis. There are important variations to be considered. A family planning a Passover Seder would probably wish to select the ingredients with time and attention at the point of sale. A young couple inviting several friends over for a social gathering might not know in advance what they wish to serve, so the shopping experience would be one of finding inspiration and ideas. In consumer electronics, the pace of technological change is so great, and the information content of the purchase so large, that we are willing to devote some time and energy to the purchase in order to assure the correct decision. Most items are not candidates for the Replenish strategy.

Now, consider your life as it relates only to those items used in your own household. How many are in the first category? How many in the second? For most of us, there are a large number of items in the first category. Each of these is a viable candidate for Replenishment.

While the Replenish strategy is not widely adopted as yet, we can see clear signs that it is on the horizon. In his book *Permission Marketing*, author Seth Godin describes the transition from traditional "interruption" marketing to "permission" marketing. Godin describes permission marketing as the state in which the consumer grants permission to receive advertising or information.[1] This is in contrast to the current situation where we have our lives interrupted by advertising or information, much of which is of no interest to us.

It is a short step from permitting a marketer to send advertising or information to granting the additional right to send us a replenishment of our inventories of physical products that meet our continuing needs. Having these products replenished "just in time," *as automatically as possible* and without unnecessary customer intervention, would seem to define the ultimate state of Simplicity Marketing. After all, we are not buying Tide detergent but clean clothes. Having Tide always available and never out of stock would be a certain step in that direction.

■ Criteria for Effective Replenishment

There are three essential criteria that must be met before the simplicity and stress-reducing benefits of the Replenish strategy can be enjoyed: an everyday low price, zero defects, and continuous supply. The absence of any one of these will block the effective implementation of this concept.

EVERYDAY LOW PRICE

One of the reasons we spend so much of our time shopping is the jungle of price incentives offered by merchants and manufacturers. We enter this pricing game and participate to do one thing: buy the desired item at the lowest possible price. The pricing game is played on several levels. Manufacturers offer periodic specials designed to temporarily lower the retail price to induce added sales. These price incentives can be made directly to the consumer in the form of a coupon or rebate or as a temporary price reduction to retailers. Retailers themselves often add to these manufacturer discounts and incentives with reductions in their normal margin structure to make the item even more appealing. Our job as buyers is to match the huge number of price reduction offers against our needs and participate with the required steps to enjoy the price reduction. We must take price-off coupons to the retail store. We are required to fill out a cash rebate form and mail in the required proof of purchase back to the manufacturers. We must join a frequent shopper program offered by the retailer and carry the identification card with us.

All of this adds complexity to our lives. In the United States alone, almost 300 billion coupons are distributed annually but only 3% are actually redeemed at the point of purchase! That means there are over 1,000 coupons distributed for every man, woman, and child in the United States and only 30 are redeemed on average. How many other marketing efforts would accept a 97% failure rate? The burden is on us to find the price incentive and take the time-consuming steps to reap the reward of the lower price.

At the retail level, the pricing and margin game is played but with a slight variation. The retailer has a mix of items for sale at any given time. The typical U.S. supermarket has up to 40,000 different items available for purchase. The astute merchant can offer a lower price on selected items, so called loss leaders, knowing full well that the average shopper will buy many additional items that are not price reduced. Many of these higher margin items are placed on prominent display at the end of the aisles thus encouraging impulse purchase. The merchant is betting on an average margin across a range of items to make up for the reduced margin on the select products offered for sale. As shoppers we intuitively understand the mathematics. We know a game is being played and we have to pick our way through this minefield to achieve a shopping basket at a fair overall price. We try to compensate by loading up on sale items; in other words, we overbuy against our immediate needs and carry excess in-home inventory. (This in turn contributes to our need to reduce the amount of stuff cluttering our homes, which the Replace strategy addressed in Chapter 4.)

Thus we enter a three-way dance: the manufacturer, the retailer, and the consumer all balancing variables of price, inconvenience, excess inventory, and complexity to average down the price of our household purchases. It is a complex and convoluted game played with almost inscrutable logic, mathematics, and intuition. But in today's stressful and time-constrained environment, we don't have the luxury of time we once had to participate in this dance. Fortunately, there is a simple answer to this puzzle.

The first and foremost requirement of Replenish is price fairness. The manufacturer must guarantee a fair everyday low price. That price is the weighted price of the item in question between the regular price and the lower prices of all the various price off incentives for that product offered during the year. We consumers want to be assured that we are paying about what we would have paid if we had played the game. Give us that assurance and we can place the product in question into the category of potential items for Replenishing. Deny us that guarantee of fairness and we are forced to play the shopping game of coupons, sales, and inventory loading.

After instituting everyday low prices, however, the retailer will want to continue to build in some element of serendipity and surprise as to pricing and overall excitement in the marketplace. In the storefront world, the consumer will find unexpected products and unanticipated sale items. The sophisticated replenishment-oriented retailer will find ways to mimic and, in fact, improve on these elements of shopping. Convenience does not mean dullness. Marketers will need to offer unexpected delights into the Replenish construct. We will naturally expect some reward from manufacturers for loyalty to their brands if we contract to make all our purchases from them. This reward may come in terms of bonus quantities of the brand in question or perhaps samples of other products from that manufacturer. Whatever form this reward takes, we will expect some quid pro quo for our loyalty.

ZERO DEFECTS

This second requirement is most critical for the nonstandard category as described earlier. Total Quality Manufacturing and Continuous Quality Improvement regimens have been so successful that the defect rate for most manufactured consumer products has been reduced to insignificance. When is the last time you found a half-filled can of Coca-Cola or a defective Gillette razor blade?

This same level of quality has not been achieved in the nonstandard category and this is especially the case in the fresh or perishable grocery category. The consumer tolerates this in a retail environment because of the ability to inspect the item and judge its suitability. These are purchases where we are concerned enough about variations and product quality to be involved in the selection process. These are typically nonstandard items.

Consider the examples in your own life: In a clothing store, we touch and feel the fabric for uniformity and absence of defects. We pick and choose produce, fruits, meats, fish, breads, and cheeses. We squeeze the loaf of bread for freshness. We examine the dry cleaning to see if the stain has been removed. We look at our developed photographs to see if all 24 pictures came out. We choose the cut of meat that appears freshest. We examine, probe, feel, and smell to weed out defects and omit unsuitable items.

The only way these nonstandard items can become candidates for the Replenish strategy is for the purchaser to be assured that the items have no defects and are in fact suitable for use much the same as if the consumer were at the point of purchase to choose or reject. Or, in the case of highly variable categories like fresh produce, where zero defects is mostly unattainable, Simplicity Marketers can at least assure customers of minimal defects well within the bounds of acceptability.

Driscoll's Strawberry Associates of Watsonville, California, has attained this for their product line. After years of genetic research and refinement with strawberry plants, this agricultural cooperative has attained a level of uniformity and quality for strawberries that approaches the level of a manufactured product. As a result, Driscoll's enjoys a 50% share of the U.S. fresh strawberry market.

The online shopping service Shoplink makes this promise:

> One of the first things you'll notice about ShopLink.com is that our quality is simply better. Our crisp vegetables and luscious fruit are the freshest you'll ever find. That's because they come directly from the best local farms and markets every day. No one has squeezed, dropped, or picked them over.
>
> ShopLink.com meats and seafood are always premium quality and impeccably fresh. Our USDA-certified Black Angus meats come from the same purveyor that supplies the finest restaurants. And our fresh fish is selected right off the docks every morning."[2]

Accordingly, there are two ways in which this level of quality can be attained:

- The manufacturer can deliver products of such uniformity and quality that these previously nonstandard items become in fact standard items with little or no variation.
- The replenishment intermediary—a function described below—takes the role of the selective shopper and eliminates or rejects unsuitable items.

Driscoll's takes the first approach and Shoplink promises the second solution. In the end, some combination of the trusted intermediary and the increasing uniformity of nonstandard products offer the likely answer.

In either case, the result to the consumer is the same: The consumer maintains an in-home inventory of a quality and appeal at least equal to what could have been obtained by actively participating in the selection at the point of purchase. Once this level is attained, there becomes little advantage or appeal to engaging in the shopping exercise itself.

In addition to the quality and defect-free nature of the product itself, we will expect this zero-defect promise to be carried over into billing accuracy and postpurchase customer support. True zero defects means our charges are accurate and without errors, omissions, and mistakes. Finally, as we have come to expect with other loyalty based programs (e.g., airline frequent flyer programs) that we will have a priority access to customer support that is faster and more convenient than is available to the more casual user of these brands.

CONTINUOUS SUPPLY

Once we have fair pricing and uniform quality for standardized and nonstandardized items, the only issue becomes maintaining an appropriate in-home inventory or an automatic provision of the service. We want no more late night trips to pick up a quart of milk. If we have contracted with Chem Lawn to maintain our yard, we want the fertilizer and insecticides to be applied when needed and in the correct quantity and we don't want to have to think about it. At this point, we enter the final stage of the final phase of Replenish: Continuous Supply.

Assume for a moment we can attain this state and consider the benefits. Shopping trips are vastly reduced. We do not have to go through the elaborate game of cutting coupons and reading food ads in our local newspaper to find where the bargains are. We do not stand in line at the checkout counter. We are given more time because many routine and unnecessary steps have been eliminated. We do not run out of things that are essentials in our daily lives. We have a more direct link to the ultimate manufacturer of those items chosen as our favorites. Most importantly, we have concluded a longitudinal relationship with a manufacturer or service provider in which we commit to a long-term relationship in exchange for an ongoing stream of products or services that meet our requirements. Numerous individual purchase decisions are replaced with one encompassing, global decision. Result: fewer decisions, less hassle, more clout with the vendor, and a reduction in stress for us.

Such manufacturers or service providers can reward us in various ways through our linked relationship. We are no longer anonymous single transactions in the marketplace but rather we become a longitudinal loyalist whose lifetime value the provider can calculate. We thus become far more important than we were before and we can expect this loyalty to be rewarded.

With the broad penetration of the Internet and the advent of several new-generation services, this ultimate goal is becoming closer to reality. By 2000 several firms had emerged in this space: Peapod, NetGrocer, HomeRuns, Shoplink, Homegrocer.com, drugstore.com, PlanetRx, PurpleTie.com, ePills, Webvan, and Streamline are examples. However, forecasts by Forrester Research and others suggest this market will penetrate the $150 billion full-service grocery markets to significant levels within the next five years. Andersen Consulting suggests that by 2007, 8% to 12% of all package goods, including toiletries, household products, dry and fresh groceries will be purchased electronically, representing a $60 to $86 billion business. These estimates may well prove to be too low.

As the personal computer becomes augmented by Internet connected appliances, this market takes on added significance. Consider a concept from Frigidaire termed the *online refrigerator*. This model has a LCD screen on the front door that can connect to the Internet. Also included is a laser wand that can scan packages and automatically read the Universal Product Code symbol and enter the item represented onto the order form on the screen. With this unit, the consumer simply scans products that are being discarded or ones that are running low and a reorder is automatically entered into the system. One can imagine such an appliance "talking" directly to an online grocer to build the next order item by item.

Anatomy of a Replenishment: Streamline

SIMPLICITY MARKETER:	**Streamline, Inc.**
SERVICE:	**Streamline Grocery Delivery**
LAUNCH:	**1998**
PRIMARY SUBSTRATEGY:	**Automatic Replenishment**

Streamline is designed to simplify life for busy families. We save you time and give you peace of mind.

Streamline Web site, October 1999

Streamline, the grocery delivery online service in the New England area, is a good example of how Replenish can work: A three-temperature Streamline box is delivered and installed in a secured and locked location, usually the garage. This device measures 60-by-30-by-62 inches and is divided into three compartments: frozen, refrigerated, and ambient temperature. A keypad access system allows entry to this area when the resident is not home.

A Streamline start-up team visits the subscriber and assists in preparing a Web-based personal shopping list. This list consists of all routinely purchased items. A standard delivery day, once per week, is chosen. Subscribers can order late at night before delivery day. The delivery is made from a 56,000-square-foot distribution center located in Westwood, Massachusetts, where items are separated and stored in the appropriate compartment. The following categories of products and services are offered:

Fresh Produce	Fresh Seafood, Poultry, and Meats
Dry Groceries	Deli Products
Fresh Baked Goods	Baby Foods, Formulas, and Diapers
Prepared Meals	Health and Beauty Supplies
Pet Foods	Video Rentals from Blockbuster
Dry Cleaning	Seasonal Items
Film Processing from Kodak	Postage Stamps & UPS Pickup/Delivery
Bottle and Can Redemption	

There is a monthly subscription charge of $30. However, Streamline requires no contract, no minimum delivery, and no delivery charge; no tipping is required. Prices are claimed to be at or below supermarket prices in the comparable geographic area. Traditional manufacturer coupons are not accepted by this service. The typical time to construct an order on the Internet for this service is expected to be less than 20 minutes. Streamline's management refers to their overall service as a *solution killer* much the same way in that storefront retailers use the term *category killer.*

Streamline offers two levels of automatic replenishment. The first is the personal shopping list which allows subscribers to quickly place orders for a list of frequently purchased items. The second level is deemed "don't run out" which automatically reorders selected items at specified intervals, for example, every week. Frank Britt, vice president of marketing of Streamline, suggests such a channel can become "the ultimate loyalty program for the packaged goods company."

By mid-1999, Streamline was averaging an 85% order frequency among its subscribers—45 weekly orders per year. Dollar value was running at $110 per weekly order or around $5,000 per year. Among those placing orders, 90% were female, 91% were college graduates, and 90% were married with at least one child.

While we have noted the need in Replenish to have a competitive price, there are two other pricing related elements that are required to make this work fully—the need for periodic elements of "marketing excitement" and the requirement to reward consumers for their loyalty. Marketing excitement in the retail world can be created by attractive displays of products, contests, sweepstakes, prizes, or free additions to the regular product. Loyalty programs are most frequently offered by the retailer in terms of preferred shopper cards that offer members special discounts. These elements will need to be incorporated into this new paradigm in some manner or form.

Replenish Checklist

The Streamline service is clearly focused on becoming a textbook example of how Replenish can work.

Does Streamline use the concept of continuous supply? How?
Streamline offers two levels of Replenishment: the personal shopping list and the "don't run out" category. The personal shopping list offers a gentle reminder of all the items and brands chosen as a regular part of the shopping experience. The don't run out list elevates this to a higher level and implicitly says that we are prepared to tolerate occasional excess inventory in the home

to absolutely ensure a critical product is never out of stock. (Think disposable diapers for families with infants.)

Does this service use the principles of zero defects?

For manufactured and standard grocery products, Streamline offers the same quality by manufacturer as found in a bricks and mortar retailer. For nonstandard products, produce, meats, and seafoods. Streamline has an economic imperative to offer high product quality and sales results show it meets these requirements. The reason for this is the higher margins found in perishables, meats, poultry, seafood, and produce, as contrasted to packaged grocery products. In the bricks and mortar world, the majority of food retailing profits are found in these categories due to their higher margins. Streamline must offer consistent quality, zero defects or suffer the risk of the online shopper ordering only the lower margin packaged grocery items online and purchasing perishables at storefront retailers.

Does Streamline offer competitive pricing?

Streamline consistently monitors grocery store prices in its delivery areas and has a policy of at least meeting the prevailing price structure in all categories. The Streamline subscriber is paying a monthly subscription fee to participate in the home delivery service and this is the only premium paid.

Is stress reduction built into the positioning?

Almost all elements of the Streamline service are targeted to stress reduction. The subscriber's weekly order is delivered on a specified day and placed securely inside the residence. A routine shopping list is maintained to gently remind the subscriber of what is likely to be needed. A special high priority "don't run out" list is offered to ensure a steady flow of the most critical products. The long physical trip to the grocery store is replaced by a 20-minute session at the PC at a time convenient to the subscriber.

■ Summary

In this chapter we have examined the 4th R of Simplicity Marketing—Replenish—and the requirements for its effective implementation (see

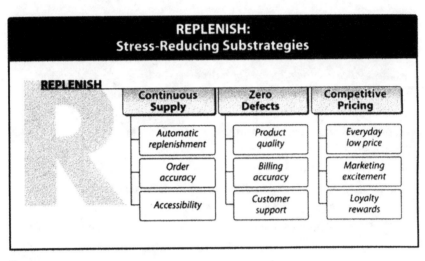

Figure 7.1

Figure 7.1). Perhaps the ultimate way to simplify our lives and reduce stress will be the ability to have a continuous supply of those products and services we prefer, faultlessly delivered to us with no defects, properly billed, and at an attractive price. The Replenish strategy offers a promise of exactly that.

PART III

Managing Simplicity

Chapter 8

Visible Simplicity, Invisible Complexity:

The Role of Information Technology

> The Industrial Revolution brought together people with machines in factories,
> and the Internet Revolution will bring together people with knowledge and
> information in virtual companies.　—JOHN CHAMBERS, President, Cisco Systems

A T ITS CORE, Simplicity Marketing revolves around what the consumer uses, sees, or acts upon and not on the underlying technology. Thus, Simplicity Marketing can be as simple as the feature AT&T offers that gives the caller the local time at the call destination. (Who among us has not gotten the time zones reversed and placed a call at a totally inappropriate time? No late night calls by mistake with AT&T.) Adding this feature was probably complex and involved extensive software modification and testing. The AT&T long distance customer is not concerned with the underlying technology that provides the time alert. The caller is offered an opportunity to hang up if she feels the local time is inappropriate.

The core issue of Simplicity Marketing is whether the marketer has structured the product or service to simplify the process and reduce the customer's stress. For example, BMW was among the first automobile manufacturers to place in its cars an onboard computer that monitors the driving cycle of each car. As the cycle progresses, a dashboard alert displays the decreasing time span until regular service is required on this specific BMW in a series of bars going from green to yellow. (Take a greater number of shorter trips in cold weather and the service requirement indicator will appear earlier. Conversely, take only long highway trips and the computer will allow the vehicle to go longer between service intervals.) The BMW owner doesn't have to worry about keeping track of oil change intervals because this is handled by the onboard computer. BMW has created a kind of electronic customer care function that silently and efficiently monitors the car and alerts the driver when service is required. The interface is even designed to gradually indicate the approach time for a service call; no sudden "service required" red light coming on unexpectedly. (This feature has also been designed by BMW as a "technology driven loyalty program." This computer activated monitoring system requires a special tool to reset the feature after an engine service has been performed. Since most non-BMW service centers do not have this tool, the owner must return to a BMW facility or have the system essentially deactivated.)

In the entire arena of "visible simplicity, invisible complexity," no platform serves to illustrate the point better than the Internet. The Internet offers a most fertile field to exploit the tenets of Simplicity Marketing and also a venue to explore innovative types of loyalty programs and customer care strategies using one-to-one marketing. We explore in this chapter the invisible complexity of the Internet and the implications for marketers.

EVOLVING SIMPLICITY: THE PERSONAL COMPUTER

From the Web's roots in academia and the defense establishment in the 1960s, the story of the Internet has been one of increasing simplicity masking a highly complex underlying technology. A similar but earlier phenomenon can be found in the evolution of the computer. Because the computer evolved first, it is useful to examine the lessons we have learned in the evolution of the computer to more fully understand how these lessons can be further applied to the Internet.

Consider the computer: Most observers would acknowledge the unveiling of ENIAC in Philadelphia in the spring of 1946 as the advent of the multipurpose, mainframe computer.[1] Filling an entire room, weighing 30 tons and containing 18,000 vacuum tubes, ENIAC had been developed during World War II to calculate trajectories of artillery shells. With the war ended, the behemoth was taken out of its cloak of secrecy and revealed to the world.

From this birth, the multipurpose mainframe computer slowly

evolved and began to penetrate large businesses, academia, and government. The hardware was housed in dedicated rooms and managed by specialists. (In the TV and film depictions, we invariably saw these people in white coats and usually holding a clipboard watching spinning tape drives.) Programs were inputted using punch cards in primitive machine language to be run in batch mode. The programmer usually waited overnight to see the results of a particular run.

By the mid-1960s, the faculties and graduate students at research universities were able to gain access to an IBM 1401 mainframe with 7 kilobytes of memory and program simple routines using FORTRAN. In 1976, Steve Jobs and Steve Wozniak created the first broadly successful personal computer: the Apple. In 1981, IBM validated the market for personal computers with the introduction of the IBM PC that preceded the introduction of the Macintosh in 1984 with its breakthrough graphical user interface. This was soon followed by Microsoft's introduction of the first Windows graphical user interface shell to sit atop of the text-based DOS operating system to simplify the command structure into a point and click environment.

Over the 50-year time horizon of the computer, we have seen a highly complex and specialized business and research tool evolve into a mass appliance with increasing simplicity. Today, one-half of all U.S. households have at least one personal computer. (We need to realize that it was not until 1945 that the telephone reached a similar penetration in the United States.) Eighty percent of household computers have a modem and the majority of those are connected to an online service and the Internet. Almost every professional or knowledge worker uses a networked computer and it is hard to find a school system without a program to make PCs available to every student. As we look at this time horizon for the computer, some central themes emerge:

- Larger became smaller.
- Limited-purpose became multipurpose.
- Stand-alone became networked.
- Time-sharing on mainframes evolved into personal computers.
- Text-based interfaces became GUIs (graphical user interfaces).
- Separate peripherals were incorporated into the PC.

Consider now the evolution of the Internet: When the Soviet Union launched the world's first earth orbiting satellite in 1957, the American defense establishment was stunned. A concerned U.S. Secretary of Defense, Neil McElroy, went to President Dwight Eisenhower and proposed creating a new government organization, the Defense Advanced Research Planning Agency or DARPA, to counter this technology threat. Along with the Rand Corporation and the defense establishment, the concept evolved of a national communications system with a distributed network infrastructure designed to survive a nuclear attack. DARPA Net was created to connect the military, the defense establishment, and research universities into a communications grid capable of withstanding a first attack.

In 1969, two computers communicated remotely for the first time—one from the campus of UCLA in Los Angeles and the other at the Stanford Research Institute in Menlo Park, California.[2] In the early 1970s, a computer engineer at MIT, Ray Tomlinson, developed the first viable e-mail program. In 1980, two scientists at the European Particle Physics Institute developed a hypertext tool to allow them to share information with colleagues. By 1988, DARPA Net was decommissioned and renamed the Internet. In 1990, scientists authored a document that organized this system into a set of fundamental protocols of the Web. In 1993, Tim Berners-Lee essentially validated the World Wide Web in his work to automate the many steps in exchanging data online. Mark Andreessen created the Mosaic Web browser, a graphical user interface to sit on top of the complexity of the Web. In July of 1995, Jeff Bezos launched Amazon.com and e-commerce came into our lives. By the close of the 1990s, the Web and the Internet browser had become indispensable components of our lives.

By revisiting the fundamental themes of the computer evolution, we can see if they reoccur in the Internet:

- Larger becomes smaller.

    Limited communication between large mainframes evolved to Internet connectivity with small handheld devices.

- Limited purpose becomes multipurpose.

    A simple text-only communications network became a multifaceted system for voice, video, text, and commerce.

- Stand-alone becomes networked.

  Forecasts call for 1 billion Internet connected computers early in this decade.

- Time-sharing becomes distributed computing.

  Web sites for large corporations evolved into personal Web sites for individuals.

- Text-based interfaces become graphical user interfaces.

  The Mosaic browser evolved into the "Macintosh GUI" of the Internet.

- Distinct peripherals are incorporated into the PC.

  The browser becomes multifunctional and is integrated with the operating system.

Part of what is powering the sustained growth of the Internet is the advent of visible simplicity sitting on top of invisible complexity. Consider some of the examples of this that follow.

SECURITY

With the growth of e-commerce, many consider ordering online a simple and convenient way to shop and order goods. But underneath a simple interface is a complex system to ensure the transaction is accomplished in private and with security. How do we protect the privacy of our order, our personal information, and our credit card numbers in a public system such as the Internet? In the old world of switched circuits, a dedicated phone line connected us to the merchant. The chance of someone intercepting our information was remote. But with the Internet and packet technology, we do not have a dedicated line but rather our communication is sent out on a public highway in numerous packets of information that are reassembled into our readable file. How then do we protect an unauthorized source from intercepting our packets and breaching the security of the transaction?

An almost invisible system known as asymmetric or public-key security is used on many Web e-commerce sites to accomplish this. One example of such a system is R.S.A., named for its founders—Ronald Rivest of MIT, Adi Shamir of the Weizmann Institute of Science, and Leonard Adleman of the University of Southern California. Here is what happens when we conduct an online transaction that uses such a system.

- The buyer enters personal information and a credit card number into the purchase form.
- To protect the information, the form is encrypted using a symmetric key that is generated by the computer sending the file. This key is a mathematical problem and uses a range of bits such as 512 or 1,024.
- When a file has been encrypted using a symmetric key, anyone who obtains that key can open the file containing, in this case, personal information and a credit card number. To allow the merchant to open this data file, the symmetric key must be sent along with the encrypted order.
- However, the symmetric key is protected by an encryption system that uses a published, or public, key from our merchant. The public key and the private key must be used together to decipher the file. The published or public key is usually the solution to a math problem such as the prime factors of a large number.
- When the encrypted file arrives, the merchant uses the private key, which contains the rest of the math problem's solution, to unlock the encrypted symmetric key and then uses that key to unlock the file and process our order.

The only way this security can be breached is to solve the math problem of the public and private key. This is where the size of the math problem creates the difficulty. Using massive computing power, a 512-bit key can eventually be solved. Increase that to a 1,024-bit key and the solution is exponentially more difficult. As processing power increases, the size and complexity of the encryption problem must be increased in a never-ending cycle.

All of this is hidden complexity to e-commerce shoppers. All of this takes place seamlessly as we click the "Order Now" button on our browser pages.

ONE-CLICK ORDERING

While not as complex or elegant as encryption, the advent of one-click ordering brings visible simplicity to the online e-commerce experience. Consider an online site that you frequent often. It could be a bookstore or a drugstore site. You find yourself satisfied with the merchant and you begin to shop with some frequency. However, each time you place an order, you must enter essential information that can become routine over time for most of your orders. In the bookstore example, you might always have the order shipped to your office because you prefer to receive it at that location. In addition, you almost always order second day delivery because the less expensive delivery option takes too long. You always use one particular credit card because you want to keep a separate record of particular types of purchases using that card.

Enter one-click ordering and this process becomes simpler. The merchant offers you an option of creating a standard order form that includes all of the options noted above. This becomes your default order and unless you want to cite an exception, next day delivery in this case, the order is processed without additional input. When you click on this option, your order is processed with no further input from you. The merchant knows who you are and what your preferences are, and keeps track of this for you.

While one-click ordering works great for a single merchant site, what about a standard order for multiple sites? For example, what if you always want to use a single credit card for all of your online purchases? What if you also wanted all purchases to come to your residence? Why is it necessary for you to reenter this information as you shop from site to site? It probably is not required and services are being offered to allow you to have a portable one-click order option. Merchants agree to accept the personal and payment system input for you as provided by a third party. The information is contained on this third-party's server and is made available to each merchant we choose.

In both systems, recordkeeping and files are maintained for us to benefit and simplify the ordering process. It is not unlike a bygone era when the local merchant knew us personally and provided many of the same functions that technology does today.

PERSONALIZED AD SERVERS

None of us particularly appreciates the interruption of advertising. This is exacerbated by an order of magnitude when the advertising is of no possible interest to us. A perfect example would be someone with all natural teeth being shown a commercial or a banner for a denture adhesive or a bald man seeing an ad for hair coloring.

Contrast this with advertising for a product or service that is of substantial interest. If you are an admirer of Harley-Davidson motorcycles, then an advertisement for the latest Harley is of likely interest and you in fact welcome the information. The same could be said for other products of interest. What we want, if we are using an advertiser-supported media, is timely, accurate advertisements that have a high probability of being of interest to us.

The San Francisco firm, MediaPlex, Inc., offers a solution to this. This organization has developed a software platform called MOJO (Mobile Java Objects). As described on the MediaPlex Web site, this is what MOJO does to solve the problem of wasted advertising:

> MOJO Works is Mediaplex's extensive line of eBusiness marketing services that delivers advertising expertise and technology for Internet sales, direct marketing and branding programs. Now, to help close the loop on the Web's promise of one-to-one marketing, we offer an exclusive capability called eBusiness Messaging. This pioneering technology allows advertisers to dynamically customize ad messages in real time depending on:
>
> - The user's profile.
> - Predefined guidelines about which product or offer to send to each user based on actual business data such as inventory and pricing.
> - The ongoing campaign's performance.

What MediaPlex is offering is a software solution to serve advertising to individual Web users; a solution that also:

1. Understands that person's profile (Do they like Harley-Davidson motorcycles?).

2. Determines if the product is in stock and available for sale.

3. Discovers the price the marketer wishes to offer to this particular Web user.

4. Evaluates how effective the particular advertising campaign being used is.

Not only are we likely to receive advertising messages of interest to us, but the product will be in stock and the marketer has the ability to offer a unique and very attractive price depending on the user's attractiveness. The consumer wins and the marketer wins; complex technology but a simple result.

INFORMATION GATHERING FOR INTELLIGENT SHOPPING

Technology can be used to aid the buyer in the necessary information gathering needed to make an informed and intelligent purchase decision in the bricks and mortar world. IPIX is a Palo Alto, California, based firm that captures and serves virtual tours of real estate properties. Using 360-degree video images of at least four scenes in a home listed for sale, IPIX allows potential buyers to take a virtual walk through the home to see for themselves the amenities and layout. The Web user goes to a real estate site on the Web and enters the search criteria for a home. The real estate site search engine sorts for these criteria and delivers the homes matching the particular request. On the static listing is a hot link titled Virtual Tour. If the buyer is sufficiently interested to click on the link, IPIX serves up a minimum of four scenes for that listing; for example, the living room, kitchen, master bedroom, and backyard. Then using only a Web browser, the panorama is displayed for the prospective buyer. Features and layout can be seen that otherwise would require a personal visit to reveal.

It is unlikely that a buying decision would be made based on a virtual tour. More likely, homes of no interest could be identified and homes of greater appeal could be identified. Unnecessary visits could be reduced and the buying process made more efficient. The real estate professional could spend more time as an advisor and counselor and less as a chauffeur. Hidden from view is the complexity of image capture/digitization, search engines, and databases. Revealed to the prospective buyer is the simplicity of a remote home visit using the Internet.

Like home buying, purchasing an automobile is a stressful and complex process. First, the buyer must select a manageable number of candidate vehicles. Next, these selections need to be researched and evaluated: How is the crash worthiness, what is the depreciation record of this model, and so on. Then the cost of the vehicle needs to be determined: What is the cost to the dealer, and what is the best price at which this particular vehicle can be purchased? Next, several questions need to be answered: Should I buy or lease, what are the insurance ratings on each vehicle, what extended warrantees are available, and so on. It is all complex and time consuming.

Enter the Web-based auto buying services such as AutoWeb.com. The prospective buyer goes to one of these sites and begins a process to answer all of these questions and accomplish this in short order. Many of the sites allow the prospective purchasers to begin the process by answering a few questions on their needs for the vehicle purchase. How many members are in the family? To what uses will the vehicle be put? How many miles per year will be driven? From those questions a set of likely selections will be offered.

The prospective buyer can then research these selections. The Insurance Institute crash worthiness rating can be accessed. The cost to the dealer for each vehicle configured exactly as desired can be determined. The most likely selling price to the buyer can be found. Is this a vehicle in great demand that commands full MSRP (manufacturer's suggested retail price), or are there likely discounts available? Is the manufacturer placing any incentives on this vehicle at this time and if so, what are they?

Next, the prospective buyer can determine the trade-in value of the present vehicle. Car buying services allow their users to access databases that give used car prices down to the exact model in particular Zip codes. (Convertibles have better resale values in Los Angeles than in Minneapolis.) Finally, the prospective buyer can investigate financing and leasing options as well as insurance costs and coverage.

All that's left is for the car buying service to refer the buyer to a nearby dealer or, as is now occurring, actually conduct the transaction on the Web. In this latter case, the new vehicle is delivered and the trade-in vehicle is picked up at the customer's location. Underneath this simple, logical, and sequential process is an enormous amount of data gathering and processing. But this is hidden from the buyer.

■ Summary

Privacy, security, ordering simplicity, personalized ads, and intelligent shopping all make use of highly complex technologies and data warehouses. However, the secret for the marketer is to make all of this complexity disappear and become transparent.

It appears that in this quest to make the technology unobtrusive, the smaller and more innovative firms are in the lead and the older and more established firms seem stuck in the old ways of doing business.

Arguably, AT&T should have created America Online. Here is a service where the average user is logged onto a telephone modem for one hour per day. Surely one of the great uses of telephony. However, it was Steve Case who made the online experience simple and entertaining, hid the underlying technology, and created a firm with a market value greater than that of AT&T itself.

Paralleling the Quicken consumer product example in Chapter 3, it was Intuit and not one of the big six accounting firms that saw the whole life context of bookkeeping in the small business sector. Intuit realized that nonaccountants did not understand double entry accounting but they did understand writing checks, creating invoices, and paying bills. So Intuit created Quickbooks which used this intuitive and simple interface and forced technology to do the required accounting protocols. Intuit carries a market capitalization of $6 billion at the time of this writing.

It was eToys that concluded the toy buying experience for parents was stressful and complex. Visiting a megaretailer such as Toys R Us with its aisle after aisle of merchandise stacked to the ceiling was not exactly a pleasant experience. EToys took this entire experience and made it fit the Web in an elegant interface. Parents responded and at the time of this writing eToys has a market capitalization of $1 billion and Toys R Us is valued at $4 billion.

The online drugstores are yet another example. None of the brick-and-mortar retailers saw the need for on-line sales or they were daunted by the technology challenges. This did not dissuade PlanetRx or drugstore. com from accepting the challenge. Shortly after its Initial Public Offering of stock, Drugstore.com was valued at more than $2 billion, offering yet another object lesson for the established marketers.

The lessons are clear. If you are an established marketer, look for ways to make technology invisible and find new ways to serve your customers. If you are a challenger or start-up firm, look to those markets with stressful and complex customer experiences, where the existing players are wedded to their current business models.

The power of Simplicity Marketing is nowhere more apparent than in those situations where complex technologies can be harnessed and made invisible in order to provide a stress-free customer experience.

Chapter 9

Integrating Simplicity Marketing into Brand and Product Strategy

> There is a property in the horizon which no man has but he whose eye can integrate all the parts, that is the poet. —RALPH WALDO EMERSON, *Nature*

IF THERE IS POETRY in Simplicity Marketing—and surely there is when it's done well—it is to be found in bringing together the 4 R's with the traditional 4 P's of marketing in one integrated process. Customer stress must be considered at every stage, in every key decision impacting how a brand or product is brought to market. It is impossible to optimize Simplicity Marketing's effectiveness if it is managed as an à la carte exercise. This chapter provides ways to ensure that every aspect of how you currently plan and execute marketing strategy is opened up along the way to the opportunities inherent in reducing customer stress. This must encompass both brand planning and product planning, from the corporate brand level down to both the design and marketing mix around every individual product and line extension, and then on through to customer care.

First, we will examine the key points of intersection between Simplicity Marketing and traditional marketing planning. Then we will provide a customizable template for self-auditing your own marketing strategy development process, to help ensure that brand-building opportunities to reduce customer stress are not missed. Finally, we will look in more depth at an example of the power of simultaneously employing multiple strategies across the 4 R's.

■ The 4 R's Meet the 4 P's

With the digital economy has come debate about whether the time-honored "4 P's" of marketing—Product, Promotion, Price, and Place (distribution)—remain an effective construct for marketing planning. Regardless of which side of that debate you're on, the 4 P's are still the foundation learned and used by most marketing managers for planning and execution. One way, then, to bring to life the intersection of Simplicity Marketing and traditional marketing would be to lay out the 4 P's and show how each can potentially leverage customer stress reduction through the simplicity strategies in this book. But managing the 4 P's has never been a linear process, and a key to integrating any two processes is the *sequence* in which those processes occur. So for practical application, our preference is to lay out instead the sequence of brand and product planning activities to help ensure that simplicity and stress will not be afterthoughts. Since managing customer stress as an afterthought is more expensive and slows time to market, the more sequential approach allows Simplicity Marketing to be managed organically as an ongoing sensibility—a way of thinking—that pervades every aspect of strategy.

■ Brand Planning and Product Development

There are many ways to illustrate brand planning and product planning processes as a framework for applied simplicity. For the purpose of integrating simplicity and stress relief, the authors choose to look at product development as part of a larger brand planning process rather than as a process unto itself. Companies that are truly market-driven and brand-conscious determine what commitment, or brand promise, they want their brand to stand for in the customer's mind so that it is relevant and unique enough to merit a long-term customer relationship. The products follow in support of that promise and the brand's core values. Enduring brands bear this out over the long haul: Historically, Coca-Cola would not put its brand on a product that didn't deliver *refreshment*, any more than IBM would put its brand on a product that wasn't *reliable*. (Since the details of product development transcend the scope of this book, product development is covered more from the perspective of how products help or hurt the delivery of the overall brand promise.)

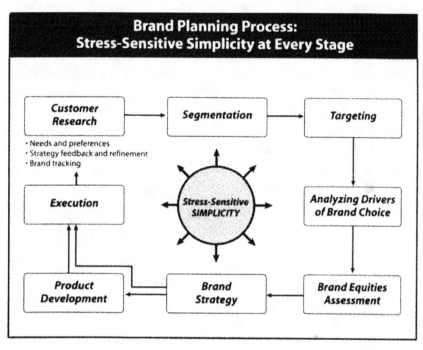

Figure 9.1

The brand planning process depicted in Figure 9.1, as a starting point for stress-sensitive strategy, acknowledges the customer-driven method of beginning with customer dialog to identify needs, both met and unmet, and preferences. It then reflects how we segment markets, target selected priority segments, analyze factors that drive brand choice in the category, assess individual brands' perceived strengths and weaknesses, and formulate brand and product strategies that are ultimately implemented, measured, and refined. This fundamental process flowchart provides a sequential loop that we can travel around together to discuss where simplicity and stress reduction fit into each stage.

CUSTOMER RESEARCH

In Chapter 1 we discussed the concept of *whole life context*. We underscored the fact that the customer's life is *not* neatly segregated into product categories the way that supermarket aisles or shopping catalogs are organized. We pointed out that marketing research for individual brands, however, tends to focus the customer on one category at a time—outside the context of the *collective* complexities of the customer's life or business. Consequently, marketing research is one of the indirect *causes* of overchoice and customer stress.

So why do customers who proclaim frustration with overchoice in their lives still so often ask for more choices and options in a specific category? The answer has a lot to do with how the questions are asked. The level of choice that may be desirable in one category, in a vacuum, compounds exponentially over dozens or even hundreds of other categories in the customer's whole life context. When we begin brand planning by identifying customer needs and preferences in a single category, or what customers want from the *ideal* brand in that category, we always run the risk of unwittingly encouraging customers to say, "Give me *more*—more flavors, more sizes, more options." After all, most consumers in highly developed economies have been trained from an early age to seek out options and have a cumulative history of amassing more things as discretionary income (or debt) permits over time. (To remind us how ingrained the more-is-better mentality is, think about how seldom, if ever, you've heard a small child exclaim, "Give me *less!*"—healthy foods notwithstanding.) Due to both natural tendencies and consumption conditioning, most of us tend to respond to open-ended questions about what we want with "more."

This is gradually changing as stress levels reach the breaking point among more customers. But except for those who have already joined the simplicity movement or are so acutely aware of their stress that they are tackling it by proactively de-cluttering their lives, we still have a tendency to relate to "more" as good and "less" as bad (unless it's less of a perceived "bad" thing, like calories or fat or nicotine content).

What is needed is further development and more widespread use of research techniques that help customers respond to alternative decision-making scenarios from more of a life-contextual perspective. Researchers at Duke University and The Wharton School of the University of Pennsylvania have recently called attention to the importance of consumers' *choice environments* in balancing four goals when making a brand or product choice: (1) maximizing accuracy in making the right choice, (2) minimizing effort, (3) minimizing the experience of negative emotions, and (4) maximizing the ease of justifying the decision.[1] These four goals are balanced differently depending not only on customer knowledge and skills but also from one choice environment to another.

Environmental context can often be better revealed through *observation* than through *inquiry*. Harvard University professors Dorothy Leonard and Jeffrey Rayport have written about the value of "empathic design," in which observing customers using products in their *own* environments rather than in a useability lab or focus groups has yielded breakthrough insights for product development at companies ranging from General Mills to Nissan to Gillette.[2] They discuss Intuit Corporation's Follow Me Home program, in which first-time buyers of Quicken software have given Intuit permission to watch first-hand their experience installing and using the software in their own homes. This has not only provided contextual cues such as seeing how the customer's personal finance-related files are organized but also has revealed how Quicken interacts (and opportunities for how it *could* interact) with other software applications that customers tend to run in tandem with Quicken on their computers. Advertising agency account planners and market research firms are also increasingly finding that getting permission to follow customers to homes or offices and observe—or loaning customers video cameras or other recording devices to document environmental experiences—yields insights that lead to more customer-relevant brand strategies and product design.

Since decision making is an abstract and inner process, observing it is obviously not possible in a literal sense like observing product use. But one way to get a life-context-sensitive window on decision making is through market research that incorporates *storytelling*—eliciting real-life stories from customers about how they behave and what they felt during various real-life decision-making events. The University of Wisconsin's Craig Thompson and others have described interpretive frameworks for deriving marketing strategy insights from the life-context details and idiosyncrasies of customers' stories about their experiences with products, brands, and shopping.[3] Thompson transcends single-category inquiry in showing, for example, how storytelling analysis revealed decision-making linkages between a customer's brand choice in the purchase of a General Motors minivan and the purchase of an Ethan Allen bunkbed—two categories which seem only remotely related at best and which each have their own distinct set of purchase behaviors.

As Thompson wrote, "Understanding how consumers interpret their product/service needs and desires in relation to their perceived life circumstances is a pressing strategic issue in the current marketing climate where competitive pressures necessitate more nuanced conceptualization of market segments."[4] Work is underway to develop next-generation research techniques that address how customers construct brand preferences in context-dependent ways. For example, in "context matching," researchers attempt to determine what customer environmental factors (such as time pressure and number of choices) influence preference, and then match those factors in the actual research environment.[5]

For a world increasingly characterized by stress and overchoice, traditional research still relies too often on old assumptions that choice is predominantly rational. Tracking studies in high-tech categories, for example, have documented the rise in emotional (vs. rational) considerations in driving brand choice even just since the mid-1990s. More life-contextual research has a better chance of identifying, understanding, and measuring emotional drivers of brand choice in ways that parallel how the customer experiences such factors.

Short of next-generation research techniques, other things can be done in the interim beyond more real-life observation. For example, certain "projective techniques" in qualitative research, such as various types of role playing, may move the customer closer to a range of whole-life context considerations that may not show up in a survey or typical focus group. With focus groups in general, moderators could often do more to remind customers about life-contextual considerations before asking for responses to questions about desired choices and options. This may include a line of questioning that helps establish what other product categories are most likely to directly interact with or indirectly impact the researched category. Such "impact categories" may or may not be related in terms of product type. For example, while an electric shaver and preshave lotion are literally related and are used together, the purchase of preshave lotion may be impacted as much or more by purchase decisions for other personal care products than by shavers. How?

Let's say that a high-stress 26-year-old man is working 80-hour weeks in a Silicon Valley start-up company and typically buys his preshave lotion at the drugstore at the same time that he buys deodorant or soap or shampoo or conditioner. His threshold for choice in preshave lotion may be lower if he is already overcome with options in these other categories that help constitute his total shopping experience during a typical store visit. If he is brand loyal on these other personal care items, he may automatically replenish them with little choice-related stress. But if he is not brand loyal, he may be sorting through multiple options of formulas, packages, and pricing in each of the other personal care categories. If you're selling preshave lotion and trying to make brand extension decisions regarding how many formulas, fragrances, sizes, and packaging varieties to offer, wouldn't you want your marketing research to reveal how brand loyalty—or lack thereof—in these impact categories might affect your customer's appetite/tolerance for options?

This is precisely the kind of issue that customer research must get better at addressing to help integrate Simplicity Marketing into the research phase of brand planning. This means better understanding of not only how one purchase decision interacts with others but also the impact of the total environmental noise level in which each decision may be made.

Altering time-honored research approaches to align them more closely to the overchoice era is not easy. As a brand marketer, you can encourage your research suppliers and call upon your marketing trade organizations to move aggressively in the development of context-sensitive research methodologies. Meanwhile, you may find competitive advantage in asking how you can make your current research more context-sensitive than your rivals', with an eye toward customer stress reduction opportunities. Context-sensitive research is a key to avoiding the customer alienation that will increasingly result from incremental, rather than replacement, products and marketing approaches (Chapter 2).

Finally, beyond evaluating preferences and choices in a whole life context, make sure you gather enough basic information from customers about their stress levels—and the nature and causes of their stress—to be able to incorporate that knowledge into market segmentation and targeting decisions. Refer to the Chapter 2 concepts of stressographics and drivers of stress to ensure that your research builds in the necessary inquiry to assess and define these critical planning elements. It is impossible to gain competitive advantage through Chapter 2's marketing mantra—*follow the stress*—if your customer research doesn't tell you where the stress is and what's causing it. (More on this in the market segmentation discussion that follows.)

MARKET SEGMENTATION

Once we have gathered enough information about customers to look for affinity groups that are predictive of buying behavior, we are ready to apply Simplicity Marketing to market segmentation decisions. This requires incorporating customer stress considerations into the foundation on which all segmentation approaches are built by identifying and profiling segments—that is, describing them in detail—so that each segment can be well understood as a fairly homogeneous group, and so that enough is known about each segment to evaluate its business potential relative to other segments.

Think about the traditional ways of identifying segments, or qualifying particular groups of customers as legitimate segments worthy of pursuit. Marketers look at segment *size* and *scale* in terms of the number of customers (large enough for marketing efficiencies, small enough to yield reasonably consistent behavior) and total purchasing power. Other factors may include *accessibility* of the segment—whether it can be cost-effectively reached and serviced, and the degree to which actionable, up-to-date customer database information is obtainable. But we are entering an era in which more and more marketers will find it useful to also consider whether a segment has significant enough *stress levels* for stress relief to be a real factor in brand loyalty.

As discussed in Chapter 2, profiling segments has been most commonly done in terms of demographics (firmographics in business markets), psychographics, and product usage levels or dollar amounts spent on category purchases. We pointed out that, as customer stress continues to rise, the level and nature of stress will likely become more and more predictive of buying preferences—to the degree that, in some product categories, stressographics may eclipse more traditional parameters as a productive way to distinguish one group of customers from another. This is the point in the brand planning process where Chapter 2's stress scan can be applied. If customer research has adequately gathered stress-related information, that information can be scanned to extract a stressographic profile for each segment that reveals the degree of stress, the drivers of stress, and customers' strategies for coping with stress.

Let's look at how this might play out differently depending on whether the product category is itself inherently stressful. In grocery products that are routinely replenished, stress may be just another of many behavioral characteristics defining a segment. As long as stress is included in the information gathering and analysis, its strategic importance relative to other profiling characteristics will become evident. But what about in categories that *are* inherently stressful due to the circumstances in which the product is used? Think about categories like over-the-counter acne medication (life or death for affected teens!), or mission-critical computer networks, or hospitals. In these cases, where the product or service is very often selected and/or used under high-stress circumstances, stress may be the *primary* characteristic that defines and distinguishes market segments. Let's examine both types of examples in more detail to see how stressographics enhance segment profiling.

For Case A, in which the product is not inherently stressful, consider dog food. Two different heavy-user market segments for Golden Bones, a fictitious premium brand that is particularly high in nutritional content and overall quality, and pricey as a result, might look something like Table 9.1 *without* Simplicity Marketing (just some selected basics for illustrative purposes).

Table 9.1

	Segment 1: Only the Best	Segment 2: Dog-Loving Sacrificers
Description	Dog owners, for whom money isn't an object, accustomed to quality	Dog *lovers*, willing to sacrifice in other areas to give their dogs the very best
Demographics		
Age	35–54	25–54
HH income	$100,000+	$25,000–$50,000
Education	College graduate/ postgraduate	High school graduate/some college/college graduate
Psychographics		
Social class	Lower upper/upper upper	Working class/middle class
Lifestyle	Busy; two-career family; live to work	Family- and community-oriented; work to live
Personality	Aggressive; analytical; ambitious	Sensitive; place priority on quality time with children and pets

[continued]

Product Usage

Usage rate	Heavy	Moderate to heavy
Occasions	Everyday; most/all feeding occasions	Everyday for some, frequent special treat for others
Brand loyalty	Moderately strong	Very strong
Media *Consumption*	Drive-time radio, news magazines, Internet	Television, entertainment and special interest magazines, newspaper, some Internet in PC households

With Simplicity Marketing, we could round out this profile by incorporating stressographics as shown in Table 9.2, based on the concepts covered in Chapter 2. While in this case stress may not *drive* segmentation strategy, it still reveals important clues to more effective marketing. The stressographics of customers in the Only the Best segment suggest that, in stress reduction context, these dog owners may perceive Golden Bones as an antidote to guilt that helps compensate for lack of time to play with and care for the dog ("Gourmet food is the least I can do for Rover, since I can barely find time to walk him—much less play with him."). This may impact the brand message to this segment in ways that would not be relevant to, or appropriate for, the Dog-Loving Sacrificer segment.

▓ **Table 9.2**

	Segment 1: Only the Best	Segment 2: Dog-Loving Sacrificers
Stressographics		
Stress levels	High	Moderate
Stress drivers	Work demands; balancing work and family; child care; guilt regarding lack of time spent with children/pets; pace of change	Bosses; job security; family money issues
Coping style	Stress tacklers	Stress escapers

The value of stressographics in segmentation is magnified in Case B, in which the product is bought or used under inherently stressful circumstances. One reason there is so much stress in the corporate computing market, for example, is that the Internet has turned the world upside down for CIOs and their technology managers in virtually every industry. For these business customers, the imperative to transform their businesses from the infrastructure they established during the 1980s and 1990s to the Internet-protocol (or IP) networks of the new millennium has created untold stress in the workplace. In Table 9.3 we show two different potential market segments, in terms of more traditional segmentation variables, for Mega-Mission Control—a fictitious brand of management software that is integral to mission-critical computing networks in large corporations.

Table 9.3

	Segment 1: Control Freaks	Segment 2: Confident Innovators
Description	Less-experienced managers in rapid-growth companies, obsessed with safe choices that provide maximum control over every aspect of network management	Seasoned managers in larger, moderate-growth companies, willing to take risks for competitive advantage—though not beyond the point of compromising the network's ability to deliver
Demographics and Firmographics		
Age	25–34	35–54
Job titles	Network manager, network administrator, information systems manager, systems administrator	Information systems director or manager, network manager, network administrator, director/manager network operations, MIS director/manager

[continued]

Industry	Professional services, small/ medium hi-tech manufacturers, small Internet services/ e-commerce providers	Financial services, telecommunications, large Internet services/ e-commerce providers, transportation, utilities, retail
Geography	United States, Europe	United States, Europe, Asia, Latin America
Media Consumption	Trade magazines, Internet	Trade magazines, Internet, trade shows/ events/seminars

With Simplicity Marketing, we could incorporate stressographics as depicted in Table 9.4. If, for example, you were selling routers—a type of networking hardware integral to the functionality of mission-critical computer networks—you could see how such stressographic profiles might impact your approach to these customers. But Case B-type examples of inherently stressful categories are by no means limited to the high-tech realm, and can just as easily apply to marketing "books on

Table 9.4

	Segment 1: Control Freaks	Segment 2: Confident Innovators
Stressographics Stress levels	Very high	Moderately high
Stress drivers	Consequences of failure; job insecurity; workload; commute (for some)	Confrontations with internal customers; workload; balancing work and family; commute (for some)
Coping style	Stress tacklers (haphazardly)	Stress tacklers (confidently, premeditated)
Impact on the job	Struggling to maintain control, but with frequent feelings of high anxiety	Very conscious of stress, but generally feeling like it's under control about as well here as in most companies

tape" to drivers with stressful commutes or selling game-day footwear to professional athletes.

Targeting

With segments defined and profiled, we can now look at stress-sensitive targeting: How we will prioritize the relative strategic importance of each segment, incorporating stress and simplicity considerations, and which segments we will choose to target. As with the segmentation process, traditional approaches to prioritizing segments for targeting are not meant to be thrown out. They are meant to be enhanced by considering customer stress as another important variable—one that may, in some circumstances, eclipse traditional variables in creating opportunity for competitive advantage. So even for Simplicity Marketers, individual segments should still be assessed and compared based on traditional factors such as segment size and structure, selling efficiencies, profitability, growth, competitive intensity, customer bargaining power, channel costs, and strategic alignment with corporate objectives and brand identity.

Where stress considerations enter into prioritizing target segments is in aligning stress levels of the segment with the stress relief benefit levels of the product/brand. Obviously, the greater the potential for a particular product to deliver stress relief benefits, the more important customer stress levels become in evaluating the relative business potential of alternative segments. Figure 9.2 represents an intentionally oversimplified but useful way to think about this. Each cell in the matrix represents potential value created by interaction between a high-, medium-, or low-stress customer segment and products capable of delivering high, medium, or only low levels of stress relief (or none at all). The numbers in each cell represent a loose rank-ordering of opportunity for Simplicity Marketers.

A key to applying this, of course, is objective self-assessment by marketers, which is as always better done by customers. It's tempting as marketers to have an inflated view of how our next new product is a stress savior. So as with everything else in product evaluation, we should let customer research help us gauge a product's real stress-relief potential to accurately place it on the matrix in Figure 9.2.

The Sweet Spot for Stress-Sensitive Targeting Decisions

Market Segment Stress Level	Product Delivers:		
	STRONG Stress Relief Benefits	MEDIUM Stress Relief Benefits	WEAK/NO Stress Relief Benefits
HIGH STRESS	①	2	9
MODERATE STRESS	3	4	8
LOW STRESS	7	6	5

Figure 9.2

ANALYZING DRIVERS OF BRAND CHOICE

With targeting decisions made and segments prioritized, we now must identify and prioritize for each target segment those factors that drive the customer's choice between Brand X and Brand Y in the category. There are two important dimensions to this before we factor in Simplicity Marketing considerations: (1) what characteristics or attributes are perceived by customers to constitute the *ideal* brand, and (2) which among those are the most important attributes that customers use to *differentiate* between brands. These are often the same attributes for (1) and (2). But sometimes the attribute that is most important in defining the ideal brand is an attribute on which two or more brands are perceived to have roughly equal strength. Then the customer drops down to the next most important characteristic of the ideal brand until finding a perceived difference between brands on which to base a preference.

With frozen pizza in the supermarket, for example, the number one attribute of the ideal brand for the majority of customers in all but the highest-stress segments is *taste*—above all, no matter how convenient, economical, or healthy/unhealthy it may be, or how many varieties and sizes it's available in, the pizza needs to taste really good. (In higher-stress segments, convenience/time-saving may eclipse taste.) But if Brand X and Brand Y are perceived to taste about equally good, the battle will more likely be won or lost on convenience (Brand X microwaves in five minutes instead of eight) or economy (Brand Y is 50 cents cheaper), so that an attribute secondary to taste in describing the ideal brand actually becomes the primary driver of brand choice.

Where does Simplicity Marketing fit into such choice dynamics? In integrating Simplicity Marketing into brand choice analysis, it is critical that stress-related factors be included in the inventory of choice drivers where applicable—and then prioritized for each targeted segment in a way that reflects the stressographics of that segment. This points back to research, where we discussed the imperative for the kind of inquiry and observation that would tell us what we need to know about the impact of stress on the customer's life.

When we simply ask customers to tell us which among a list of brand attributes are most important to them, their responses tell us only what they *say* is important, but often don't reflect actual behavior—or the full impact of stress. In any quantitative research that attempts to prioritize the strategic importance of brand choice drivers, we will almost certainly miss the boat if the list of attributes being prioritized doesn't adequately reflect stress impact. For example, a full-time working Mom with three kids may rank nutritious as the most important attribute of the ideal fruit juice brand (after all, that's not just a politically correct response but is also what she emotionally wants for her children); yet, independent of that question, she may rate the brand she actually *buys* lower than another brand on nutrition but higher on packaging convenience—because when she's in a big rush every morning, it's easier and faster to handle the sculptured 64-ounce plastic bottle that fits in her hand and that has an attached cap which doesn't have to be placed on the counter and then picked up again. So when we analyze how these same customers rate their *preferred brand* on the same attributes, the true drivers of brand preference—and the impact of stress—are more likely to surface.

Of course, this assumes that any list of attributes has included stress-related factors gleaned from qualititative research as previously discussed. Consider the category of hotels geared to business travelers. Among the attributes driving brand choice, besides location and price, are some factors that are not particularly stress-related (like whether the hotel gives frequent flier miles for the airline of choice, or whether the food is good) and some factors that can be directly related to stress (easy/good Internet connections for checking e-mail, dependable room service, a good shower head, a gym and/or pool, or a special feeling of warmth and comfort in the club- or concierge-level rooms). As stressful as business travel can be, being in a hotel underscores the feeling of "not being at home" even more than does an airplane, so there is great opportunity for stress relief related to mitigating discomfort and inconvenience. Some hotel brands have found this sort of dynamic a useful way to segment markets, marketing differently to customers who find being away from home significantly more stressful than do other customers—and whose brand choice is driven by a different heirarchy of attributes.

BRAND EQUITIES ASSESSMENT

Once we understand the attributes that describe the ideal brand in the customer's mind, and which of those attributes are most important in differentiating between brands, we can assess the customer-perceived strengths and weaknesses of individual brands on those attributes. Even if the category is not inherently stressful for the customer, and even if the most important category-driving attributes are not ostensibly stress-related, it is still strategically important to ensure that brands and products are both evaluated based on whether they are perceived as *sources* or *relievers* of stress. This is because brands are certainly capable of creating stress even in low-stress categories.

As an example that purposely borders on silly in order to make the point, stress-related attributes are not likely to show up in routine customer research on socks. Neither wearing socks nor, say, buying socks on the Internet is inherently stressful (especially when you already wear that particular sock and know that it's what you want), but when the Internet retailer sends you the wrong color or size for the second time, it's a pretty good bet that the retailer's brand will be perceived as a source of stress.

So in assessing brand equities and tracking shifts in brand health over time, Simplicity Marketing requires that we understand the degree to which a brand's presence in the customer's active brandscape (Chapter 6) is a comfort or is a source of anxiety, uncertainty, or concern. This again impacts customer research design to incorporate inquiry or observation that will reveal whether a brand and its competitors are adding to or reducing the amount of stress in the customer's life—and why. *Every customer experience with every product falls somewhere on a continuum that runs from stress producer to stress reliever.* The higher the stress levels in the targeted market segment, and the more stressful the circumstances under which the product is used, the more integral a measure such as this will be to understanding customer satisfaction.

If part of the stress-relevant value of a brand lies in its perceived image, then another part lies in brand familiarity. A key component of brand equity is brand *knowledge*—the combination of the customer's awareness of and perceptions about a brand.[6] A familiar brand can reduce stress just by virtue of its familiarity (as often occurs in Discontinuous Repositioning as covered in Chapter 6). So a brand's familiarity relative to competitor brands is an essential component of assessing brand equities—not just for the usual, obvious reasons but also as one gauge of a brand's stress-reduction potential and comfort factor. In particular, measures of unaided awareness (brands mentioned by a customer when asked to name brands in a category) and especially top-of-mind awareness (first brand mentioned), viewed in conjunction with the degree and nature of positive or negative associations with the brand, help paint a picture of what strategies will be required to maximize customer perceptions of the brand as a stress-reliever.

BRAND STRATEGY

On the Figure 9.1 planning loop, it is here in the strategy phase and in product development that decisions are made about which of the 4 R's and their substrategies are most relevant to maximizing marketing effectiveness. After all, this is when marketers decide what face the brand or product is going to present to the customer, so this is the time to pin down the ways in which the brand's identity should embody simplicity and the ways in which each product will deliver stress relief. It is here that the checklists from Chapters 4 through 7 can be used to assess strategic potential for each of the 4R's.

It is also typically here that a strategy brief is prepared (sometimes called a brand brief, product brief, or creative brief) which, based on marketing objectives, lays out *what to say* to customers before deciding *how* to say it in the execution phase of brand planning. Typically, the brief summarizes the brand's current situation, including the state of brand health and its competitive environment, and describes the target customer and the desired impact of brand communication in terms of customer attitudes and behavior. It also attempts to distill key insights from customer research to reveal the hot buttons connected to unmet needs, and to summarize facts and products/features that serve as reasons to believe that this brand can meet those needs better than any other. Throughout this process of developing a brief, the Simplicity Marketer will look to incorporate relevant stress considerations at every turn.

We are approaching the point when *no brand positioning document or creative brief should be considered complete unless it has asked and answered the question of what the product or brand will do to reduce customer stress.* To put this into action, the customer research, segmentation, and targeting phases of brand planning must incorporate the considerations discussed earlier in this chapter. The Simplicity Marketing audit in the second half of this chapter will help you do just that. Then when you get to this strategy phase, you will have already assessed your opportunity relative to competitors' to use each of the 4 R's and any of the Simplicity Marketing substrategies within each R.

PRODUCT DEVELOPMENT

A persistent core issue in the product development process is optimum allocation of resources to develop certain features and functionality. Typically, customer feedback has generated a wish list of everything the perfect product should be able to do. Teams of engineers scramble to respond while management scrambles to prioritize and pay for development efforts. But more and more, customer stress can be an effective arbiter of priorities for product development and R&D.

To see a very specific example of this in practice, let's return to the case of Hewlett-Packard enterprise storage solutions for managing data on large computer networks.[7] HP's development of next-generation products in a category with highly compressed cycles of new product launches created the usual conundrum—not having the resources to develop all the features the customer wants and still bring products to market in a timely manner. Among the potential product features fighting for development resources was greater configuration flexibility, which would simplify the task of configuring system installation; another was an "active hot spare" which, in the event of a system failure, would allow the customer to quickly swap out components without completely shutting down the system for repair. Customers said both of these features were important, but what if there had been sufficient time and money to incorporate only one?

Given the relative high-stress target segment (remember, we've already discussed the nature of mission-critical corporate computing) and the stressful circumstances under which enterprise storage products may be deployed, the choice becomes easier. Configuration flexibility is a real plus and an obvious simplifier as well, but configuration happens under less stressful circumstances than recovery from a system failure (which creates more stress for the customer than any other product-related situation)—so the active hot spare becomes the must-have for an enterprise storage brand that wants to be a hero in the customer's fight against stress. This was especially true in the case of the HP brand, which was already running advertising in support of its then-new brand promise, "Stress-free storage. Guaranteed."

Stress reduction may largely take care of itself when simplicity is made the overriding core value of the product development organization. Germany's Mittelstand—mid-size companies that collectively account for roughly half of German GDP and most of the country's new job creation—has many shining examples of this in the manufacturing sector. A study of 39 of these companies showed that the most successful make a narrow range of products with up to 50% fewer parts than competitors' products.[8] Fewer things to go wrong, along with a narrower range of options, have helped these companies reduce customer stress.

Once a stress-sensitive brand strategy has been established, products and specific product features can be mapped to the strategy to help evaluate the degree to which each product and feature supports—or becomes a proof point for—the brand's positioning strategy. This can then be a primary input for how to talk to customers about these products and where they fit into high-level brand messages such as in brand advertising campaigns.

For example, in the case of Hewlett-Packard where the brand promise was stress-free data storage, it made sense that the products that did the best job of reducing stress should be the products most prominently featured in advertising. So even at the tactical level, when the advertising manager was trying to decide how many of the campaign's total magazine ad pages should be devoted to each product, or which products should be most prominently featured on the HP Enterprise Storage Web site, stress relief was a primary consideration. Within each product, the same logic followed through to focusing on the features that most obviously addressed customer stress throughout the marketing communications mix.

The result was that sometimes a product that was clearly a stress reliever would be featured more aggressively than another product with a larger potential revenue stream or higher margin, so that the brand promise would have the best chance of being credibly received by customers—who would then be more predisposed to buy any storage solution that the HP sales force or channel partners might try to sell them. And sometimes a product feature that was totally unique to HP would take a back seat to a more "me-too" feature that was more obviously connected to customer stress. To further telegraph that HP products were designed to reliably deliver on the stress-free promise, HP enterprise storage products were even branded with the prefix Sure- (SureStore E for the total line of solutions, SureSoft for software, SureGear for hardware, SureGuide for services). While this ran counter to brand streamlining (Chapter 6), the comfort factor promised by a stress-free brand positioning justified the extra reassurance provided by this particular sub-branding strategy.

Another key aspect of customer stress on both the business and consumer sides of technology has been protecting investments already made in the products currently being used. "Future-proofing" has been a particularly contentious (read *stressful*) issue in developing and marketing products in the software category and in certain categories of computer and networking hardware, as well as in the consumer electronics arena. Will the next generation of hardware still run my old software? is a question as applicable to video games as to NASA's mainframe computers. Will a new DVD (Digital Versatile Disc) player still play my CD's? Stress-sensitive customer care programs reduce customer anxiety about what the migration path to newer technology will be—and how painless and affordable—as the endless crush of upgrades become available after the initial purchase.

Future-proofing is one way that Lucent Technologies maintains its leadership in the communications equipment business. Lucent has been especially successful leveraging this in selling equipment to wireless phone service providers such as Sprint PCS, since evolving wireless technologies have long been in flux. Companies that buy equipment for their wireless networks have tremendous anxiety about protecting their capital investments in equipment as next-generation technological shifts continue to occur. To nurture its brand leadership as a stress reliever, Lucent product development focuses heavily on backward- and forward-compatibility with each new wave of products and each flavor of technology.

As compelling as future-proofing and stress-reduction upgrades to existing products may be, there may be times when stress-sensitive positioning strategy (Chapter 6) for "as-they-are" products can altogether replace the need to actually improve or upgrade the product—at least for some period of time. Consider this: Analysis by Booz, Allen & Hamilton found that 44% of new product launches are to defend market share.[9] In an increasingly stressed-out world, surely there will be more and more occasions when being the first in a category to reposition an existing product on its stress-relief potential could make as much or more marketplace impact than product development itself—usually with the advantage of getting to market sooner with a defensive strategy (since product development typically takes longer than initiating a shift in positioning).

EXECUTION

In executing Simplicity Marketing, we start by acknowledging that solid brand strategies are most effectively executed when carried through at the brand's every point of contact with the customer—extending far beyond advertising and other marketing communications to encompass how every customer-facing employee presents the brand in person. This ranges from sales presentations to how the company's phone is answered.

The importance of stress-sensitive advertising has been covered in earlier chapters (3 and 6), as has stress-sensitive pricing (Chapters 4 and 7), and promotion (Chapter 3). But complementary, stress-sensitive PR can also lend itself well to stress-reducing marketing events. In the Hewlett-Packard example, a "Stress-Free NYC" customer and press event was held in New York City to kick off a major new product launch, replete with palm trees, island music, and shoulder massages all staged smack in the middle of midtown Manhattan on a busy Wednesday (and was Webcast to busy IT professionals all over the world). HP even sponsored the creation of a permanent Stress-Free Garden in a New York city park frequented by businesspeople. But what about stress sensitivity in personal selling and in postsale customer care?

In the personal selling process, brand loyalty starts with stress-sensitive lead development and carries through with stress-sensitive direct marketing, sales presentations, order taking, and fulfillment. Direct marketers who best understand how to build customer relationships know that customer database management skills are paramount in minimizing stress when developing leads. Sloppy lead management almost guarantees unnecessary customer stress.

In direct marketing, there are three sources of potential stress for customers before a sale is ever made: *selling approach, timing,* and *frequency.* Any one of the three, if insensitive to stress, can sabotage a customer relationship. Inexperienced and/or poorly trained telemarketers can produce customer stress just by being too persistent or pushy. A perfectly pleasant approach delivered at an unacceptable time, however, such as the middle of dinner, may produce just as much stress. An acceptable approach at an acceptable time may still produce stress if attempted too frequently. The combination of all three executed without stress sensitivity can preclude any possibility of a relationship with that customer. That's what happens when overly aggressive telemarketers from a long distance phone company call the same customer during dinner (or while the business customer is having lunch at her desk) three times in a two-week period.

This author was a preferred Platinum credit card customer of a large bank until its database management ran amok and was sometimes sending me two or even three mail solicitations on the same day. When this persisted, I was so annoyed that I cut the credit card in half and mailed it to the president of the company (with a demand to be removed from their database). The brand had provided otherwise acceptable service but had become a stress villain.

In face-to-face personal selling, selling approach and timing are potential sources of customer stress just as they are in direct marketing. In personal selling situations, the presentation approach is often a greater source of customer stress than presentation content. Very early in my career, I sat in the waiting room outside a buyer's office at a supermarket chain's headquarters, along with several other salespeople from different companies. A large sign on the wall read, "We require you to limit your sales presentations to 10 minutes." 10 minutes was italicized *and* underscored *and* painted in red, as if one or the other wouldn't have been sufficiently intimidating. I remember imagining what this buyer's day must be like if he was hearing an endless stream of compressed 10-minute presentations in which every eager young salesperson was seeing how much information and persuasion could be crammed into that little slice of the clock. The point lost on me then was that I had the opportunity to ask myself what I could do to make that buyer's day less stressful. I was exclusively focused on what he would need to hear from me to say yes, so I never even asked myself questions like, "What if one compelling idea could be conveyed in even less time than allotted?" or asking him, "What can our company do that would make things less stressful for you?" Being on the receiving end of a stressful sales presentation can undermine any of the 4 R's no matter how well Simplicity Marketing is executed outside the selling space.

In order-taking and fulfillment, stress reduction comes in the form of both *simplicity* and *accuracy*. For simplicity, making it simple to order can be a critical complement to a stress-sensitive marketing mix. Early leaders in business-to-business marketing on the Internet leveraged ease of ordering into real competitive advantage. Companies such as Dell Computer and Cisco Systems not only recognized early on that the Internet was inherently easier for customers as an ordering tool than were other channels but also recognized that within the Internet there were formidable, complex ordering systems cropping up everywhere that they could significantly improve upon. Amazon.com mastered this as we show later in this chapter. These companies were all among the great stories of shareholder value creation during the late 1990s, and low-stress ordering was a cornerstone of those stories.

Regarding accuracy, there are few marketing tragedies as great as having gotten so far down the line—having made the sale—only to create customer stress at the time of delivery/fulfillment. For telecommunications companies, for example, service order defects—when an order is inaccurately recorded or fulfilled—are the number one reason for customer dissatisfaction, as they always create stress in any market segment.

The final and sometimes most daunting challenge in executing Simplicity Marketing is after the product is in the customer's hands. Stress-sensitive customer care encompasses postsale service, customer retention programs, and—for certain products—a future-proof, smooth migration path through future product upgrades. Entire books have been written about postsale service and support, with the focus on making it easy for the customer, so we won't attempt to deal with the executional issues here. Much of customer care in Simplicity Marketing is just common sense applied by stress-sensitive marketers.

Special attention must be given to simplicity in loyalty-building retention programs. The heaviest users of many products and services are often the busiest people in the customer base. Airline and cell phone customers are cases in point. In striving to differentiate rewards programs, marketers keep adding bells and whistles—and more complexity along the way. (Remember the overstuffed, overwhelming Mileage Plus mail package described in Chapter 1?) Meanwhile, more and more customers experience a sense that being a rewards program member can sometimes just be more trouble than it's worth. In the overchoice era, common sense dictates that less is often more in retaining loyal customers—less complex point schemes and award structures, less complex award redemption, even less mail.

MEASUREMENT AND REFINEMENT

Measurement and refinement brings us full circle, back to customer research on the Figure 9.1 brand planning loop. The old adage, "You can't manage what you don't measure," certainly applies to customer stress.

Incorporating indicators of customer stress into brand tracking metrics and identifying needs has been covered above—both in the discussion of customer research and brand equities assessment. We encourage you to incorporate Chapter 2 concepts, including drivers of stress, stressographics, and coping styles and strategies, as well as the market research approaches discussed, to gain competitive advantage through a superior, ongoing understanding of the nature and impact of customer stress.

In marketing to higher-stress segments, stress measures may also be especially relevant in customer satisfaction research, as well as in further dimensionalizing product testing, creative/copy testing, promotion testing, and even media research (e.g., how stressful are the environments in which different media are consumed?). Stress measurement is essential to stress management and continuous refinement of strategy, especially in gauging which of the 4 R's and their substrategies hold the highest potential for effectiveness at each stage of the brand's, product's, and category's evolution.

■ The Simplicity Marketing Audit

As a final coalescing tool to integrate marketing planning around customers' stressful lives, let's now take the key considerations covered in this chapter and in Parts I and II of the book and distill them into a Simplicity Marketing strategic audit. The questions in the audit template provided in Figure 9.3, when thoughtfully answered, will provide a stress-sensitive strategic road map for the Simplicity Marketer. Used in combination with the checklists provided for each of the 4 R's in Chapters 4 through 7, this template ensures that simplicity and stress reduction are much more likely to be optimized for your customers (resulting in *optimum* choice rather than maximum choice).

You may wish to customize this to capture simplicity- and stress-related strategy considerations unique to your particular industry, or to eliminate some considerations that may be less relevant to your category or target market segments. But this provides a generic starting point, beginning with the first stop on the brand planning loop: customer research.

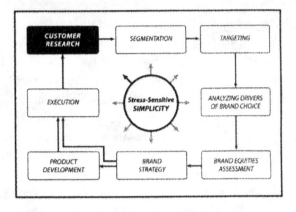

Customer Research

The following should be asked and answered in developing a customer research agenda, as well as in establishing research objectives, evaluating research design, and interpreting research findings.

- Does our customer research incorporate inquiry that reveals enough whole life context to understand customer stress (which, in qualitative research, may include storytelling and/or projective techniques such as role playing)?

- Does it incorporate contextual *observation* (where applicable)?

- From each of the following types of customer research, how much do we really know about customer stress levels, nature, sources, and impact?

	Knowledge/Understanding of Customer Stress		
	Good Knowledge	*Moderate Knowledge*	*Little/No Knowledge*
__ Customer needs identification	___	___	___
__ Drivers of brand choice	___	___	___
__ Product testing	___	___	___
__ Creative/copy testing	___	___	___
__ Promotion testing	___	___	___
__ Media habits	___	___	___
__ Customer satisfaction research	___	___	___

[Continued]

- Do we know what "impact categories" are most likely to influence purchase dynamics—especially *stress*—in *our* category?

Impact Categories	Brief Description of Nature of Impact

- In tracking brand health, are we measuring the degree to which our brand is perceived as a stress-reliever or stress-producer?

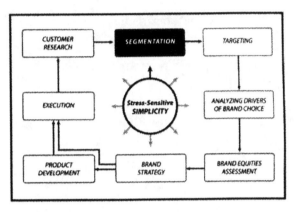

Market Segmentation

The following should be asked and answered in developing segmentation approaches and specifically in developing profiles of each segment (to augment traditional considerations such as segment size, scale, purchasing power, accessibility, etc.).

- **Do we have a stressographic profile of each segment?**

- **Describe customer stress for each segment:**

  Stress Level: __ Extreme   __ High   __ Moderate   __ Low

  Consistency: __ Persistent   __ Variable   __ Occasional

  Stress Drivers (sources of stress):   _____

  Stress Nature (stressful behaviors):   _____

- **Describe customers' coping strategies (for each segment):**

  Coping style: __ Stress Tacklers   __ Stress Escapers

  Relevant coping behaviors: _____

- **Beyond helping us understand each segment better, can level of stress, nature of stress, drivers of stress, or coping strategies provide a more effective basis on which to segment the market than the basis on which we are segmenting it now? How?**

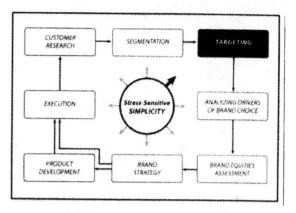

Targeting

The following should be asked and answered in prioritizing alternative segments for targeting (along with traditional considerations such as segment growth, profitability, size, structure, selling efficiencies, competitive intensity, customer bargaining power, channel costs, and strategic alignment with corporate/brand objectives).

- **How do market segment stress levels align with stress relief benefits of the product/brand?**

    Product(s) delivers: __ Strong stress relief benefits

    __ Moderate stress relief benefits

    __ Weak/no stress relief benefits

    Level of match with segment stress levels:

    __ Good match (sweet spot, Figure 9.2)

    __ Moderate match

    __ Mismatch

- **Should this change how we have prioritized our market segments for targeting? If so, how?**

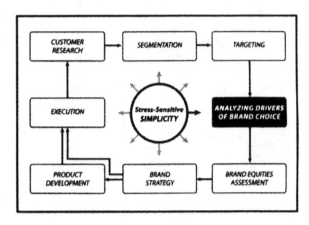

Drivers of Brand Choice

The following should be asked and answered in developing a prioritized list of: (1) the most important attributes—both rational and emotional—that describe the ideal brand in the category, and (2) the attributes on which customers are most likely to differentiate between brands in arriving at a preference.

- **Which choice-driving brand attributes (how a brand is perceived) in this category are most directly related to customer stress? (Examples: Reliable company? Easy-to-use products? Excellent service? Superior guarantees/warranties?)**

- **Historically in the category, which aspects of product purchase, product use, or customer service have been especially frustrating/stress-producing for customers?**

    To what degree are these frustrations unique to our brand?

    How are we addressing these?

- **How would customers in each segment answer the question, "Why does choosing Brand X *make me more comfortable* than choosing Brand Y in this category?"**

(Note: The answers to the above questions about drivers may produce somewhat duplicative answers, but are all included because of the importance of ensuring that stress-related factors are not underestimated relative to the other drivers of brand choice that typically surface in customer research.)

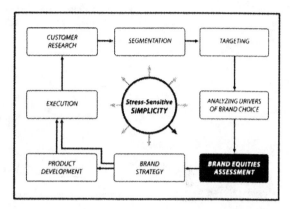

Brand Equities

The following should be asked and answered as part of the ongoing assessment of your brand's strengths and weaknesses relative to each key competitor brand, in terms of brand awareness, perceptions, purchase intent, and customer satisfaction/loyalty.

- Since brand familiarity can reduce customer stress, how familiar is our brand relative to other key competitor brands (especially in terms of unaided and top-of-mind awareness)?[10] In other words, to what degree does each brand live in each segment's *active brandscape* (Chapter 6)?

- How is our brand currently perceived on the stress-related attributes that are the most important drivers of brand choice identified above? On which of these attributes are our biggest perceptual advantages and our biggest disadvantaged gaps?

- Overall, how is our brand perceived relative to key competitor brands on a "stress-producer ↔ stress-reliever" continuum? What is our standing, and what is our trend?

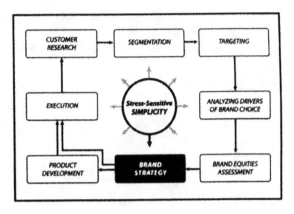

Brand Strategy

The following should be asked and answered in the development of the brand positioning strategy brief that lays out what unique, relevant, and credible position in the customer's mind you aim to own, and what you will say to customers and do for them to establish or fortify that position.

- **Which of the 4 R's of Simplicity Marketing will be our primary strategy for reducing customer stress?**

  __ Replace   __ Repackage   __ Reposition   __ Replenish

- **Which will be our key substrategy or substrategies?**

  If primary strategy is . . .

Replace:	__ Substitution	__ Consolidation	
Repackage:	__ Aggregation	__ Integration	
Reposition:	__ Brand Streamlining	__ Vertical Extension	__ Discontinuous Repositioning
Replenish:	__ Continuous Supply*	__ Zero Defects	__ Competitive Pricing

  (*Is Automatic Replenishment feasible and appropriate?)

- **Which other of the 4 R's can be employed as secondary strategies, and which attendant substrategies?**

  [Continued]

- For the primary strategy, attach the appropriate completed checklist from Chapter 4 (Replace), 5 (Repackage), 6 (Reposition), or 7 (Replenish). This will serve to summarize the primary Simplicity Marketing strategy and what the brand and/or product will do to reduce customer stress—as well as the degree to which simplicity and/or stress reduction will be an overt part of the brand communication strategy.

- Competitive Advantage Audit: For each Simplicity Marketing substrategy that is relevant to the category, place an X in the cells below to indicate on which substrategies we have an advantage over competitor brands, and on which we are disadvantaged:

SIMPLICITY MARKETING SUBSTRATEGIES	SUPERIOR	PARITY	INFERIOR
REPLACE:			
Substitution			
Consolidation			
REPACKAGE:			
Aggregation			
Integration			
REPOSITION:			
Brand Streamlining			
Vertical Extension			
Discontinuous Repositioning			
REPLENISH:			
Continuous Supply			
Zero Defects			
Competitive Pricing			

Briefly explain, where strategically significant:

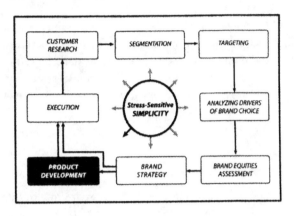

Product Development

The following should be asked and answered in identifying and prioritizing product development priorities.

- Is there sufficient knowledge about customer stress from market research to prioritize development initiatives, or is additional stress-related product testing required?

- Has customer stress reduction as a buying behavior dynamic been adequately considered in establishing product development priorities and resource allocation (both human and financial)?

- In what ways will the priority products being developed support, or become proof points for, the promise of customer stress reduction?

[Continued]

- For each priority product, which features/functionalities are most relevant to delivering customer stress reduction?

Priority Products and Features	Likely Stress Reduction Value			Relevance to Brand's Positioning Strategy			Relevance to Key Drivers of Brand Choice		
	Hi	*Med*	*Lo*	*Hi*	*Med*	*Lo*	*Hi*	*Med*	*Lo*
Product 1									
Feature A									
Feature B									
Feature C									
Product 2									
Feature A									
Feature B									
Feature C									

- To the degree that future-proofing is a driver of brand choice in the category, how well will the priority products and features that are in development—and planned for the future—address this from the customer's perspective? (Also consider the impact on future-proofing of postsale service policies and upgrade/trade-in policies.)

- From the customer's perspective, in whole life context, does our product line offer *optimum* choice rather than *maximum* choice?

- Could a more overt stress-reduction positioning strategy replace or delay the need for any of the new product features or feature upgrades planned?

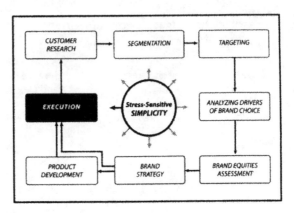

Execution

The following should be asked and answered to assess the stress-reducing versus stress-producing potential for every communication that touches the customer.

- In executing customer communications in each of the following categories, what is currently being done that might reduce *or produce* customer stress? What more could be done to reduce it, and to simplify rather than complicate?

	Stress Reducers/ Simplifiers	Stress Producers/ Complicators	Best Opportunities to Improve
Media Advertising			
Direct Marketing			
Internet Presence			
Public Relations			
Promotions			
Retention/ Loyalty Programs			
Customer Events/ Shows			
Personal Selling			
Customer Service			
Product Documentation			
Guarantees/ Warranties			
Corporate Identity			

[Continued]

- Are we training *all* customer-facing employees to interact with customers in a stress-sensitive way?

- Are the company's most senior brand stewards (including the CEO in marketing-oriented companies) sufficiently empathetic to customer stress and how it impacts purchase, loyalty, and brand equity? If not, what could be done internally to raise awareness and improve sensitivity to customer stress?

The desired outcome of conducting a Simplicity Marketing audit for your brand is that senior marketing officers, their managers, their agencies, and even their CEOs will be able to respond to, and get in the habit of asking: How does this product look from a Simplicity Marketing perspective? and How does our *brand* look from a Simplicity Marketing perspective? The result will keep you at the forefront of the opportunities and challenges that customer stress presents.

DIGITAL-AGE PLANNING REALITIES

In the fast-moving digital age, there seems to be less time than ever for thorough discipline in marketing—including any kind of marketing audit, such as the one prescribed above. In more traditional, established categories, we would like to think that taking the time to conduct all aspects of a Simplicity Marketing audit and take action based on its results would pay handsome rewards. But we also recognize that in technology and other ultra-dynamic categories characterized by daily market shifts and violently compressed product cycles, intuition and decisiveness must often prevail over a linear planning discipline that there simply isn't time for—without risking being too late to market or too late to react to competitors. So the reality for many companies may be to cherry-pick those aspects of Simplicity Marketing strategy development that are more implementable "on the fly."

For example, during its first few years, e-commerce pioneer Amazon.com certainly didn't have the luxury of disciplined planning. In the Internet's good old days of the mid- and late '90s, Amazon was a company at the bleeding edge of a warp-speed revolution—submerged in a scramble to keep up with explosive growth while inventing, and then reinventing, e-commerce every day. More and more companies today are in frighteningly similar circumstance in terms of finding time for methodical planning or processes such as audits.

If we audited Amazon.com, however, we'd find that they didn't do Simplicity Marketing by the numbers, but they did do it intuitively. In market research, they paid a lot of attention to customers' storytelling, and spent a lot of time on "reducing *friction* in the customer experience" (as they like to say internally at Amazon) while shopping online. (They might have just as easily said "reducing *stress*.") They segmented the market in stress-sensitive ways, recognizing that anyone shopping online was more likely to be busy and stressed than customers who had time for a trip to the mall. They quickly discerned that, among these customers, the lesser-stressed segment tended to be more subject-focused (e.g., interested in the history of baroque music, and open to a multiple-media solution including recommendations for relevant books, CDs, and videos), meanwhile the more-stressed segment tended to be medium-focused ("I need a book on baroque music," or "Do you have *this* book on baroque music?"). They learned how their female customers had different coping styles than men, making much more use of reading other customers' reviews to reduce uncertainty about whether a book was good or not. They recognized that, by the end of the 1990s, when hordes of Internet newcomers were ready to enter the market, these second-wave customers would need more security and privacy assurance to trust cyberspace with their credit card information and to reduce e-commerce anxiety. And in terms of targeting, Amazon's strong-to-moderate stress relief benefits were a great match for the strong-to-moderate stress levels of its customers—putting it squarely in the targeting sweet spot described in Figure 9.2.

Even if your company doesn't have all the customer research in place, or the time and resources to do everything suggested by a Simplicity Marketing audit, there can still be huge opportunity in intuitive-style Simplicity Marketing when planned and executed by managers who carry stress sensitivity in their consciousness. As evidence, next we look at how Amazon.com's stress sensitivity translated to action in leveraging the 4 R's to deliver simplicity.

■ Putting It All Together: Simplicity Marketing at Amazon.com

The Amazon.com story has been told so many times in so many places, we won't reprise it here. But what hasn't been revealed about the first e-commerce megabrand is how—even back when it was merely "Earth's largest bookstore," before diversifying its brand across other retail categories—it implemented more of Simplicity Marketing's tenets behind one brand than possibly any other brand ever had, online or off.

Sometimes this was the result of strategic brilliance and great instincts, and other times it was unwitting good fortune and the simplicity potential of the Internet itself. But the "sixth sense" of simplicity that founder Jeff Bezos and some of his chief lieutenants shared was a key reason why this upstart was able to weather strategic broadsides from deep-pockets competitors while innovating daily in uncharted e-commerce seas. That sixth sense was a key reason why Amazon dared to continue showing huge operating losses to invest in creating and re-creating the simplest, lowest-stress experience possible for customers. Amazon was building a brand in the ether of the new economy, and applied simplicity would quickly create the kind of loyalty that presented a huge barrier to successful market entry for competitors. The Amazon story has relevance far beyond the online world, as this brand raised the bar in shoppers' total frame of reference for what would be considered a simple, stress-free shopping experience.

While the Amazon story is still unfolding, we can look back now with 20/20 hindsight and reconstruct how this brand instinctively deployed all four of the 4 R's of Simplicity Marketing and 9 of the 10 stress-reducing substrategies that we have covered in this book. One lesson here is in thinking about how Amazon could accomplish this much with the 4 R's "on the fly." Just think what would be possible in a category that moves a little slower than Internet retailing if Simplicity Marketing were done in an orchestrated strategic fashion—as an ongoing commitment in every stage of brand planning and execution.

Briefly examining Amazon.com in the context of each of the 4 R's as covered in Chapters 4 through 7, we can see how many things Amazon did in parallel to reduce customer stress." Taken together, all of these created an extraordinarily stress-free shopping experience for some very, very busy consumers. Throughout this examination, it's also worth thinking about how many aspects of the Chapter 8 discussion about simplicity-savvy use of information technology were operative in Amazon's ability to bring this experience to life for shoppers.

REPLACE

Amazon.com started as a replacement for a time-consuming trip to a brick-and-mortar bookstore—a trip that often ended in frustration when the book sought by the customer was not in stock. Or sometimes Amazon just substituted for telephone calls to bookstores that would have often ended with the same unsatisfying result.

SUBSTITUTION

Offering a complete, exhaustive collection of virtually all unused books that were not out of print, as well as access to many out-of-print titles, Amazon substituted a high degree of predictability in place of uncertainty by assuring customers that they would find the book they were looking for—or the broadest possible selection of books on a topic of interest. (As advertising touted, "If it's in print, it's in stock.") Another aspect of predictability was in pricing, with everyday 30% discounts offered on best-sellers (raised to 50% in 1999). And yet another aspect of predictability was in timing, allowing the customer to choose three to seven days by standard delivery, or overnight by expedited delivery (substituting for a brick-and-mortar bookstore's saying something like, "It usually takes about two or three weeks—we'll call you when it's in.") Finally, as part of a Customer's Bill of Rights, Amazon's safe shopping guarantee assured customers from the beginning that they would have no liability for any unauthorized charges to their credit cards as a result of shopping at Amazon.com, which was a significant stress reducer especially for novice buyers online.

Consolidation

Just as Barnes & Noble had done in the brick-and-mortar world, Amazon consolidated shopping for books and music into one shopping destination before it further diversified into the video, grocery, drugstore, electronics, software, and toy worlds. In Chapter 4 parlance, the customer benefits were to reduce the number of steps and the number of stops, as well as the number of purchase transactions when books and CDs were purchased in the same online shopping trip. One-click ordering, which Amazon pioneered for repeat customers, further reduced the number of steps by replacing the need to fill out electronic forms or even reenter a credit card number. Simply find what you're looking for and, when you do, click on the one-click ordering box and the order fulfillment process has already begun and will be seen through to delivery.

REPACKAGE

Of the 4 R's, Repackage was Amazon's primary strategy: aggregating all those books in one easy-to-visit place, and integrating the entire shopping experience around a single-mouse-click transaction.

Aggregation

On the day Amazon first opened it "doors," it boasted an "inventory" of nearly 2 million book titles under one virtual roof—Chapter 5's many-in-one aggregation on a grand scale. You'll also recall from Chapter 5 that Aggregation typically enhances the value of the individual items being aggregated, which Amazon soon did by allowing customers to post their own reviews of books and allowing authors to comment on their own books as well. Having these other perspectives easily accessible online added value for those shoppers who wanted to know more about a book before deciding to purchase. Beyond its ongoing diversification, Amazon further aggregated in 1999 with its addition of zShops—a multitude of specialty merchants in 19 categories ranging from antiques to sports, pulled together in one place where customers could trust doing business.

Integration

As Amazon extended its brand horizontally across media categories, it was able to integrate multiple-media solutions around customer preferences. If you were interested in a certain topic, for example, Amazon—by virtue of lever-aging its IT capabilities to *understand* customer needs as well as to fulfill them—could instantly recommend books, videos, music, and sometimes even computer software that related to the subject. The customer could also elect to be automatically notified by e-mail when other related titles in any medium became available. Preference-based integration was not only a great time-saver, but added value by introducing solutions that customers would have never thought of on their own. Especially for repeat customers, the value of integrated one-stop shopping was further magnified in gift-giving problem solving, as one very time-efficient stop on the Internet found gift recommen-dations, an electronic gift card, packaging, and delivery to the gift recipient—all without ever having to even reach for a credit card.

REPOSITION

Amazon correctly decided that, in the beginning, it should not directly position the brand on simplicity for two reasons: First, selection and price were more crit-ical drivers of brand choice in choosing a place to buy books, and selection would be Amazon's most obvious competitive advantage at first glance. Second, even without an overt simplicity positioning, Internet users (particularly online shop-pers) would immediately grasp the stress-reduction benefits of less time and effort required. But online shoppers were still a small group of early adopters when Amazon launched in mid-1995—and to the rest of the world back then, any purchase dependent on the Internet and computers would seem sufficient-ly formidable that the promise of simplicity could strain credibility. Though Reposition was the least used of Simplicity Marketing's 4 R's by Amazon, the company still intuitively took advantage of some of the positioning-related sub-strategies covered in Chapter 6, including Brand Streamlining.

BRAND STREAMLINING
Amazon kept brand clutter to a minimum to create a low-stress, streamlined shopping environment in two ways: First, it resisted the temptation to create proprietary sub-brands on its site. For example, by 1999, an Amazon competitor was branding its e-mail card services (e-nouncements™), while Amazon simply called its e-mail cards by a generic name (e-Cards). Second, there were no pro-prietary-sub-branded cybercafes on Amazon's site or proprietary-branded spe-cial promotions (just the occasional use of their promotional partners'

names). Amazon put all its branding wood behind one arrow, and the Amazon.com brand shone through clearly and simply to reinforce the notion of a simple-to-use service.

VERTICAL EXTENSION

This is one substrategy that, in terms of how it was explained in Chapter 6, was not particularly relevant to Amazon. However, though the cases of vertical extension discussed in Chapter 6 dealt mostly with bringing upscale brands downmarket, there was an element of Amazon.com bringing the online shopping experience downmarket in a different way: Amazon mainstreamed it from the early Internet elite (not incomewise, but as in an elite group of very early adopters of e-commerce) to make it safe and attainable for the average Internet user, who could then grow with it over time.

DISCONTINUOUS REPOSITIONING

By 1999, as one of the strongest brands in any category ever built in less than four years, it was already easy to see many possibilities for discontinuous repositioning of the Amazon brand. At this writing, how that unfolds remains to be seen. But while not so discontinuous as the repositioning of Tums or Arm & Hammer Baking Soda discussed in Chapter 6, Amazon did leverage a "soft" discontinuous repositioning in 1999 when it moved into online auctions to compete with auction innovator eBay. Auctions were still the wild, Wild West of the Internet where a shopper couldn't touch or feel what they were bidding on. Anxiety was high, and Amazon already had enough brand equity among heavier online shoppers to be a stress-reducing comfort in the auction arena. This was further reinforced when Amazon offered free insurance of up to $250 ($50 more than eBay's insurance at the time) on any item purchased at auction on Amazon.com if the customer was dissatisfied with the item compared to how it had been described, or if it was not delivered in a timely manner.

REPLENISH

Amazon plunged headlong into the Replenish strategy when it acquired stakes in both Homegrocer.com and Drugstore.com, both brimming with staple categories ideally suited to automatic or at least semiautomatic replenishment. But even before that, in its bookselling business Amazon had incorporated aspects of the Replenish strategy.

CONTINUOUS SUPPLY

On the surface, Amazon.com certainly had an unfair advantage in being more accessible than brick-and-mortar bookstores by virtue of the Internet: $24 \times 7 \times 365$ perpetual availability for customers anywhere in the world who had Internet access and a credit card. But plenty of Internet marketers in other categories had still managed to compromise availability by having more frequent outages of their servers (the computers that manage the information on their Web sites), or having difficult-to-navigate Web sites and cumbersome, time-consuming online ordering processes. Also, many offered no easy way to reach a human being by telephone if something on the Web site interfered with customers achieving their goals. During the year most of this book was written, Amazon's site actually "went down" for a total of only five minutes, so its round-the-clock availability for the year was 99.999%—exceeding that of even major online brokerage firms. (No matter that most would agree that executing a stock trade deserved more reliable technology than buying a book.) Furthermore, Amazon's telephone representatives were also available 24×7, and typically with very short hold times compared to most toll-free service lines.

ZERO DEFECTS

From the beginning, Amazon put tremendous energy and a very significant portion of its resources into ensuring that it shipped the right book to the right place at the right time. In spite of how dramatically its business scaled up in years two and three, greatly taxing its infrastructure, Amazon.com's order defect incidence was less than .00025. And importantly, when Amazon did make a mistake, it usually excelled in service recovery—the art of turning a complaining customer into a loyal one—through earnest, attentive service reps who telegraphed that the customer is always right.[12]

COMPETITIVE PRICING

Amazon's pricing strategy ensured that price would not be a hurdle for most customers interested in replenishing their reading supply. In its first few years its prices averaged 5% to 10% below that of brick-and-mortar stores even including shipping costs (depending on order size, since shipping cost per book would be less with more books in the order). Amazon also offered competitively deep discounts on best-sellers. In May 1999, Amazon became the first among major online booksellers to institute 50% discounts on best-sellers as "everyday low pricing," further greasing the wheels of its Replenishment strategy.

Automatic Replenishment

Before getting into staple goods businesses, the opportunity for automatic replenishment seemed remote at best and irrelevant at worst in a category like books in which the same title is seldom bought twice. But that didn't stop Amazon from trying. Amazon realized that by mastering two core competencies—customer preference database management and IT-enabled order fulfillment—it could still semiautomate a flow of appealing books, music, and video to a loyal customer with highly personalized services. It set up a service called Book Matcher and used affinity algorithms in its computers to predict what a customer would like based on past purchases and expressed preferences, and then used e-mail to notify customers who elected to use this service when something of interest became available—offering the opportunity to say yes with a mouse click right there in the e-mail without even visiting Amazon.com. That click then automatically replenished the customer's supply of content for reading, listening, or viewing. As Amazon continues to learn more about its customers' habits and preferences over time, it will be well positioned to incorporate other elements of automatic replenishment in its Simplicity Marketing efforts.

■ Summary

In this chapter, we have examined where and how Simplicity Marketing and traditional marketing come together. In encouraging this fusion, we have looked at how sensitivity to the level, nature, and sources of customer stress can enhance the value of customer research and tracking brand health. We have discussed how it can also enhance market segmentation, targeting, understanding of the drivers of brand choice, assessment of individual brands' strengths and weaknesses, and how it can streamline product development and resource allocation. We have provided a tool—the Simplicity Marketing audit—that can help you assess opportunities and challenges in leveraging the 4 R's to reduce customer stress more effectively than your competitors. Finally, we looked at how one brand, even a hyper-growth brand with little time for disciplined marketing planning in its early years, brought these strategies to life to become a model of success for the promise of the digital economy.

Chapter 10

The Bottom Line: Converting Customer Stress Relief to Shareholder Value

> Saying that we work for our shareowners may sound simplistic—but we frequently see companies that have forgotten the reason they exist.... they miss their primary calling, which is to stick to the business of creating value for their owners.
> —ROBERTO C. GOIZUETA, Former Chairman and CEO
> The Coca-Cola Company

PETER DRUCKER has sagely schooled us for decades with the simple tenet that *creating a customer* is every company's foremost mission. This book thus far has been about how to do just that, creating customers through simplicity and stress relief. Now we must look at a final perspective: the essential link between simplicity and every public company's foremost *financial* mission—creating shareholder value.

If we create customers and retain customers, then shareholder value most always takes care of itself. But the companies that best understand the impact of each marketing strategy on shareholder value will have a value-creation edge. Simplicity Marketing is not exempt from such fundamental metrics, and so in this final chapter we ask and answer two questions:

1. What are the real business benefits that executive management can expect from de-stressing customers?

2. How can managers who adopt Simplicity Marketing as a way of doing business link its benefits to shareholder value creation?

STRESS, BRAND EQUITY, AND VALUE CREATION

The relationship between Simplicity Marketing and shareholder value is not transparent, much as the direct linkage between corporate brand advertising and the resulting share of market cannot be precisely determined. We can, however, examine the linkage between Simplicity Marketing and building brand equity and then assess brand equity's impact on shareholder value. (Mathematically speaking, if A is a function of B and B is a function of C, then A is a function of C.) We will review the concept of brand equity, how it is enhanced by the customer loyalty that Simplicity Marketing engenders, and how that equity impacts shareholder value as manifest in the market capitalization of various companies. To see this logic chain in action, we will then look at a broad-based program from the grocery products industry—the Efficient Consumer Response initiative (ECR). Finally, we will examine how one participating firm, Procter & Gamble, implemented ECR and how P&G's resulting simplification strategies created additional shareholder value by strengthening brand equity and improving the bottom line.

■ Brand Equity: The Bridge Between Simplicity and Shareholder Value

In previous chapters we have cited many examples of how Simplicity Marketing strategies build stronger brands. But to connect brand equity to shareholder value, we need to back up for a moment and look at where brand equity comes from. In the first of three books on this subject, *Managing Brand Equity*, brand equity expert Professor David Aaker at the Haas School of Business of the University of California at Berkeley defined brand equity as the sum of four key inputs as shown in Figure 10.1.[1]

In this context, brand awareness, perceived quality, and brand loyalty are self-evident concepts. Brand associations, as viewed by Aaker, are things that connect or link the consumer to the brand, such as user imagery, use situations, and symbols. The ultimate *direct* business benefit of brand equity is the extent and intensity of brand loyalty. But very significant *indirect* benefits of brand equity also accrue from that loyalty.

INDIRECT BENEFITS OF BRAND EQUITY FEED SHAREHOLDER VALUE

Enhanced loyalty increases the customer's long-term value to the firm and drives the customer's willingness to pay a price premium. It also increases the customer's interest in selecting the brand in other related (and sometimes even unrelated) categories as the brand extends into

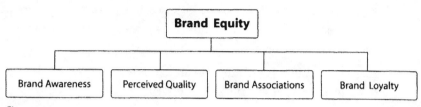

Figure 10.1

additional lines of business. Furthermore, a strong brand creates market-ing efficiencies and leverage in the distribution channel. Such benefits in turn feed the key drivers of shareholder value: generating and protecting revenue, reducing operating costs, increasing margins, reducing cost of capital, and enhancing future cash flow.

Throughout this book we have discussed how Simplicity Marketing strategies, and resulting customer stress relief, can positively influence the customer's perceptions of a brand (encompassing Aaker's perceived quality and brand associations boxes in Figure 10.1). The metrics chal-lenge is in measuring how shifts in perceptions of the brand relate to quantifiable changes in brand equity, and then measuring how the bene-fits of that equity relate to each of the shareholder value drivers. For example, increased lifetime value of a customer translates not only to increased revenue and future cash flows, but also to reduced operating costs because customer retention costs are generally much lower than customer acquisition costs. And the loyal customer's willingness to pay a price premium speaks directly to improved margins driving yet addition-al shareholder value.

BRAND VALUATION

The good news is the ongoing advances in techniques for quantifying the dollar value of brand equity. In their recent book, Aaker and Joachim-sthaler suggest that it is possible to estimate a rough value for a brand to within plus or minus 30% of actual value.[2] This estimate is derived from measuring the earnings stream of major products or markets using the brand, and breaking that earnings stream into three composite parts:

1. The total earnings attributable to the brand itself are identified by calculating the earnings stream from the major markets/products carrying the brand's name.

2. Earnings attributable to those fixed assets like plant and equipment are estimated by placing a fair return, say 12%, on the value of the fixed assets associated with the brand.

3. Earnings attributable to other intangible assets such as people, systems, processes, or patents are estimated.

From total brand related earnings, we then deduct earnings attributable to fixed assets and other intangibles and what remains are earnings driven by the brand itself. This figure is the key to estimating the value of the brand's equity.

The firm Interbrand estimates brand values using a process similar to this logic as shown in Table 10.1. Interbrand's data illustrates the extent

Table 10.1 Interbrand Valuations

Brand	Brand Value $ in Billions	Brand Value as % of Market Capitalization
1. Coca-Cola	83.8	59
2. Microsoft	56.7	21
3. IBM	43.8	28
4. General Electric	33.5	10
5. Ford	33.2	58
6. Disney	32.3	61
7. Intel	30.0	21
8. McDonald's	26.2	64
9. AT&T	24.1	24
10. Marlboro	21.1	19
11. Nokia	20.7	44
12. Mercedes	17.8	37
13. Nescafe	17.6	23
14. Hewlett-Packard	17.1	31
15. Gillette	15.9	37
16. Kodak	14.8	60
17. Ericsson	14.8	32
18. Sony	14.2	49
19. American Express	12.6	35
20. Toyota	12.3	14
21. Heinz	11.8	64
22. BMW	11.2	77
23. Xerox	11.2	40
24. Honda	11.1	37
25. Citibank	9.1	22

Source: www.interbrand.com, August 1999

and importance of shareholder value created by brand equity. As of mid-1999, as posted on Interbrand's Web site, here are the 25 most valuable brands on the globe as well as the importance of each brand in the total market capitalization of its respective owner.

The role brands play in the total market capitalization of these firms is substantial. Table 10.1 shows the degree to which shareholder value is being created and driven by the power of these brand franchises. As illustrated, brand value ranges from a low of 10% of market capitalization for General Electric to a high of 77% for BMW. Firms such as Coca-Cola, Ford, Disney, McDonald's, Kodak, and Heinz each have over half of their market capitalization based on this brand value.

If General Motors could enjoy the value creation multiple of BMW's brand equity impact, its market capitalization would increase from $41 billion to $73 billion. It is in this ability of brand equity to significantly increase the firm's total market capitalization that we have the ultimate reward from using Simplicity Marketing strategies. Simplicity Marketing becomes a key filter for success in the implementation of effective brand building that, in turn, yields increases in brand equity as stress relief engenders loyalty.

We can now explore in a more tangible context the relationships discussed above by looking at an overall industry and then, within it, one well-known company and its brands.

■ The Efficient Consumer Response Initiative: Simplicity Marketing for the U.S. Grocery Industry

An excellent laboratory in which to examine Simplicity Marketing and the creation of shareholder value is the U.S. grocery products industry. The industry is large, approaching $400 billion annually, and touches almost everyone. It is the home territory for some of the world's great brands and it is a market of intense competition and fierce rivalries.

We begin at the start of the last decade because in the early 1990s the U.S. grocery products industry found itself with a serious problem. The root cause of this began even earlier as grocery retailers gained increased power over manufacturers based on the use of scanner data to understand customers better.[3] Grocery marketers began to court the retailers with more programs and larger discounts and began cutting back on brand advertising to fund these programs. Retailers imposed so-called slotting allowances, the fee ostensibly imposed to offset the cost of adding a new item to the warehouse. Manufacturers were asked to fund shelf stocking fees, allowances for secondary displays, and temporary price reductions. As the grocery retailers gained even more knowledge of customers' buying patterns and habits, they demanded even more consideration from manufacturers. This process began a subtle but certain shift on the part of grocery retailers from being good merchants to becoming proficient at getting funds from manufacturers.

The extent of this shift can be seen in the reallocation of the aggregate marketing budgets in the industry. In 1981, advertising represented 50% of total marketing costs for the manufacturers in the grocery products category with trade promotions and consumer promotions each getting about 25% of the total. In acknowledgement of this power shift, advertising declined to only 25% of total marketing expenditures by 1991, and the funds offered to the retailers increased from about 25% of expenditures to almost 40%.

Vast amounts of money were being offered to entice the grocery retailer to give particular brands and manufacturers preferential treatment for short-term benefits such as temporary price reductions. These funds became the primary focus of the grocery retailing community. The primary mission of being an efficient distributor and merchant was relegated to secondary consideration.

The results were disastrous. Many grocery retailers were buying up to 80% of their volume on promotional deals. Many such purchases were made for quantities well beyond that needed for immediate sale. This so-called forward buying phenomenon disrupted the natural forces of supply and demand and, in so doing, created yet additional complexity.

COMPLEXITY BREEDS INEFFICIENCY

Inefficiencies in the supply chain grew. Manufacturer discounts became so enticing that many grocery chains forward purchased such large amounts of inventory that they had to rent additional storage space to store the "deal price" inventory for future sale. Inventories soared and on average a grocery product took 104 days to reach the checkout counter due to these bloated inventories. Inventories became so large that grocers were forced to create reclamation centers for manufacturers to pick up damaged and out-of-date merchandise. Products were moved and relocated so often that damage due to multiple handling increased substantially. Total inventories in the grocery industry supply chain grew to $90 billion.

In this chaotic environment, a new business emerged to conduct a form of arbitrage in the emergence of "diverter wires." This opportunity occurred when manufacturers had unequal discount levels in different parts of the country. For example, Gillette might offer a deeper discount on razor blades in Boston than in San Diego. The diverter wire would highlight this and grocery buyers in San Diego would purchase product in Boston and arrange shipment across the continent.

Others provided software packages termed *float management programs* which were designed to use the banking system to delay the processing of payments to manufacturers thus increasing the days of float for the retailers.

The deals and price discounts became so impactful at retail that the consumer began switching brands at each purchase depending on whose product was on "deal" that week. If Coca-Cola and Pepsi Cola two-liter bottles gyrated between a regular price of $1.69 and a deal price of 99¢, the consumer became convinced that paying the regular price for either brand made no sense. Marketers came to refer to this as "insult pricing," meaning that it was an insult to think a customer would pay the regular price. Brand loyalty was being systematically destroyed.

Deal offers became so complex and convoluted that the essence of the buying function itself became imperiled. Invoices were so laden with deal conditions that accounts payable could not discern what was actually owed the manufacturer.

In modeling a typical 100 store grocery chain, the ECR working group estimated that a total of 25,000 annual invoices would be received in the dry grocery category during a typical year. By 1992, the deal terms, allowances, and discounts had become so complex that 70% of these invoices, 18,000 in total, would need to be rejected from routine payment and would require manual audit and handling. The estimated cost of this auditing process for one chain was $360,000 per year. One manufacturer reported offering a total of 110 separate and unique invoices at any given time.

The deal offers themselves became so complex that specialists arose to take advantage of this situation. These "invoice audit" businesses were outside consultants who attempted to reclaim additional deductions from manufacturers based on a more detailed and comprehensive audit of the deal terms on each invoice. This extra-audit function became such an accepted routine that some chains implemented a process called deduction anticipation. Their logic was this: We are going to audit this invoice and we believe we will find additional deductions in our favor so we are going to withhold a part of this face payment in anticipation that this will occur.

The point of contact and stress between the manufacturer and the retailer was in the buying office. The only communication was between the salesperson and the buyer. Supply chain logistics were not considered. The efficiencies of Electronic Data Interchange were not on the table. The benefits of Electronic Funds Interchange did not come up. Automatic replenishment and better shelf management were not the priorities. The almost single focus was "What's your deal today?"

The buying contact became a continuous one-on-one battle. The conversation was focused on "What's your price today and how many weeks inventory can I buy?" The supplier/customer relationship became stressful and confrontational. The emphasis was on deal negotiating and not on the replenishment of shelf stocks and the display of inventory as efficiently as possible.

COMPLEXITY ANTIDOTE: THE BIRTH OF EFFICIENT CONSUMER RESPONSE

Into this situation came a visionary leader in the form of David Jenkins, at the time CEO of the Shaw's Supermarket grocery chain based in New England. In June of 1992, Jenkins began his talk to a meeting of the Grocery Manufacturers of America by saying: "The title of this session is 'Grocery Industry Technology—Fallen from Leading Edge to Trailing Edge.'" He went on to outline the problems faced by the industry and he

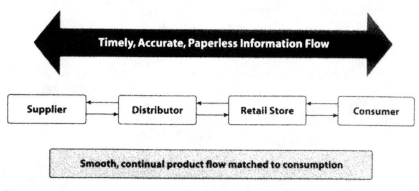

Figure 10.2

proposed the formation of an interindustry group to study the issues and recommend solutions.

As a result, the Grocery Manufacturers of America, the Food Marketing Institute, and the Uniform Code Council formed what was to become the Efficient Consumer Response initiative. Representatives of the major grocery manufacturers[4] and the major grocery chains[5] sat down to study the problems and recommend solutions. From these sessions, a mission and vision arose for the Efficient Consumer Response depicted in Figure 10.2.

Based on a yearlong study and extensive analysis and research, the ECR Working Group crafted the overall strategies listed in Table 10.2. As summarized in the final report, the benefits of these strategies were projected to be very significant:

> The benefits of ECR are substantial, with total savings in the warehouse-supplied dry-grocery segment of $10 billion. The savings in this segment, which represents approximately one-quarter of total sales volume, will also be found in other segments (e.g., frozen, HBC, general merchandise, dairy) and, to a lesser extent, in perishables. It is projected that the total potential supply chain savings are in excess of $30 billion. Because the grocery supply chain is a highly competitive system it is likely that ultimately all of this cost savings will be passed through to the consumer. This is exactly what has happened with Quick Response in the general merchandise segment.[6]

▓ Table 10.2 ECR Strategies

Strategy	Objective
Efficient store assortments	Optimize the productivity of inventories and store space at the consumer interface
Efficient replenishment	Optimize time and cost in the replenishment system
Efficient promotion	Maximize the total system efficiency of trade and consumer promotion
Efficient product introductions	Maximize the effectiveness of new product development and introduction activities

We have painted a picture of ECR's evolution at this level of detail for three reasons: First, in the picture of the pre-ECR grocery industry it is not difficult to imagine how marketing complexities led to customer confusion, frustration, and more complicated buying decisions and processes. Second, the glimpse inside the complexities of one industry are a reminder to every other industry that it is likely sitting on top of its own undesirable complexities which can be streamlined to reduce customer stress and improve business performance. Finally, the entanglements described in the grocery products industry of the early '90s provide a setting in which the efforts of one company can be better understood and appreciated in the case that follows.

■ Procter & Gamble: Where Simplicity Marketing Drives Simplicity Management

A funny thing happens when a company's assets and processes are reengineered around the customer's need to simplify: Simplifying things for customers can require a complex set of tough decisions initially, but then stimulates simplicity in management and tremendous efficiencies that result. The impact on brand equity and shareholder value is striking.

This story has vividly come to life at Procter & Gamble. Bastion of best practices in marketing, P&G further enhanced its marketing leadership cache in the 1990s by becoming a Simplicity Marketing pioneer. P&G was one of the first important companies to tackle customer stress reduction with a vengeance, and to do it so thoroughly and organically that it transformed the company to its core. In doing so, P&G reinvigorated its brands, reduced stress for its retailers as well as its customers, and increased brand equity across its vast brand architecture.

Procter & Gamble is the largest manufacturer of household products in the United States, with annual revenues approaching $40 billion—primarily from packaged foods and beverages, laundry and cleaning products, health and beauty aids, and paper goods sold in more than 140 countries. During the 1990s, P&G came to view simplification as its primary imperative in preparing for the next wave of innovation and global competition. In the words of Durk I. Jager, P&G's president and CEO:

> Since the railroad and telegraph first broke humans free of the top speed of a horse, the world has been getting ever faster and smaller. And today, we stand poised for another great leap, another breakthrough in business growth, success and profitability—*if*. What is the *if*? *If* we dramatically simplify the way we do business in a rapidly emerging global marketplace.[7]

For P&G, simplifying meant embracing Efficient Consumer Response with a breathtaking strategic commitment.[8] ECR at P&G has encompassed worldwide streamlining initiatives to simplify both brand management and supply chain logistics. ECR has required the reversal of a long history at P&G of ever-increasing product introductions, line extensions, and variations from country to country in brand names, packaging, and product formulations. It has also required a seismic shift in pricing and promotion strategy. From a shareholder value perspective, the rewards of simultaneously simplifying things for consumers, for retailer and wholesaler customers, and for P&G internal processes were very significant and relatively swift: During 1995–1998, when the most sweeping of P&G's ECR initiatives were implemented, P&G stock outperformed the Dow Jones Industrial Average by *nearly 50%* even though many other stocks among the 30 industrials were in categories growing faster than packaged food and household products.[9]

Let's take an instructive look at the basic elements of P&G's implementation of Efficient Consumer Response and the impact on specific drivers of shareholder value. In doing this, we will see how this efficient response is actually a response to both the consumer's and channel customer's need to reduce confusion, complexity, and stress.

STRESS-REDUCING ELEMENTS OF P&G'S ECR STRATEGY

When ECR first got the attention of the grocery industry in the early 1990s, complexity-driven stress among retailers and wholesalers was arguably even more obvious to manufacturers than was the rapidly rising stress at the consumer level. Only later would the resulting rewards of reducing *consumer* stress become clear. Yet we can readily see how the following ECR initiatives would simplify life not only in the distribution channel but also for consumers both in shopping and in product usage at home:

- Fewer products and product variations, or fewer SKUs (stockkeeping units).
- Everyday value pricing in lieu of frequent special promotions.
- Reduced use of coupons.
- Less ambiguity due to increased brand loyalty.

Fewer SKUs meant not only cutting back on product variations by standardizing product formulas and packaging but also cutting back on new product introductions. In just three years, 1996–98, P&G globally reduced its total number of SKUs by a staggering 20%. It also significantly reduced its number of new product introductions, especially "me-too" products that would further crowd the shelves in established categories, focusing on fewer but more innovative new products for which benefits would be more readily apparent to consumers. And while P&G sold some brands to other companies (for example, Aleve pain reliever, Lava soap, and Duncan Hines), it actually killed and buried others—such as White Cloud toilet tissue, Citrus Hill orange juice, and Clarion cosmetics—forever removing them from the customer's overcrowded brandscape (see Brand Streamlining in Chapter 6). Employing the Replace strategy of Simplicity Marketing (Chapter 4), P&G further streamlined consumers' purchasing and product use by building on its earlier success in 2-in-1 product consolidation with conditioning shampoo (Pert Plus, Chapter 3) and laundry detergent with fabric softener (Bold II). It extended the Pert Plus concept to its Head & Shoulders brand with Head & Shoulders 2-in-1, and also consolidated purchases for consumers with 2-in-1 products in other categories (such as cosmetics, under the Olay brand).

It is impossible to overstate the enormous impact on the industry—and on customer stress—of everyday value pricing. The grocery products business had long been driven by a perpetual cycle of promotional pricing and forward selling, through which manufacturers significantly discounted price to stimulate sales of large quantities of goods to wholesalers or retailers. This practice was so common that it trained consumers and the channel to expect discounted prices, and in fact for many products the discount was the rule rather than the exception. Andersen Consulting reported that half the time consumers bought an item on special, they didn't even realize it.[10] By the mid-'90s, P&G's Value Pricing Initiative broke the endless circle of promotional pricing by reallocating trade promotion funds to lower everyday list prices. Dramatically fewer promotions not only reduced consumer confusion about the value of P&G brands but enormously simplified manufacturing, order fulfillment, and channel logistics.[11]

Compared to the breadth of issues surrounding fewer SKUs and value pricing, couponing may seem a trivial arena. But millions upon millions of coupons increase clutter for the consumer, and each coupon adds three steps (Chapter 4) to the purchase process (clipping, carrying, redeeming) while adding both logistical and accounting complexity at the retailer and manufacturer levels. By 1996, P&G had cut its use of coupons by half, and even test-marketed total elimination.

What all this has meant for consumers is better value and less stress: a less bewildering, more manageable, more efficient shopping experience and streamlined brand choice decision making. Reducing promotional complexity and smoothing pricing has also introduced more predictability into these processes. Reduced uncertainty, less brand clutter, and less promotional clutter have all contributed to the increasing likelihood that P&G begins the new millennium as stress hero rather than stress villain—with consumers and channel customers as well.

But how have the simplifying elements of ECR impacted shareholder value? Let's look at each value driver individually, starting with the most obvious area of benefit to P&G, reduced operating costs.

REDUCING OPERATING COSTS

Though promotional pricing and forward selling enabled economies of scale for the manufacturer and often displaced the wholesaler's or retailer's purchase of a competitor's brand, they eroded brand loyalty and created tremendous complexity both in the supply chain and in the retail shopping environment. They also created inefficiencies for manufacturers like P&G. For example, factories ran inefficiently as they constantly endured the changeover time and scaling required for 12-week runs of producing special price packs and promotional SKUs.

Complexity-borne costs were everywhere. Ralph Drayer, vice president of efficient consumer response for Procter & Gamble Worldwide, explains: "The company realized that the proliferation of product, pricing, labeling and packaging variations necessitated by extensive promotions translated to an explosion of SKUs and UPC [Universal Product Code] changes. This further burdened the order, shipping, and billing activities throughout the supply chain—without producing value for retail customers or consumers. In addition, the bloating of the supply chain with product, together with the proliferation of product variations related to promotions, increased manufacturing costs by generating erratic demand patterns."[12] In discussing the value-creating power of simplicity and standardization in pricing and in supply chain procedures, and the relationship between cost and revenue impact, Drayer goes on to say, "Procter & Gamble determined that the overall costs of the 'gaming' associated with promotional pricing actually defeated any short-term gains that might be realized."[13]

Since every SKU adds cost and time to the marketing process, substantial reduction in SKUs over a relatively short time has been the most obvious driver of P&G's dramatic operating cost reductions attributable to simplification and standardization. Product cost overall has been reduced by more than $2/case since paring SKUs, accounting for nearly $3 billion in savings. By 1999, simplification had enabled P&G to announce the closure of 10 plants, yielding annual savings of nearly $1 billion.

Cost reduction benefits of simplification came in many other forms, including $325 million in supply chain savings and well over $100 million from standardizing pricing and promotion policies and reducing the number of price brackets across all brands in the five retail operating divisions. In fact, prior to simplification initiatives, P&G's credit department had been receiving from its channel customers more than $400 million in unauthorized deductions each year because of confusion over pricing and promotional variables. Also saved were countless and costly sales organization hours previously spent haggling with customers over trade allowances, rebates, stocking fees, and retail assistance. Fewer new product introductions also meant reduced payments of slotting allowances.

The impacts of simplification on inventory and order fulfillment also generated very significant savings. Finished-product inventory was reduced 10% as ECR initiatives improved just-in-time inventory management for more efficient replenishment of product to the channel. Inventory turns increased and out-of-stocks declined since the replenishment process became driven by consumer demand rather than by promotional forward selling. Before simplifying, more than 27,000 orders taken by P&G each month required manual corrections; afterward, the order error rate had been reduced by 80%, saving some $20 million a year. Shipping costs were reduced as fewer fractionalized orders across too many SKUs facilitated a significant increase in full truckloads (which now occur 98% of the time). And logistical handling of fewer products and fewer package variations reduced damaged goods by 25%, yielding another $15 million in savings. Millions more have been saved through reductions in couponing, from administrative and logistical costs as well as redemption costs.

Finally, there were organizational cost reductions and improved efficiencies as P&G moved from a brand management to a category management structure. Streamlining enabled a reduction in individual brand managers within the same product category competing with each other for market share, as P&L and marketing responsibilities were consolidated at the category level. There, marketing across each portfolio of category brands could be optimized, which brings us to the topic of revenue generation.

GENERATING AND PROTECTING REVENUE

Conventional wisdom at the time suggested that eliminating products would reduce sales, regardless of what happened to costs. But consumers and channel customers responded enthusiastically to stress reduction: During the first five years of ECR, P&G's total market share across all categories increased from 24.5% to 28% in an industry where each aggregate all-category share point is worth $500 million in annual revenue in the United States alone.

Head & Shoulders shampoo SKUs were slashed from more than 30 to just 15, but sales per item more than doubled. P&G's Max Factor in Japan went from 1,385 items to 828 in 1995, but Max Factor revenue increased 6%.[14] Overall at P&G, volumes are now growing two to three times faster than before ECR. In fact, even though value pricing initially reduced revenue, P&G's total revenue increased by nearly $7 billion, or more than 20%, during the first four years since the SKU-slashing really kicked in. How can this be?

ECR ushered in an era in which P&G finally went to market as a single company, giving the channel customer a single point of contact (Repackage, Chapter 5) across its five divisions. Retail customers began using the savings from simplicity and standardization and more efficient transactions to increase merchandising on P&G products to drive incremental volume. Meanwhile, the consumer applauded. Stronger brand loyalty accrued to fewer brands with more stable, predictable marketing, and the real value and quality of these brands were more readily perceived.

INCREASING MARGINS

Incremental revenue from the chaotic pre-ECR promotion approach was ultimately determined to be insufficient to cover promotional costs. So value pricing directly increased profitability, even while it initially reduced total revenue. In just three years of simplification, P&G increased its margins from 6.4% to 9.5%—the highest in nearly a half century.

Enhanced brand loyalty and perceived quality have also translated to price forgiveness, improving margins. And even with value pricing passing along to consumers some of P&G's operating cost savings, a significant portion of the huge savings discussed above have been returned to bottom line profitability.

REDUCING COST OF CAPITAL

There are two important ways in which simplicity has reduced P&G's cost of capital to improve long-term financial performance. First, the more capital required, the more expensive capital tends to be. The dramatic reductions in operating costs have lowered P&G's capital requirements per dollar of revenue over time. Second, cost of capital tends to be inversely proportional to investor confidence.

Since confident investors part with capital more willingly, it's important to look at how simplicity impacts the drivers of investor confidence. Beyond the financials, investors like to see industry leadership, innovation, speed, and efficiency in going to market, and operational shrewdness. Enhancement of P&G's image on these attributes, fueled by simplification and standardization—and the resulting customer response—has not gone unnoticed on Wall Street. (Most analysts agree that, with all its operational improvements, P&G stock would have outperformed the market by an even more dramatic margin if it had recently been more successful in introducing a few blockbuster, breakthrough new products. The internal streamlining resulting from reduced complexity has now increased the odds that it will do just that, with recalibrated allocation of resources and focus on simplicity in product development.)

Of course, investors also like to see a high return on equity—the measure of efficiency with which the firm deploys owners' capital. Since ECR, P&G's return on equity had risen to 38%, about 20% higher than the industry average.

ENHANCING FUTURE CASH FLOW

In evaluating cash flow potential, investors look at not only the *amount* of potential cash flow but also the *predictability* of cash flow over time. P&G

enhanced the loyalty of its consumer, retail, and wholesale customer bases through simplicity-driven improvements in customer satisfaction, securing greater *and* more reliable future cash flow (besides further reducing cost of capital).

Before value pricing brought more stability to the marketing process and contributed dramatically to SKU reduction, retailers and wholesalers were receiving from P&G an average of 55 price and promotion changes a day. This was not only a formidable administrative and logistical challenge in the channel but also manifested consumer confusion and bewilderment at the shelf. But fewer SKUs and fewer promotions meant significantly fewer out-of-stocks at retail, allowing P&G to do a better job on the 4th R—Replenish—ensuring continuous supply for repeat buyers. Efficient replenishment to a more loyal customer is now feeding both present and future cash flow. Meanwhile, with value pricing training consumers to buy on quality rather than on promotion, the resulting long-term behavior will feed future cash flow as well.

■ Summary

Throughout this book we have seen the power of Simplicity Marketing to build stronger brands. In this chapter, we examined how Simplicity Marketing's positive impact on brand equity connects to the traditional financial drivers of shareholder value. We saw how Efficient Consumer Response analysis in the grocery products industry revealed the kind of underlying complexities that can create customer stress in any industry, and how that stress could be reduced to strengthen the components of brand equity. Finally, in looking at Procter & Gamble's tough decisions of recent years, we witnessed the potential of simplification to create value for a company's owners and customers (see Figure 10.3).

Beyond providing a competitive edge, Simplicity Marketing's ability to reduce stress can simultaneously benefit your customers and the people in your own organization. Less stressed buyers are better equipped, both psychologically and physically, to make informed and more confident buying decisions. And when Simplicity Marketing translates to "Simplic-

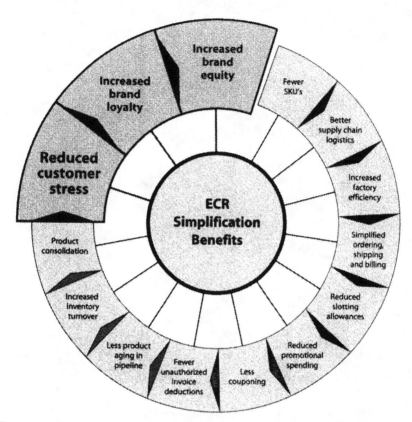

Figure 10.3

ity Management," as we saw it do at Procter & Gamble, it yields a more streamlined organization and brand management. That's a big win-win for the people at both ends—and in the middle—of the marketing process. Applied collectively across many companies, the overall result can be a healthier marketing economy and selling environment.

We hope you will use Simplicity Marketing, both as a suite of stress-reducing strategies and as an attitude in doing business, to build stronger brands and to create value. The authors wish you the best of luck—and so do your customers!

Chapter 1: Too Much Choice

1. Various references in this chapter to the number of SKUs for total super-market and selected items/brands come from retail store checks conducted in 1999, U.S. Marketing Services Trend Report data, the Food Marketing Institute, and individual manufacturers' data. References to number of new product intro-ductions are based on *New Product News* tracking data.

2. Alvin Toffler, *Future Shock* (New York: Random House, 1970).

3. Hilton Time Survey, as reported by University of Maryland sociologist Dr. John P. Robinson in "Your Money or Your Time," *American Demographics*, November 1991.

4. Jennifer Steinhauer, "Forget Conspicuous Consumption, Today's Cus-tomers Shop Across Class Lines," *The New York Times*, March 15, 1998.

5. Consumer research conducted for 3Dfx Interactive by Goodby Silverstein & Partners, 1998.

6. David Kuntz, *Stopping: How to Be Still When You Have to Keep Going* (Berkeley, CA: Conari Press, 1998).

7. Nicholas Negroponte, *Being Digital* (New York: Knopf, 1995).

8. National Sleep Foundation, Washington, DC, 1998 survey.

9. Biobehavioral Institute of Boston, Web site *www.bbinst.org*, 1998.

10. Arno Penzias, "Revenge of the Have-Littles," *Forbes ASAP*, December 1, 1997, p. 53.

11. Lyle H. Miller and Alma Dell Smith, *The Stress Solution* (New York: Pocket Books, 1994).

12. Raju Narisetti, "How IBM Turned Around Its Ailing PC Division," *The Wall Street Journal*, March 12, 1998, p. B1.

13. PaineWebber, Inc., analysis by Andrew Shore.

14. George Gilder, "Life Span vs. Life Spam," *Forbes ASAP*, April 6, 1998, p. 76.

Chapter 2: Becoming Part of the Solution

1. Based on Dun & Bradstreet Corporation data as reported by the U.S. Small Business Administration, December 1998.

2. Pamela W. Henderson and Joseph A. Cote, "Guidelines for Selecting or Modifying Logos," *Journal of Marketing*, April 1998, pp. 14–30. It should be noted that the research also suggests there are exceptions to "simpler is better"; an example is with certain logos depicting real objects, such as Prudential's rock, in which oversimplification can make the logo too abstract and risk losing some communication effectiveness.

3. Christopher Power et al., "Flops," *Business Week*, August 16, 1993, p. 76.

4. Herbert A. Simon, *Administrative Behavior: A Study of Decision-Making Processes in Administrative Organizations* (1945; reprint, New York: The Free Press, 1997).

5. Interview with Dr. William Deaton, ConStat, Inc., February 1, 1999, conducted by Steven Cristol.

6. *Toyota Product News*, Toyota Motor Sales U.S.A., Inc., June 10, 1999.

7. Attributed to Edward Fredkin by Marvin Minsky in *The Society of Mind* (New York: Touchstone, 1988), p. 52.

8. One such body of research is the work of Dr. Thomas Holmes and Dr. Richard Rahe, which produced the Holmes-Rahe Social Readjustment Scale. This scale attempts to rank the stress contribution of more than 40 life events, ranging from death of a spouse (number 1) to Christmas (number 40).

9. Yankelovich Partners, *The Daily Grind*, a client newsletter reporting on the findings of *Monitor* consumer research, 1998.

10. William Finnegan, *Cold New World: Growing Up in a Harder Country* (New York: Random House, 1998).

11. Yankelovich, *The Daily Grind*.

12. R. S. Lazarus and S. Folkman, *Stress, Appraisal and Coping* (New York: Springer, 1984).

13. Stephen A. Auerbach and Sandra E. Gramling, *Stress Management: Psychological Foundations* (Upper Saddle River, NJ: Prentice Hall, 1998).

14. Lee Gomes, "QWERTY Spells a Saga of Market Economics," *The Wall Street Journal*, February 25, 1998, p. B1.

15. Ibid.

Chapter 3: The 4 R's of Simplicity Marketing

1. Internal Procter & Gamble data.

2. Stephen Dowdell, "Value-Added Fresh Growth Will Continue, Study Finds," *Supermarket News*, February 16, 1998, p. 23.

3. Michael E. Porter, *Competitive Advantage: Creating and Sustaining Superior Performance* (New York: The Free Press, 1985), pp. 36, 130.

4. Ibid., p. 132.

5. Ibid., pp. 130–140.

6. Ibid., p. 4.

Chapter 4: REPLACE: Substitution and Consolidation

1. Emily Nelson, "Why Wal-Mart Sings, 'Yes, We Have Bananas!'," *The Wall Street Journal*, October 6, 1998, p. B1.

2. Christopher Powers et al., "Flops," *Business Week*, August 16, 1993, p. 76.

3. This overview of iMac's launch is based on information provided by Apple Computer, Inc., plus reporting by *Interactive Week* and *MacWEEK Online*.

Chapter 5: REPACKAGE: Aggregation and Integration

1. G. Christian Hill, "War! The Battle for the Telecommunications Dollar Is Turning into a Free-for-All," *The Wall Street Journal*, September 16, 1996, p. R1.

2. Reference to the fifth wave based on comments by Alan Greenspan, chairman of the Federal Reserve Bank, and data from the Hudson Institute (Indianapolis, IN), reported by Peter Brimelow in *Forbes*, August 10, 1998, pp. 102–103.

3. Arno Penzias, *Ideas and Information: Managing in a High-Tech World* (New York: Simon & Schuster, 1989), p. 138.

4. Bose story based in part on internal information furnished by Bose Corporation, November 1998.

5. Based in part on an interview with William Fenimore, Jr., CEO of Integrion Financial Network LLC, conducted by Steven Cristol on December 17, 1998, and subsequent conversations with Integrion managers and with Washington Mutual Bank.

Chapter 6: REPOSITION: Aggregation and Integration

1. Two sport roadster models are identified as the Z3 and M3 with the latter being a higher performance model.

2. Steven Kerr, "On the Folly of Rewarding A, While Hoping for B," *Academy of Management Journal*, 1975, pp. 769–83.

3. *The New York Times*, December 3, 1998, p. C–6.

4. *The Wall Street Journal*, December 3, 1998, p. B10.

5. *The Wall Street Journal*, March 25, 1998.

6. For Porsche drivers this presents one major problem: From the front view, the two models are in fact indistinguishable. True to Porsche heritage, the easiest way to tell the Boxster from the 911 is from the rear view.

7. The Porsche Spyder 550 has attained almost cult status since film actor James Dean was killed on September 30, 1955, while driving this model from Los

Angeles to Monterey, California, where he was to drive in a race at Laguna Seca Raceway.

Chapter 7: REPLENISH: Continuous Supply, Zero Defects, Competitive Price

1. Seth Godin, *Permission Marketing: Turning Strangers into Friends, and Friends into Customers* (New York: Simon & Schuster, 1999).

2. Shoplink Web site, October 1999.

Chapter 8: Visible Simplicity, Invisible Complexity: The Role of Information Technology

1. ENIAC is an acronym for Electronic Numerical Integrator And Calculator.

2. Historians now agree that the Internet was in fact born on October 26, 1969, at 10:30 P.M. when a UCLA graduate student successfully logged onto a computer at the Stanford Research Institute in Menlo Park, California, and successfully communicated via packet technology. His notation read: "Talked to SRI host to host." Thus the Internet came into being.

Chapter 9: Integrating Simplicity Marketing into Brand and Product Strategy

1. James R. Bettman, Mary Frances Luce, John W. Payne, "Constructive Consumer Choice Processes," *Journal of Consumer Research*, December 1998, p. 210.

2. Dorothy Leonard and Jeffrey F. Rayport, "Spark Innovation Through Empathic Design," *Harvard Business Review*, November–December 1997, p. 102 ff.

3. Craig J. Thompson, "Interpreting Consumers: A Hermeneutical Framework for Deriving Marketing Insights from the Texts of Consumers' Consumption Stories," *Journal of Marketing Research*, November 1997, p. 438 ff.

4. Ibid., p. 439.

5. Bettman, pp. 209–210.

6. Dartmouth College's Dr. Kevin Lane Keller has written a definitive book about brand equity which discusses brand knowledge in more detail, as well as many other important brand equity-related concepts relevant to Simplicity Marketing. See Kevin Lane Keller, *Strategic Brand Management: Building, Measuring and Managing Brand Equity* (Upper Saddle River, NJ: Prentice Hall, 1998), p. 46 ff.

7. In the spirit of full disclosure, Hewlett-Packard is one of the author's consulting clients, and the author has been very involved in the development of HP's stress-sensitive strategy in the enterprise storage category.

8. Gunter Rommel, Felix Bruck et al., *Simplicity Wins: How Germany's Mid-Sized Companies Succeed* (Boston: Harvard Business School Press, 1995).

9. Philip Kotler, *Marketing Management: Analysis, Planning, Implementation and Control*, 7th ed. (Englewood Cliffs, NJ: Prentice Hall, 1991), p. 314.

10. A brand's "unaided" awareness refers to a measure of the incidence of customers identifying a particular brand in the category without being prompted. For example, in athletic shoes, each brand's unaided awareness measure would be the percentage of customers who recall the brand without a prompt when

asked the question, "When you think about athletic shoes, which brands come to mind?" A brand's "top-of-mind" awareness measure refers to the percentage of customers who name that brand *first* (e.g., "When you think about athletic shoes, what's the *first* brand that comes to mind?"). Both of these measures are generally stronger predictors of brand preference than is "aided" awareness, which is measured by prompting the customer (e.g., "Have you ever heard of Adidas?"), because both unaided and top-of-mind awareness represent greater degrees of brand familiarity.

11. Based in part on information furnished by Amazon.com and on an excellent chronicle by John M. Jordan of The Ernst & Young Center for Business Innovation, Cambridge, Massachusetts, entitled, "Web Commerce at Amazon.com," *Perspectives on Business Innovation: Issue 3, Electronic Commerce*, pp. 20–27.

12. When marketing mistakes cause customer stress, excellence in service recovery is critical for Simplicity Marketers to get back on track. For further reading about service recovery importance, rewards, and strategies, and how to not only retain temporarily dissatisfied customers but also make them even more loyal than before, see "The Profitable Art of Service Recovery," by Hart, Heskett, and Sasser in *Harvard Business Review*, July–August 1990, pp. 58–66.

Chapter 10: The Bottom Line: Converting Customer Stress Relief to Shareholder Value

1. David A. Aaker, *Managing Brand Equity* (New York: The Free Press, 1991).

2. David Aaker and Erich Joachimsthaler, *Brand Leadership* (New York: The Free Press, 2000).

3. The bar code scanner was introduced by the NCR Corporation on May 5, 1974. The first product to be scanned at the checkout counter, a 10-pack of Wrigley's Juicy Fruit gum, was swiped at a Marsh Supermarket in Troy, Ohio, six weeks later.

4. Borden, Inc.; Campbell Sales Company; The Coca-Cola Company; Crown/BBK Inc.; Kraft General Foods; Nabisco Foods Group; Oscar Mayer Foods Corp.; Procter & Gamble Company; and Ralston Purina Company.

5. Kroger Company; Safeway Inc. Sales Force Companies; Scrivner, Inc.; Shaw's Supermarkets, Inc.; Supervalu, Inc.; and The Vons Companies, Inc.

6. "Efficient Consumer Response: Enhancing Consumer Value in the Grocery Industry," published by the Research Department of the Food Marketing Institute, January 1993, p. 3.

7. Durk I. Jager, "Preparing for an Emerging Global Retail Supply Chain," *Forum*, Summer 1999, p. 40.

8. Much of the information in this chapter regarding Procter & Gamble is courtesy of Ralph W. Drayer, vice president of efficient consumer response for Procter & Gamble, who was interviewed by Steven Cristol on June 25, 1999.

9. On March 7, 2000, subsequent to the writing of this chapter, Procter & Gamble stock tumbled 31% in a chaotic market that had already seen the Dow

Jones Industrial Average lose more than 20% of its value in less than two months. P&G's slide that day was triggered when its CEO delivered to the already jittery financial community an earnings announcement in which a range of largely temporary problems were revealed—including significant increases in raw material costs, deferred income due to pharmaceutical-related regulatory delays, and intensified competition and margin pressure in Latin America. This followed weeks of investor concern about P&G's potential acqustion of two major drug companies (which never materialized). These issues notwithstanding, P&G's execution of Simplicity Marketing during the five preceding years stands as exemplary, as does its impact on shareholder value. Indeed, without those simplicity initiatives in place, P&G stock would not have had as far to fall that day after the sustained excellent performance that ECR and Simplicity Marketing had helped drive.

10. Zachary Schiller, Greg Burns, and Karen Lowry Miller, "Make It Simple," *Business Week*, September 9, 1996, p. 102.

11. Ralph W. Drayer, "Procter & Gamble's Streamlined Logistics Initiatives," *Supply Chain Management Review*, Summer 1999, pp. 32–43.

12. Ibid., p. 34.

13. Ibid., p. 36.

14. Schiller, "Make it Simple," p. 99.

STEVEN M. CRISTOL is a brand strategist and brand equity management advisor to leading technology companies. Drawing on 25 years of client-side and consulting experience in both business-to-business and consumer marketing, his consultancy provides decision intelligence in brand positioning, brand extension strategy, brand equity metrics, organizational issues impacting effective brand communications, and strategic integration of the Internet into the marketing mix. With a focus on telecommunications, computing, and the Internet, he has in recent years helped shape strategy for some of the world's most successful technology brands, including Commerce One, Hewlett-Packard, Lexmark, Netscape, Pacific Bell, Sony, Southwestern Bell, Tektronix, 3Com, and 3Dfx.

Mr. Cristol was formerly a senior marketing executive at Pacific Bell (acquired by SBC Communications) and in Silicon Valley start-ups, and earlier in his career managed consumer packaged goods accounts at major advertising agencies. He is principal author of *Essentials of Media Planning: A Marketing Viewpoint,* now in its third edition and translated in five languages. He now lives in Seattle, Washington, and can receive e-mail correspondence regarding *Simplicity Marketing* at *smc@cristol.com.*

PETER SEALEY is Adjunct Professor of Marketing at the Haas School of Business at the University of California-Berkeley and Co-Director at the school's Center for Marketing and Technology. He has served as a management consultant for leading firms including Sony New Technologies, Inc., the Anheuser-Busch Company, Visa U.S.A., United Parcel Service, ImproveNet, Johnson & Johnson, Hewlett-Packard, The Eastman Kodak Company, Nokia and A.T. Kearney, Inc. He serves on the Boards of Directors of AutoWeb.com, USWeb/CKS, Encanto Networks, Inc., CyberGold, Inc., United Parcel Service Capital Corporation, L 90, Inc., MediaPlex, Inc., T/R Systems and Kinzan.com. He serves on the Boards of Advisors of Purpletie.com, HomeGain.com, Bamboo.com, Space.com and eVoice.com. He is a special partner in DigaComm Ventures, LLC, a venture capital firm. He is a speaker at over 30 industry conferences each year.

The majority of Sealey's career was spent at The Coca-Cola Company during which he held senior positions in virtually every business sector of that corporation including soft drinks, wine, and filmed entertainment. He was appointed that Company's first Global Marketing Director in 1990 and introduced the successful "Always Coca-Cola" global advertising campaign in association with Hollywood's Creative Artists Agency in 1993.

Professor Sealey and his wife, Elizabeth, live in Silicon Valley with their four cats and three dogs. There he can often be found riding his motorcycle on the back roads of the Santa Cruz mountains. He can be reached at: *sealey@haas.berkeley.edu.*

Printed in the United States
By Bookmasters